THE
FAMOUS
LADY
LOVERS

GENDER AND AMERICAN CULTURE

Martha Jones and Mary Kelley, editors

Editorial Advisory Board

Cathleen Cahill	Tamika Nunley	Noliwe Rooks
Rosalyn LaPier,	Annelise Orleck	Nick Syrett
University of Montana	Janice A. Radway	Lisa Tetrault
Jen Manion	Robert Reid-Pharr	Ji-Yeon Yuh

Series Editors Emerita

Thadious M. Davis	Linda K. Kerber	Nell Irvin Painter
	Annette Kolodny	

The Gender and American Culture series, guided by feminist perspectives, examines the social construction and influence of gender and sexuality within the full range of American cultures. Books in the series explore the intersection of gender (both female and male) with such markers of difference as race, class, and region. The series presents outstanding scholarship from all areas of American studies—including history, literature, religion, folklore, ethnography, and the visual arts—that investigates in a thoroughly contextualized and lively fashion the ways in which gender works with and against these markers. In so doing, the series seeks to reveal how these complex interactions have shaped American life.

A complete list of books published in Gender and American Culture is available at https://uncpress.org/series /gender-and-american-culture.

THE FAMOUS LADY LOVERS

Black Women
and Queer Desire
before Stonewall

~~~~~~~~~~

COOKIE WOOLNER

THE UNIVERSITY OF NORTH CAROLINA PRESS

Chapel Hill

Set in Scala, Harlie, and Zipnut
by codeMantra

Manufactured in the United States of America

Chapter 1 is based on an article by the author originally published in the
Journal of African American History. Cookie Woolner, "'Woman Slain in Queer
Love Brawl': African American Women, Same-Sex Desire, and Violence in
the Urban North, 1920–1929," *Journal of African American History* 100, no. 3
(Summer 2015): 406–27, https://doi.org/10.5323/jafriamerhist.100.3.0406.

LIBRARY OF CONGRESS CATALOGING-IN-PUBLICATION DATA
Names: Woolner, Cookie, author.
Title: The famous lady lovers : Black women and queer
desire before Stonewall / Cookie Woolner.
Other titles: Gender & American culture.
Description: Chapel Hill : The University of North Carolina Press, 2023. |
Series: Gender and American culture | Includes
bibliographical references and index.
Identifiers: LCCN 2023014310 | ISBN 9781469675473 (cloth ; alk. paper) |
ISBN 9781469675480 (paperback) | ISBN 9781469675497 (ebook)
Subjects: LCSH: African American lesbians—Social life and
customs—20th century. | Sexual minority culture—United States. |
BISAC: HISTORY / African American & Black | SOCIAL SCIENCE /
Ethnic Studies / American / African American & Black Studies
Classification: LCC HQ76.27.A37 W66 2023 |
DDC 306.76/6308996073—dc23/eng/20230420
LC record available at https://lccn.loc.gov/2023014310

For my mother,

ANNE KASSEL WOOLNER

(1943–2006)

CONTENTS

ILLUSTRATIONS

THE
FAMOUS
LADY
LOVERS

INTRODUCTION

Have We a New Sex Problem Here?

In November 1920, the Black newspaper the *Chicago Whip* ran a front-page article with the provocative headline, "Have We a New Sex Problem Here?" The short article detailed an incident involving a married couple and another woman, describing the situation as "one of the most peculiar divorce cases to yet be heard in Chicago." After six years of "marital peace and harmony," Ida May Robinson had "forsaken" her husband, Sherman Robinson, when "she left him without any cause" for a woman whom she "had formerly known in Paducah, Kentucky."[1] According to their landlord, the two women had been living together in a boardinghouse prior to the official divorce. The possibility that a woman would leave her husband to enter a romantic relationship with another woman and live with her as a family unit was a new concept for the anonymous journalist. So shocking was this notion that the author wondered whether Ida May Robinson and her partner heralded a "new sex problem."

The "here" to which the headline referred was the rapidly growing Black district of Bronzeville on Chicago's South Side, now filled with recent southern migrants like Ida May Robinson who were escaping the Jim Crow South. By 1920, the Great Migration, a mass exodus of African Americans from the South to the North and West, was in full swing.[2]

1

The Black population of Chicago had more than doubled since 1910, and women now outnumbered men.[3] Most of these Black southern migrants were young and single, and they often lived in boardinghouses like the one in Bronzeville where Robinson and her partner made a home.[4]

The *Chicago Whip*, like many Black newspapers, was started and run by college-educated, middle-class African Americans from the North. Often referred to as "old settlers," their families had lived above the Mason-Dixon Line for a number of generations.[5] For this more established and educated class of northern African Americans, the sexual deportment of an ever-growing population of "new settlers" like Ida May Robinson was of great concern, not least because it clashed so strikingly with an established politics of respectability designed to present Black people as fit for full citizenship in the age of Jim Crow.[6] Respectability in this context demanded hewing to traditional gender roles, which did not involve women leaving their husbands for other women.

Black women's historians have long attended to the lives of African American queer women before the era of gay liberation. Prior historical work has delved into the political, intellectual, and artistic lives of some of these women, but their intimate lives remain unexplored. This book, in contrast and complement to this rich tradition, places Black queer women and their intimate lives at the center of the narrative.[7] The Stonewall Uprising of 1969 is normally used to demarcate the emergence of modern gay communities, but this book reveals a queer world that Black women crafted many decades prior, which coalesced in the 1920s. Black "lady lovers"—as women who loved women were then known—fashioned modern new identities, social networks, and gathering spaces in the interwar era. This book examines the lives of well-known women like popular blues singer Bessie Smith along with many "everyday" women uncovered in the archives, like Ida May Robinson. Utilizing a wide array of sources such as Black newspapers, vice reports, blues songs, memoirs, sexology case studies, manuscripts, and letters, I show that Black queer women were emergent cultural figures in the new Black districts of the urban North. To the Black press and other male authorities, they came to symbolically represent the social chaos of increasingly racially heterogeneous modern cities, as sexually active women separated from the domestic sphere and the heteronormative family unit. However, despite the multiple oppressions that Black lady lovers experienced, they created careers, relationships, cultural texts, and networks that enriched interwar American culture. Black women's queer relationships in the urban North modeled new forms of modernity: they reveal that many women prioritized romantic relationships with other women over or alongside traditional marriage and motherhood. Black lady lovers strategically created queer networks inside and outside of the Black entertainment industry and intellectual circles that allowed them to take part in the newly emerging sexual subcultures of the early twentieth century.

The story of Ida May Robinson touches on multiple key themes raised in this book: the role of the Great Migration in creating Black queer networks and gathering spaces, how Black women's mobility contributed to their ability to take part in queer relationships, the growing visibility of Black lady lovers in the urban North, the role of the Black press in disseminating information about them, and the "sex problem" that these women represented to the larger Black community. While this 1920 opening article implicitly suggested that Ida May Robinson's leaving her husband was a form of rhetorical violence that wounded the Black family and the race, soon literal acts of violence would saturate portrayals of lady lovers in the Black press. Throughout the 1920s, multiple attacks and murders involving women occurred that journalists and police declared were caused by "unnatural" desires for the same sex.[8] Many of the women embroiled in these events were recent southern migrants, but not just old settlers were concerned; recent immigrants and migrants who adhered to the traditional gender roles prescribed through immensely popular Black nationalist channels like Marcus Garvey's newspaper, *Negro World*, were also incensed.[9] According to these sources, Black women needed to birth and raise the next generation of Black men, and lesbianism displaced men as well as put the future of the race in peril.[10] There was no room for women's nonreproductive sexuality in an increasingly masculinized struggle for racial equality and full citizenship. The popularity of masculinist Black nationalist thinking was another reason that Black lady lovers could not be embraced as modern, sexually liberated women in the Black community in the interwar era.

However, at the dawn of the 1920s, there were other milieus where Black women could literally take center stage, such as the popular entertainment industry, which increasingly encompassed segregated forms of Black vaudeville, the spectacle of Black musicals, and the rapidly expanding market for "race records"—later to become known as "rhythm and blues."[11] Beyond creating new work opportunities for thousands of talented women, these industries also served as central meeting places for lady lovers. Women's live performances attracted diverse audiences, particularly southern migrants, who identified with blues songs that often discussed the hazards of northern living and nostalgia for life back in the South.[12] Black performing women were constantly mobile, which facilitated queer liaisons, such as those of blues singer Bessie Smith, who initiated multiple relationships on the road with the dancers in her show.[13] Smith, like many women in the industry, was married to a man but still enjoyed queer relationships that she sought to hide from her husband while touring. Black performing women's increasing mobility and sexual fluidity helped them fashion new relationships and social networks in the interwar era.

Whether rehearsing performances, socializing backstage, touring on trains, or staying overnight at segregated boardinghouses, day-to-day forms of sociability offered myriad potential opportunities for women to take part in same-sex relationships or flirtations. While most women sought to keep their queer behaviors out of the public eye, this was even more of a concern for highly successful performers, who did not want to damage their celebrity status. Therefore, singers like Bessie Smith developed a range of strategies to make their queer behaviors illegible to those who would not approve. Similarly, the songs, performances, and record ads of the "famous lady lovers" engaged with queer themes both subtly and overtly—and in ways that increasingly hailed queer counterpublics.[14] These performing women accessed the freedoms of mass migration and the new mobility of the twentieth century and in doing so crafted new sexual subjectivities.[15] This market-driven mobility, in turn, allowed them to bring cultural texts and performances crafted in the urban North to the rural South (and vice versa), thereby circulating texts and performances about Black women's changing conceptions of gender and sexuality.

This story traces the formation of Black queer women's networks, which could not fully emerge until the 1920s through the interaction of the Great Migration, Prohibition, a national Black press, the popular entertainment industries, and changing notions of gender and sexuality in the interwar period. As John D'Emilio and Estelle Freedman note, "The 1920s stand out as a time when something in the sexual landscape decisively altered and new patterns clearly emerged. The decade was recognizably modern in a way that previous ones were not." The "values, attitudes, and activities of the pre-Depression years unmistakably point to the future rather than the past."[16] This modernity was expressed through an increasingly national mass culture that disseminated northern Black newspapers, such as the *Chicago Defender*, throughout the North and South via Pullman train porters; through the "race records" segregated music industry that brought the emotional blues songs of women like Bessie Smith into living rooms; and through the house parties, speakeasies, buffet flats, and Black vaudeville circuits where these singers performed for enthusiastic crowds. Blues women subtly hailed their audiences with veiled references to queerness and took advantage of the privacy and liminal spaces of touring life to enact same-sex relationships on the road. Not only were performing women viewed regularly on Seventh Avenue in Harlem and State Street in Chicago, but so too were "sophisticated ladies" with "boyish bobbed hair" who wore men's "brogan shoes."[17] "Young women bedecked in male attire" could be seen "perambulat[ing] with a distinctive and well practiced swagger" down the main thoroughfares of Black urban districts.[18] Black lady lovers were full participants and historical actors in the vibrant, urban working-class Black neighborhoods that southern migrants helped fashion.

While queerness was more visible in this milieu, Black women who were college-educated also took part in same-sex relationships in the interwar period. While Black lady lovers of different class backgrounds will be focused on separately at times in this book, it is nonetheless important to note that just as sexuality was often fluid for these women, so too was social class. It has always been more difficult to define social class categories for Black Americans than for white Americans, as lack of economic and educational opportunities due to racial discrimination meant that one's job did not always determine one's class. Further, many of the "elite" women to be discussed here came from families only a generation removed from slavery or sharecropping, and they saw manners and morals as just as critical to one's class position as wages and salaries.[19]

Since middle-class women often had more leisure time to document their inner worlds through letters and diaries, there is more evidence of their relationships and queer desires before the 1920s than that of working-class women's. At the same time, college-educated Black lady lovers' social networks continued to grow and flourish more than ever before in the interwar era. Indeed, prior to the 1920s, the available evidence suggests that Black women's relationships were more likely to be isolated and not part of a larger social world of like-minded women. However, by the 1930s, queer couples such as writers Dorothy West and Marian Minus started Black literary journals, while Howard University's first dean of women, Lucy Diggs Slowe, and her partner, playwright Mary Burrill, regularly entertained female Howard students in their Washington, DC, home.

Women in this milieu connected through ideas and literature, sharing intellectual, political, and artistic interests as well as physical attraction. Not only did these women make a home together, but their relationships also forged new avenues for Black women's expression and education. For couples such as Slowe and Burrill, earlier nineteenth-century conceptions of women's emotionally intimate, yet sexless, relationships gave cover to their socially transgressive partnerships.[20] While all of Slowe and Burrill's friends were aware of their relationship, it was never referred to openly as romantic or akin to a marriage; they were merely "dear friends" who shared a life together. As the two were in their forties by the time the Jazz Age arrived in the 1920s, the more modern conceptions of women's active sexual desires and lesbianism that the decade wrought were not applied to them.

While the notion of lesbianism became more visible in this era, Black women's increasing autonomy to create and define their own relationships was met with disapproval from Black male authorities such as journalists, religious leaders, theater producers, college administrators, and sociologists, who saw such women as threatening for subverting norms of gender and sexuality. By the end of the 1920s, sermons against homosexuality in the Black community were held in churches and documented in newspapers. One religious leader who spoke out against lesbianism was the powerful and popular pastor of the Abyssinian Baptist Church in Harlem for almost thirty years, Adam Clayton Powell Sr. The *New York Age* quoted a 1929 sermon in which he singled out the harm caused by lady lovers. He exclaimed, "Homo-sexuality and sex perversion among women" has "grown into one of the most horrible debasing, alarming and damning vices of present day civilization." Powell "asserted that it is not only prevalent to an unbelievable degree but that it is increasing day by day."[21]

In his autobiography, Adam Clayton Powell Sr. noted that almost every Black newspaper in the country had reprinted excerpts or commented on this sermon, which was one of the first ever given on this topic in the Black church.[22] The following week, he declared that he had "struck a chord" with congregants, who had sent him letters concerning sex perversion in their local communities.[23] He argued that much of this behavior came from "contact and association" and not "inherent degeneracy," which offered the prospect of correcting or avoiding such "vicious habits" in the future. Powell suggested that "the seeking for 'thrills' of an unusual character by the modern youth is responsible" for some of the emerging sex perversion problem, which resulted in debasing "the race."[24] Powell decried homosexuality for "threatening to eat the vitals out of America" as "wives leave their husbands for other women" and girls "mate with girls instead of marrying."[25] Church leaders sought to promote ideologies of respectability, morality, and racial uplift and did not approve of homosexuality, which they conflated with other vices they saw as infiltrating and weakening Black communities.

The overlap of Black neighborhoods and vice districts in the early twentieth century was another reason that old settlers were concerned with new settlers' behavior, as the lure of immorality was seen as never far away in the urban North.[26] At the same time, the geographic proximity of Black districts to vice "underworlds" allowed for illicit queer recreational spaces to emerge in the 1920s, furthering the association between same-sex behavior, crime, and immorality.[27] Progressive Era reformers and religious leaders had worked hard to shut down vice districts nationally in the 1910s, but soon after, prostitution, gambling, and then bootleg alcohol began to seep into Black urban neighborhoods with the arrival of Prohibition.[28] Police generally turned a blind eye to these illegal activities in order to keep vice out of white neighborhoods and because they lacked concern for the well-being of African American communities.[29] This "wide open" atmosphere allowed for a multitude of queer behaviors and networks to emerge and momentarily thrive in the Prohibition era.[30] New and more liminal spaces opened up in the 1920s that straddled older definitions of "public" and "private," such as "buffet flats"—parties held in residential apartments—which were typically hosted by entrepreneurial Black women.[31] It was precisely these sorts of environments, found outside of traditional commercial establishments, where women gathered, flirted, and enjoyed their leisure time. And among more elite circles, hostesses like A'Lelia Walker—the heiress daughter of millionaire Madam C. J. Walker—entertained Black artists, intellectuals, and white patrons in Harlem salons, where lady lovers and queer public affection were welcome.[32]

While Black queer women have historically socialized in their homes for reasons ranging from economics to safety, private parties became even more central to their leisure time during Prohibition, as white thrill-seeking "slummers" descended upon Black districts for entertainment, bootleg liquor, and interracial dancing and sex.[33] Some of the most famous clubs of the Harlem Renaissance era, such as the Cotton Club, allowed as patrons only white and very light-skinned African Americans; otherwise, Black people were permitted only as employees and performers.[34] Frustrated that they could entertain and serve white people but not sit among them as equals, Black women opened up residential spaces, such as buffet flats, which became important sites for working-class leisure and amusement. One of the most popular performers whom white slumming audiences came to Harlem to see was Gladys Bentley, a large, masculine Black woman often sporting a tuxedo who expertly played the piano and sung dirty ditties all night long in various speakeasies. Bentley became so popular that she eventually performed in Times Square and on Broadway. One of the most infamous figures of the Harlem Renaissance and Pro-hibition eras, Bentley was also unashamedly open about her lesbianism; she flirted with white women in her audience and proudly told a white newspaper critic that she was marrying her girlfriend in Atlantic City.[35]

The visibility of queer figures such as Gladys Bentley to the white slumming crowd was an embarrassment to the Black middle class. White audiences sought out performers like Bentley, who represented to them the "primitivism" of "Jungle Alley," which offered a momentary release from their routinized daily lives.[36] However, Black journalists and critics were concerned that their neighborhoods were being used like a trip to the zoo or the circus. As W. E. B. Du Bois wrote in his magazine *The Crisis* at the height of the slumming vogue in 1927, white people "must be made to remember that Harlem is not merely exotic, it is human; it is not a spec-tacle and an entertainment, it is life; it is not chiefly cabarets, it is chiefly homes."[37] Du Bois and others feared that outrageous figures like Gladys Bentley were representing the race, which was doing a disservice to the cause of racial uplift and to the dignity of the community.

As these tensions between lady lovers and the larger Black community suggest, the formation of Black queer women's networks in the urban North was political for multiple reasons. African American women's sexu-ality has been circumscribed by histories of slavery, segregation, and labor that often allowed for little sexual autonomy. Under chattel slavery, repro-duction was prioritized by white planters and overseers, who benefited from the creation of future laborers. Mothers were often separated from their children, and the law did not acknowledge bondspeople's marriages, while rape and sexual violence at the hands of white overseers was com-mon.[38] Antebellum ideology and laws viewed Black women as not fully human nor able to consent. In this context, the early twentieth-century mass migration of single Black women to urban centers, the creation of queer networks, and the increasing visibility of lady lovers show how women only a couple of generations removed from slavery prioritized their desires, ambitions, agency, and autonomy. This book examines historical subjects who, despite the fact that remaining within solely heterosexual relationships could grant them a modicum of privilege and respect, nonetheless chose to resist or subvert the social norms of their day to fulfill their romantic and sexual desires and bring joy and pleasure to their lives.

Journalists who discussed lady lovers in the Black press often utilized the language of sexology—the science of sex—to explain newly emerging sexual identity categories, demonstrate their cultural awareness of medical discourse, and distance themselves from such "deviant" subjects. Since the late nineteenth century, European sexologists such as Richard von Krafft-Ebing and Havelock Ellis had noted the violence of female "inverts," a medical category that preceded "homosexuality."[39] Such women were believed to have an inverted, masculine soul, which explained their desire for women.[40] Thus, the medically created identity category that preceded "lesbianism" saw one's sexuality as an outgrowth of one's gender expression, which led to the association of queerness with masculine women rather than with feminine women. A series of "lesbian *love* murders" at the end of the nineteenth century helped usher in a new, modern conception of lesbianism to a national newspaper audience and codified the association between female homosexuality and violence.[41] These cases also saw the emergence of feminine women—whose normative gender expressions did not meet the old definition of an "invert"—who desired women. Such women were viewed as even more threatening, as they were more likely to be the objects of desire for men, which later became the subject of popular plays like *The Captive*.

The rise of sexology led to increased discourse on the pathologization of queer desire and further conflated the bodies and sexualities of all Black women with those of lesbians and criminals.[42] Richard von Krafft-Ebing introduced the theory of degeneration, under which the Victorian sex/gender system was the pinnacle of civilization and only primitive societies embraced lust and non-monogamy, same-sex behavior, and sex outside of marriage, which were all degenerative signs.[43] Havelock Ellis also argued that female same-sex behavior was more likely to occur within what he called the "lower races." He documented sources that found same-sex practices to be common among women in "Brazil, Bali, Zanzibar, Egypt, French Creole countries, and India," among other non-Western locales.[44] Sexologists tended to dwell on the sexual perversions found in "primitive cultures," which allowed them to develop arguments justifying the superiority of white European culture.[45]

The association of Black lady lovers with violence at this time came from both the medical realm and the racial antagonisms of the Jim Crow era. As southern African Americans migrated North, their increased proximity to northern white people in overcrowded cities heightened white anxieties and led to their further association in the white imaginary as violent criminals. Racist caricatures of Black men as violent, ignorant, and immoral were propagated through blackface minstrel shows, songs, and other forms of popular culture to justify such beliefs; practices like lynching took the lives of thousands of African Americans in the late nineteenth and early twentieth centuries at the hands of white vigilante mobs who adhered to such ideas.[46] While the available crime statistics from the early twentieth century reflect the bias of a white police force and court system that arrested and imprisoned Black people in increasing numbers, white social scientists read these statistics as objective reports that demonstrated African Americans' innately violent natures.[47] Black women were frequently arrested for solicitation, disorderly conduct, petty theft, and "crimes of passion" that were often acts of self-defense against abusive partners.

By 1923, Black women constituted 64.5 percent of the women in American prisons, even though they made up less than 10 percent of the nation's female population.[48] Against this background, lesbian historian Lillian Faderman notes that "a Black lesbian subculture" emerged "fairly early" because of the prison "demiworld" that so many Black women were subjugated to in the Jim Crow era. Here, Black women who had been incarcerated learned not only about queer sexuality but also about the particular gendered sexual roles that emerged in single-sex environments, such as referring to female partners as "mama" and "papa," which developed in prisons and reformatories by the beginning of the twentieth century.[49] In the 1910s, authorities were particularly concerned with the growing prevalence of Black and white girls' queer interracial relationships in reformatories and women's prisons. One infamous 1913 report by psychologist Margaret Otis noted, "The difference in color, in this case, takes the place of difference in sex" when "both races are housed together."[50] While this report suggested that the white inmates saw Black inmates as inherently masculine and aggressive, Otis did not speak to many inmates of color, nor did she address how often such relationships took place between two white girls or two African American girls.[51] At the same time, some Black women who took on a masculine role in reform schools and prison regarded their masculinity as "a point of pride to be embraced rather than a shameful expression of deviance or inversion."[52] As Cheryl Hicks argues, whether or not young Black women had experience with women before being imprisoned, same-sex relationships in these settings provided opportunities to more fully embrace their queer desires, and as many women sought to keep in touch once released, they furthered the creation of queer social networks in the process.[53]

Black lady lovers' networks began to grow right after World War I, when the New Negro era had begun, bringing the promise of a renewed commitment to fight the racial inequities of Jim Crow. However, this new race consciousness was infused with a masculinization that prioritized Black men and male leadership over women.[54] This outlook was consolidated not only through the success of Black military personnel in World War I but also in response to national race riots and massacres that were spawned by mounting racial tensions in the North, as Black populations rapidly grew during the early Great Migration. The aftermath of these events led to an increasing masculinization in the rhetoric of the struggle for racial equality and heightened community policing of the behavior of southern migrants in the North. Women's behavior "became a trope for the race, their public deportment and carriage the basis by which some assumed the entire race would be judged."[55] A 1922 editorial in the *Chicago Whip* accused Black South Side women of being "too familiar" with men of other races in their neighborhoods, which would give them the wrong idea. Southern migrant women needed to learn that they were "under constant and continual surveillance" and "must stand in position to satisfy the critical eye of the public."[56] While Black lady lovers had new freedoms and opportunities in northern cities, they could not fully escape the watchful eye of neighbors and local authorities who would not approve of their way of life.

In the private sphere, however, women could make a home together, which came to the public's attention only when something extraordinary occurred, such as a violent crime. As more and more southern migrant women lived in boardinghouses or rented out a room from a family, fewer living arrangements in the urban North came to look like the traditional domestic sphere, which added confusion over what it meant for women to live together. Indeed, several of the murder cases that will be discussed in the next chapter occurred between women who were married or separated and rented rooms out to other women. In each case, the Black press claimed that "perverted love" was to blame for these crimes of passion, and yet little solid evidence is given to confirm that queer desires were actually the cause of the homicides. As more women of all races and classes sought out birth control and nonreproductive sex; remained single, separated, or divorced their husbands; and had relationships with both men and women, lady lovers became less marginal and more symbolic of a system of gender and sexuality in the midst of upheaval.[57]

In the nineteenth century, relationships between women were often viewed as innocent "practice" for later marriage to men or merely as platonic friendships.[58] However, by the early twentieth century, proponents of "companionate marriage" and of psychoanalysis all emphasized women's active sexual desires, which meant that women's relationships could be more than platonic and might be a threat to heterosexual marriage and the family.[59] The creation of nonnuclear families and living arrangements by Black lady lovers was part of a long tradition in Black women's history of creating kinship forms and ties that were differentiated from white ideals and their legal standards.[60] This will be examined in more detail in chapter 4, where the alternative kinship structures of middle-class Black lady lovers are discussed, and also in the conclusion, which looks at the new forms of family arrangements created by lady lovers in the interwar era.

While journalists, reformers, religious leaders, and others sought to regulate Black women's sexuality, by the 1920s growing numbers of women, whether single or married, took part in queer relationships. However, espousing an "open" queer or lesbian identity was not an ideal championed in this time period. Indeed, it would be considered a privilege that few women—especially Black women in the Jim Crow era—were in a position to freely claim, as most people still viewed queerness as a type of sickness at this time. Open homosexuality could only serve to harm the fight for racial equality and the struggle for full citizenship, which led to heightened resistance against lesbianism by the Black critics most concerned with the "race question." And since representations of the Black family as female-dominated and lacking a male breadwinner were cemented long before the studies and critiques by congressman and sociologist Daniel Patrick Moynihan and Black social scientists like E. Franklin Frazier, lady lovers' growing visibility was further viewed as harmful to the future of the race.[61] Long-standing European notions of the pathology of Black female sexuality were only reinforced by the growing representations of Black queer women. For these reasons, queerness was a topic often not discussed outright but generally accepted as an open secret that was mutually and quietly understood. Yet at the same time, the multiple discourses condemning lady lovers served to bolster their visibility and cultural power. Each article in the Black press decrying lady lovers' growing presence let curious female readers know where to find such women. Despite the increasing concern over women's relationships, many nonetheless sought such connections, demonstrating the lengths that lady lovers would go to in order to create the type of relationship that satisfied their desires and brought them happiness.

For decades, scholars have discussed the methodological difficulties in carrying out historical work on African American women, and the search for sources on Black women who loved women is an even more daunting task. Finding these women's stories often requires consulting sources that were created to regulate and reprimand them and then reading them "against the grain" in order to parse details of their lives that have rarely been saved for posterity in institutional archives. As George Chauncey has shown, for better or worse, the creation of subaltern histories demands relying heavily on "outsider sources" usually written by authorities instead of sources like diaries that reveal the contours of Black women's everyday lives and inner worlds.[62] Whenever possible I have drawn on autobiographies, biographies, and oral histories: sources that are still mediated but also offer an "insider" perspective on the experiences of Black lady lovers. Yet this work has also been crucially formed by newspaper articles from the Black press, vice reports, and sociological studies that have represented Black lady lovers with all the qualities that the Black middle class sought to refute. The danger here then becomes overestimating the role of policing and violence in the lives of these women, who often did not enter the official record unless they were charged with committing a crime.

When it comes to queer sexuality and relationships, yet another dilemma of the archives emerges: when middle-class Black women's lives have been documented for posterity, concerns over respectability have often led to the hiding of details regarding same-sex relationships. As Matt Richardson argues, "Black middle-class pleas for citizenship and humanity have resulted in a capitulatory politics of inclusion and respectability that has distorted and suppressed memories of variant genders and sexualities."[63] For example, when literature scholar Akasha (Gloria) Hull was researching clubwoman Alice Dunbar-Nelson, who began to have relationships with women at the turn of the century, Hull found that Dunbar-Nelson's relatives did not want any details about this aspect of her life to be discussed in her study. Eventually Hull was able to convince Dunbar-Nelson's niece that her attraction to women was only one aspect of her identity and was important enough to be included, but not every scholar and historian has taken such a viewpoint.[64]

These often-conscious silences in the archives can be further understood through Darlene Clark Hine's theory of dissemblance, a key concept in the study of African American women's history and the history of sexuality. Hine argues that the long-standing myth of Black women's hypersexuality—which white men used to justify their sexual abuse of women in the antebellum era and beyond—greatly contributed to the notion of "dissemblance," under which "the behaviors and attitudes of Black women . . . created the appearance of openness and disclosure but actually shielded the truth of their inner lives."[65] Dissemblance also helps explain why primary sources by Black male journalists, scholars, and religious leaders are much more plentiful on the topic of lady lovers than those authored by Black women. While many of the intellectual women discussed in chapter 4 wrote and published extensively, queer desire was a topic they avoided mentioning in public, including in their published writing.[66] Therefore, undertaking queer African American women's history prior to the overlapping eras of gay liberation and Black feminism in the 1970s involves hypothesizing and filling in the blanks with possibilities, as these subjects so rarely spoke outright of their queer desires and relationships. By reading their sources against the grain, the relationships that professional Black women had with each other can become more visible, helping us understand how queer, socially "elite" women lived their lives both beyond and within respectability.[67]

In part due to painful historical legacies, Evelynn Hammonds noted thirty years ago, "the restrictive, repressive, and dangerous aspects of Black female sexuality have been emphasized by Black feminist writers while pleasure, exploration, and agency have gone under-analyzed."[68] Jennifer C. Nash has called for a turn to "ecstasy as a corrective to injury" in order to organize "around the paradoxes of pleasure rather than woundedness" and "possibilities rather than pain."[69] This book seeks to find these moments, when women wrote about each other in their diaries, danced together in speakeasies, flirted at bus stops and in theaters, and sang and listened to the blues women's stories of desire and heartbreak. Following this, I use the identity category of "lady lovers" both to ground my language in the historical terminology of the early twentieth century and to highlight that it was love that brought these women together, despite the wider cultural focus on their violence and jealousy.

The first chapter, "Woman Slain in Queer Love Brawl: The Violent Emergence of Lady Lovers in the 1920s Northern Black Press," argues that the Black queer woman was introduced to the northern public as an innately

criminal and immoral figure. The chapter focuses on newspaper articles about Black lady lovers in the Jazz Age against the backdrop of the
Great Migration. Multiple cases of "queer love brawls" between women
occurred among southern migrants and were written about sensationally
in the Black press. This chapter analyzes four such stories in New York
and Chicago, arguing that these narratives revealed the growing networks
of Black lady lovers and their private socializing to the greater public in
the 1920s. Sources such as Black nationalist newspapers and sociological
studies also offer further context and examples of how lady lovers were
depicted at the time by Black male authorities. The reported crimes always
took place exclusively between women, revealing that in the urban North
amid the Great Migration, women's queer relationships no longer existed
in isolation, as they had tended to in earlier decades. While such women
became associated with violence and immorality, I argue that read against
the grain, these articles introduced newspaper audiences to the emerging
world of Black lady lovers' social networks and gathering places, which
helped them continue to grow.

The second chapter, "The Famous Lady Lovers in the Early Twentieth-
Century Black Popular Entertainment Industry," focuses on the theatrical
world and its important role as a source of financial support for many Black
queer women, a meeting place for queer performers, and a site where
Black queer cultural representations were crafted. The chapter begins
with an overview of Black performing women in vaudeville before they
became recording artists, focusing on the dangers of touring in the South
and the difficulties in securing the first recordings of Black female singers
in a white-dominated music industry. Then I turn to the specific strategies
that Black lady lovers used to prosper in this industry, which, while employing many queer people, was still primarily run by heterosexual white
men. For example, popular singer Ethel Waters brought her girlfriend on
tour with her because her girlfriend was a dancer and Waters was able to
add her to her show. Other successful blues singers such as Bessie Smith
and Gertrude "Ma" Rainey purchased their own train cars, which allowed
them to avoid segregated Jim Crow seating while achieving privacy to enact
queer affairs with women in their shows. Performers attracted queer as
well as straight fans through their use of devices like double entendres,
which gave their songs multiple meanings for different audiences. This
chapter concludes with analysis of some of the explicitly queer recorded
songs that the industry allowed in this period, such as Rainey's "Prove it
on Me Blues." This 1928 song included themes that echoed the negative

newspaper representations of Black lady lovers as criminal and violent yet also inserted a first-person account of a masculine woman unashamed of her desires and her gender.

The third chapter, "A Freakish Party: Black Lady Lovers, Vice, and Space in the Prohibition Era Urban North," turns to the particular context of Prohibition and how the illicit spaces that opened up from 1920 to 1933 affected Black queer women and the formation of their networks. Using vice records from the New York–based organization the Committee of Fourteen, I examine the milieu of rent parties, speakeasies, and buffet flats, which were spaces serving illegal alcohol during Prohibition that often allowed same-sex and interracial dancing and flirtation along with live music, gambling, and sometimes commercial sex. I argue that the conflation of lady lovers with vice districts—which were a product of segregation and Progressive Era reform—was another reason that the larger Black community looked down on queer women at this time. Using the oral history of Harlem resident and lady lover Mabel Hampton, this chapter also demonstrates the importance of residential sites for Black queer women's gatherings and shows how single Black women and queer women were regulated by their communities and conflated with prostitution and criminality. Gladys Bentley is also an important figure here, as by the late 1920s she was one of the most popular performers in the speakeasy milieu, which catered to white slummers. The 1933 repeal of Prohibition changed the landscape of Black queer counterpublics, as many illicit spaces closed when the sale of alcohol became legal again. The advent of the Great Depression also furthered concerns about nontraditional gender norms and contributed to an increasingly hostile landscape for lady lovers, but Black women were nonetheless able to continue socializing in private.

The fourth chapter, "Intimate Friends and Bosom Companions: Middle-Class Black Lady Lovers Crafting Queer Kinship Networks," turns to a different setting to examine the experiences of queer women in interwar era "high society," focusing on women such as writer Dorothy West, author and activist Alice Dunbar-Nelson, heiress and arts patron A'Lelia Walker, and educator Lucy Diggs Slowe, the first dean of women at Howard University. These women were part of educated and artistic Black social circles in northern and mid-Atlantic cities such as New York, Boston, and Washington, DC, and they mingled with intellectual luminaries like anthropologist Zora Neale Hurston and writers Langston Hughes and Richard Wright. While Hurston was not known to have had any same-sex relationships herself, she ran in queer circles and formed close relationships with lady lovers such as Ethel Waters and Dorothy West.[70] As writers, artists, educators, and intellectuals involved in same-sex relationships, the women discussed in this chapter generally hid this aspect of their lives from work colleagues and the larger Black community. They kept their relationships as "open secrets" by not speaking of them publicly or as anything other than platonic. While it was often easier for more economically secure women like educator Lucy Diggs Slowe and writer Dorothy West to make a home with another woman, it still was not deemed socially acceptable, and women in queer relationships often faced resistance from authority figures despite their best efforts at dissemblance. Nevertheless, educators like Slowe opened up new opportunities to Black female college students, and West and Walker started important literary journals and salons that were crucial to the formation of Black queer intellectual networks.

This story of the famous lady lovers ends right before World War II, as that moment ushered in a new era in queer history and American life. The short conclusion focuses on the central issues raised in the book, from how Black lady lovers crafted new types of identities, families, and partnerships in the interwar era to the significance of their sexual agency and autonomy and their role as culture makers and leaders. By centering Black lady lovers as historical subjects, their cultural contributions to the Great Migration, Prohibition, and Great Depression eras come to the fore. This book reveals the courage of Black queer women from a century ago who actively crafted unconventional lives to suit their desires and, in doing so, influenced generations of women and American culture at large.

A NOTE ON TERMINOLOGY

Historians of sexuality agree that while same-sex behavior is not a modern phenomenon, our contemporary sexual identity categories are.[71] The growth in early twentieth-century terminology referring to women who loved women—from "lady lovers" to "bulldaggers"—reveals the increasing visibility of queer women, but newspapers and medical discourse often gestured more to the imaginary trope of "the lesbian" at a time when few women of any race self-identified as such. In this study, very few women referred to themselves with labels suggesting they saw themselves in a sexual identity category based on their desires. However, this may speak more to the codes of respectability that limited what educated Black women wrote about and to the small number of archival sources that allow Black lady lovers' inner worlds to be accessed.

The oral history of Mabel Hampton, who socialized almost exclusively with queer women in 1920s and 1930s New York, suggests that while various terms were used, many did not emerge until later decades. When Hampton was asked in the late twentieth century what she called lesbianism back in the 1920s, she responded, "I didn't call it anything but to say they liked women."[72] At the same time, in her recollections she referred to all-women parties where "the bulldykers would come and bring their women with them."[73] This shows that Hampton used the term "bulldyker" to refer specifically to masculine women, as was common at the time. However, vice reports from the 1920s also documented feminine women who referred to themselves as "bulldaggers," and Black performer Maud Russell claimed, "Lesbians weren't well accepted in show business, they were called bull dykers." She recalled, "Girls needed tenderness, so we had girl friendships, the famous lady lovers. . . . I guess we were bisexual, is what you could call it today."[74] "Lady lovers" was also used in the Black press interchangeably with "women lovers," and as this term was used in the urban North in the early twentieth century, in Black as well as in white circles, I use it whenever possible. This term is also important considering that Black women were rarely allowed the status of "lady" in American history, which was reserved for white women. While many of the women in this study had relationships with both men and women and were, as Russell noted, therefore "bisexual" in contemporary parlance, I rarely use this term since it was not utilized at the time. I refer to "lesbianism" throughout this study as the concept of women loving women and the act of building a life with a female partner, while "lesbian" is generally referred to as a trope in discourse, since few women in this time identified with the term.

Lastly, there is the complex term "queer," which first emerged in the 1930s to signify same-sex behavior and identity—as an act or a category—and was primarily used in a negative way, but some sources also show it was used as self-identification.[75] While "queer" is not a word that the women in this study used themselves, I have taken the liberty of using it throughout this study as a shorthand term for "women loving women" and "same-sex behavior." Since the advent of queer theory and queer studies in the early 1990s, "queer" has been used as an expansive, umbrella term that refers to both non-heteronormative behavior and resistance to respectability vis-à-vis "assimilation" into heteronormative life.[76] Aside from the issue of the terminology for individual historical subjects, there is also the question of how to view their group formations at this time.

I refer to queer or social "networks" instead of "communities" because, while same-sex desire was a commonality between some women at this time, it is not clear whether they truly saw it as a significant part of their identities or personalities.[77] As gay-identified Harlem Renaissance author Richard Bruce Nugent recalled, "Harlem was very much like [Greenwich] Village. People did what they wanted to do and with whom they wanted to do it. You didn't get on the rooftop and shout, 'I fucked my wife last night.' So why would you get on the roof and say 'I loved prick.' You didn't. You just did what you wanted to do."[78] Similarly for women, even those who made a life together in the 1920s and 1930s rarely spoke publicly about their partners in a romantic sense. And yet, by reading sources about them against the grain, the world of the "famous" (and infamous) lady lovers of the interwar era comes into view.

ONE

Woman Slain in Queer Love Brawl

～～～～～～～～～～～

The Violent Emergence of Lady Lovers in
the 1920s Northern Black Press

In 1926, the Black newspaper the *New York Age* published a front-page article with the graphic headline "Woman Rivals for Affection of Another Woman[,] Battles with Knives, and One Has Head Almost Severed from Body." The lengthy opening sentence read,

> Crazed with gin and a wild and unnatural infatuation for another woman, Reba Stobtoff, in whose Manhattan apartment her friends and acquaintances had gathered for a Saturday night rent party, grabbed a keen-edged bread knife and with one fell swoop, severed the jugular vein in the throat of Louise Wright after a fierce quarrel in which Reba had accused Louise of showing too much interest in a woman named Clara, known to underworld dwellers as "Big Ben," the name coming from her unusual size and from her inclination to ape the masculine in dress and manner, and particularly in her attention to other women.[1]

The article went on to note that "when the police arrived, only women were present, and it is said that no men had attended the affair."[2] This suggests that a full decade into the Great Migration, Black women who loved women had forged social networks in the urban North that allowed them to socialize without men. While gatherings like rent parties took place in residential apartments, an act of violence in such spaces could quickly bring a private event to the forefront of the community through a front-page story in the Black press.[3] Newspaper articles such as this one illustrated the double-bind of the Black middle class at this time: while stories about sex and violence were also popular fodder for white newspapers in the 1920s, the Black press carried the burden of not just reporting the news but setting aspirations and policing behavior as well. These newspaper stories often read like lurid dime novels, drawing the reader in and then moralizing over the subjects' deviant behavior.

The area in which this murder occurred, Columbus Hill—known as San Juan Hill before World War I—had rapidly become the largest Black neighborhood in Manhattan in the first decade of the twentieth century.[4] However, by 1920, practically every major Black institution had moved uptown to Harlem, and areas such as Columbus Hill had become "terrible rundown backwash communities" inhabited by poor and working-class African Americans who could not afford to pay the high prices charged by white realtors to Black renters in Harlem.[5] By 1923, Columbus Hill was considered the second-most crime-dense area of New York City.[6] Given this, a murder at a women-only gathering in Columbus Hill was not that unique, aside from its queer aspect, as similar articles about men who attacked or killed women out of jealousy, and vice versa, were regular features in both the Black and the white press during this era.[7] Newspapers in the 1920s specialized in attracting readers through provocative headlines, suggestive images, and shocking quotes. The site of the murder suggests that some of the participants were recent southern migrants, as the neighborhood was one of only three sections of Manhattan in which Black southerners were allowed to rent at the time.[8] "Old settler" Black journalists who grew up in the North were often the authors of such newspaper articles, and they critiqued what they perceived as the immoral leisure of recent southern migrants. Relationships between women were becoming a more visible disturbance in Black communities of the urban North, which the opening *New York Age* article described in vivid and sensationalistic language.

This chapter will examine newspaper articles in the Black press documenting acts of violence that allegedly took place between Black lady lovers throughout the 1920s. These cases will be further contextualized with other negative coverage of Black lady lovers by Black male authorities in this era of changing ideas of gender and sexuality. Indeed, not only journalists but also religious leaders and sociologists disseminated texts that depicted Black lady lovers as actively destroying northern urban Black communities. The chapter looks at the press's coverage of four cases—one attack and three homicides—concerning women only. While statistically speaking, these acts of violence made up a very small fraction of the murders in New York and Chicago throughout the decade, they nonetheless serve as important narratives describing the growing networks of African American women who loved women in the urban North at this time.[9] While two of the cases discussed can be traced through criminal records, the other two have not been located in official reports, and notably, none of the available criminal records specifically mention same-sex love as a motivation for the murders.[10] Regardless, representations of crime influence people's conceptions of their lives and communities quite out of proportion to actual occurrences of criminal activity.[11] Therefore, whether or not these acts of violence all actually occurred between Black women who loved women, they had a separate function as cultural texts. These articles thus helped shore up heterosexuality as the correct form of sexuality, through representing lesbianism as inherently violent, criminal, and immoral. Taken together, these documents reveal that in the 1920s, Black queer women constituted a new "type," one with established and growing social circles in the urban North.

While a handful of newspaper articles from the 1890s and early 1900s also discussed murders between women who loved women, there was one major difference: these earlier cases always involved love triangles between two women and a competing male suitor. An 1892 Memphis "lesbian love murder" involving young middle-class white women made national news when Alice Mitchell killed Freda Ward after Ward left Mitchell to marry a man. Several alleged "copycat" murders occurred in the wake of the Mitchell trial, one of which involved African American women, but most known similar cases involved white women.[12] While these pre-1920s murders show women struggling with the difficulties of desiring women in isolation from queer communities, the Jazz Age murders I will discuss reveal women negotiating life in newly emerging Black queer networks. The anonymity of northern cities created new opportunities for women to be together romantically, but they now had to compete with other women for partners.

While the Black press argued that queer desires were to blame for these acts of jealous violence, many of the women involved in these cases were in most ways just like their neighbors in Harlem, midtown Manhattan's Columbus Hill, and Chicago's Bronzeville: dealing with difficulties finding work; laboring long, hard hours for little pay; confronting the psychic toll of de facto segregation in the North; navigating overcrowded apartments and high rents; and dealing with problems caused by easy access to poorly made, highly intoxicating bootleg liquor during Prohibition.[13] Black women who were convicted of murder—of men or women—in the 1920s and 1930s had typically killed lovers or husbands in the heat of passion. Such deaths usually occurred during the course of drunken arguments or physical fights, in momentary explosions of rage or jealousy, or in reaction to domestic violence, so few of these attacks were premeditated.[14] Black sociologist E. Franklin Frazier saw such violence as indicative of the changing landscape wrought by the Great Migration. He wrote in 1928, "The mass which is being uprooted from the plantation system has been set adrift in a world without a moral order. . . . In the city where most primary group relations are dissolved we find illegitimacy and sex delinquency as indices of this lack of social control."[15] While female same-sex behavior represented a new "sex problem" to the Black community, at the same time it was also seen by elites as a symptom of the larger issue of "sex immorality" among recent southern migrants, which the old settlers of the northern Black press often railed against.[16] In this way, Black lady lovers' increasing visibility made them symbols of what many viewed as the growing deviance and excess of northern urban life.

Other sociological studies by E. Franklin Frazier examined northern Black districts in the Prohibition era and corroborated the criminal representations of lady lovers that the Black press circulated. His 1932 study, *The Negro Family in Chicago*, included a description of a "terrible" building in Bronzeville known for queer female tenants who gambled, fought, sold bootleg alcohol, and engaged in sex work. A young woman whose cousin had lived in this building recalled a time when two women said to be "homo-sexuals" "got to fighting and one pulled the other's clothes off." Notably, the interviewee used a different term, most likely the then-commonly used "bulldagger," which the publisher redacted and substituted with "female homo-sexual." At one point, the narrator recalled, "I tried to get her to tell me what a [female homo-sexual] was but she never did tell me," which suggests the concept was then deemed unspeakable to children. Frazier's interviewee also told him, "There was an old woman there who used to come up to my cousin's [apartment] and she said to me one day, 'Say, honey, when are you [com]ing up to my house [to] sleep with me?' She used to pat me down, and I turned around to her and one of the men in the house told her to let me alone[;] I was a little girl." Due to the reputation of the building's illicit goings-on, "police used to go up there and raid the place all the time." Frazier noted the young female narrator had learned about "abnormal" sexual matters, vice, and "demoralized behavior" in this building, which was located in a neighborhood that was home to "cabarets, pleasure gardens, gambling places, night clubs, hotels, and houses of prostitution."[17] Here, the "female homosexual" represented the chaos of southern migrant life in the North and the very worst problems plaguing the city in the Prohibition era.

Undergirding such negative representations of lady lovers disseminated by sociologists like Frazier and the Black press were similar messages from religious leaders.[18] Reverends Adam Clayton Powell Sr. and James M. Gates also wrote and even recorded sermons that spoke out against women who loved women and "mannish women" in this era. They put forth the idea that those who cared about racial uplift in the interwar era should view female homosexuality as a threat to the cause. As noted in the introduction, Powell gave a 1929 Harlem sermon that "centered upon the prevalence of sexual perversion and moral degeneracy," which, he declared, was "steadily increasing in all the large cities in the United States."[19] This sermon is particularly significant as it is the first known speech made specifically against queer people documented in the Black church. It served as a blueprint for the future, with some arguing that it initiated a vigorous campaign against homosexuality.[20] The *New York Age* noted that Powell's sermon brought him a slew of letters from people revealing their knowledge of "moral sex-perversion," "particularly with reference to some of the institutions of learning and of community welfare work attended by large numbers of girls and women."[21] The Black press also picked up the theme of predatory lesbians that Powell's sermon emphasized and ran with it.[22]

Reverend James M. Gates was from rural Georgia and preached in Atlanta for a decade before becoming nationally known by 1926, after spending a month of that summer on a New York City preaching tour. Gates went north specifically to record his sermons, after his first release for Columbia Records of an Atlanta sermon became successful.[23] In 1930, he recorded a sermon titled "Manish Women," in which he admonished modern women for trying to do everything men did. While his complaints seemed more concerned with women taking over men's jobs, an image accompanied the advertisement for his new single featuring a "mannish woman" in men's clothing, which raised the specter of lesbianism by 1930.[24] All of these negative depictions created by Black men in positions of authority provide further context for how the articles about violent Black lady lovers disseminated in the Black press were received by the public.

As the majority of the newspaper articles about Black queer women concentrated on their occasional violent acts, the dominant image that came to represent lady lovers in the urban North was that of a murderer—or a victim of one. The impossibility of Black women's relationships was further underscored through these representations in the Black press, and the pathological language of sexology that such texts often used just reinforced this idea. Notably, it was quite rare during the 1920s to come across similar articles about the violence of Black or white gay men or white women, which makes these sources involving Black lady lovers a unique site to explore.[25] Through their deft use of sexological theories, Black male journalists demonstrated their expertise in the latest scientific language while simultaneously using such discourse to moralize and distance themselves from the working-class southern migrants they singled out for taking part in such deviant behavior.[26] These articles were further informed by concerns over a proliferation of single migrant women, as well as by the popular ideology of Black nationalism, two issues that will give further context to the representations of violent Black lady lovers that will soon be discussed.

SINGLE BLACK WOMEN IN THE GREAT MIGRATION

Between 1910 and 1920, 1.5 million African Americans left rural southern areas for cities in the South, North, and West.[27] Chicago's Black population grew from some 44,000 to over 109,000 during this decade, while New York's grew from roughly 92,000 to more than 152,000.[28] These northern cities offered the hope of freedom and equal citizenship for southern African Americans who had been disappointed and disenfranchised by the failed promises of Reconstruction. The institutionalization of "separate but equal" segregation in 1896 under *Plessy v. Ferguson* and increasing rates of lynching, along with the rise of the Ku Klux Klan and racial violence and intimidation, provided further motivation to leave the South.[29] World War I also played a large role in this mass migration. As the military effort became American industries' priority, the Great War became central to all aspects of the domestic front. Immigration from Europe was shut down

at the same time that more factory workers were needed to make ammu-
nition and other supplies, which created even more of a need for southern
Black men to head North for industrial jobs, although Black women were
able to secure such work only temporarily in the case of drastic worker
shortages.[30] African Americans had already begun to move from rural
areas to southern cities to escape the exploitative sharecropping system,
yet in the urban South they still had to negotiate repressive Jim Crow
segregation laws and racial violence, which made the North look more
attractive. While these compounded factors "pushed" them away from the
South and "pulled" them toward the hope of opportunity and freedom in
the North, Isabel Wilkerson also emphasizes the agency of the migrants,
noting that the Great Migration was "the first mass act of independence
by a people who were in bondage in this country for far longer than they
have been free."[31] Indeed, the Great Migration was a case of mass voluntary
displacement.[32] However, many women who came north were soon disil-
lusioned by the combination of exploitatively high rents in the segregated
areas of the cities and limited work opportunities beyond domestic service.

Black women migrating north were not necessarily welcomed, either,
by white northerners or by the established Black old settlers of the middle
class. As Hazel Carby argues, migrating Black women were simultaneously viewed as threats to the progress of the race, to the establishment
of a respectable Black middle class, and to the formation of Black urban
masculinity.[33] Black newspapers' sensational reports of these murders
may have served as warnings to single Black female newcomers in northern cities, who were deemed an urban problem requiring intervention by
reformers. Their alleged sexual availability, it was feared, would lead to
disease, miscegenation, and prostitution. While many southern migrants
had friends or family in the North, whom they often first visited before
determining whether to move, the majority of Black women who left the
South for the North in the early twentieth century were single, divorced,
separated, or widowed.[34] Since Black women could usually find domestic
work in urban settings while Black men had a better chance of securing
agricultural work in more rural areas, uneven sex ratios soon emerged in
northern cities.[35] It was also difficult for new settlers to find work in Black-
owned businesses due to the biases of old settlers, who often saw recent
migrants as uneducated, lazy, and untrustworthy.[36]

Even before the Great Migration had begun, in 1906 Howard University
professor Kelly Miller wrote about the notion of "surplus women," contend-
ing that there was an "enormous preponderance of colored females over

males, especially in our large cities," which he saw as "perhaps the most striking phenomenon of the urban Negro population" since a "preponderance of one sex over the other forebodes nothing but evil to society."[37] Miller was concerned primarily with how these uneven demographics would lead "comely" women to be made into "the easy prey of the evil designs of both races." In the following decades, same-sex behavior and relationships would soon become another possible outcome of such unbalanced sex demographics.[38] It would not be until the 1920s that Black leaders would also speak of women treating one another as "easy prey," but how single Black women were perceived in the urban North and the lecherous influences they might encounter were of concern to reformers even before the Great Migration began, and this later intensified.[39]

Another reason that single Black women migrating north were focused on by reformers was that by World War I, vice districts in major cities were concentrated in the segregated areas also populated by African Americans. This occurred because Black southern migrants were often forced to live in "the sections of least desirability in the city," where "the disorganized condition" of neighborhoods "enabled white vice resorts to hide from law enforcement."[40] Vice industries now had a more difficult time operating in urban white neighborhoods because reformers' concerns in the 1910s over "white slavery"—prostitution and trafficking involving young white women—had led to increased surveillance and regulation of vice in white districts while leaving communities of color to fend for themselves.[41] In Chicago, as the South Side's Black population grew and spread southward, so too did commercial vice travel south "in consequence of the efforts at public suppression."[42]

It was thus that newly arriving single Black women were at a higher risk of falling into illegal activities than white women, as the latter had more choices over where to reside and work in a new city. The structural inequalities in these northern Black districts allowed such neighborhoods to emerge as central vice and leisure zones for burgeoning queer populations.[43] Therefore, it was in part the disenfranchisement suffered by African Americans in areas like Harlem that created the opportunity for "deviant" behaviors to flourish there. As journalist Edgar M. Grey noted in the *New York Amsterdam News* in 1927, "In the old days it was possible for many of the Negroes of the city to escape the contact and stigma" of vice districts, "but today this advantage of escape is not possible, for the colored population of the City of New York is almost canned up into a prescribed area—Harlem."[44] Similarly, a *Chicago Defender* journalist complained in 1920 that "police wink at crime and immorality in South Side cabarets" but took little action against the problem.[45] As a result, the Chicago Commission on Race Relations conducted a poll and found that white Chicagoans believed that "Negroes willingly tolerate vice and vicious conditions in the midst of their residential districts" and also, notably, that white people saw recent migrants from the South as "more likely to offend them than the Negro who has resided longer in the North."[46] Thus, the racialized geography of the urban North that de facto Jim Crow and the early Great Migration set into motion contributed to the Black press's concerns over female southern migrants' immorality.

BLACK NATIONALISM AND RACE SUICIDE

As sex for pleasure and not just reproduction became more socially acceptable in the early twentieth century, the use of birth control began to alter Black birth rates. Public support for birth control among African Americans was evident from the beginning of the fight for family planning in the 1910s. Due to advances in medical technology, social changes, and the influence of feminism, African Americans practiced and advocated for birth control in the early twentieth century in increasing numbers, which led Black birth rates to decline 50 percent from 1880 to 1940.[47] Many in the community were troubled by these decreasing birth numbers, which, along with fluctuating infant mortality rates and Black morbidity levels, all contributed to heightened concerns about the future of the race.[48] The rise of Black lady lovers' visibility was therefore seen by many as yet another obstacle to creating stronger Black families.

One channel where such concerns could be aired was the newspaper *Negro World*, the official organ of the immensely popular Black nationalist organization the Universal Negro Improvement Association led by Jamaican immigrant Marcus Garvey. At its peak in the early 1920s, the Garvey/Universal Negro Improvement Association movement was one of the most powerful Black organizations in the world, with more than 800 chapters on four continents and over 1 million members. Garveyism espoused the worldwide liberation and self-sufficiency of all people of the African diaspora and derived much of its support from the Black working class.[49] Garveyism emerged as a mass social movement in the United States in the post–World War I environment of Black radicalism and cultural revitalization, bolstered by the racial pride of Black soldiers returning from military service abroad.[50] Garveyism's proponents expressed particular concern over nonreproductive sexual practices in the Black community, especially regarding the increasing use of birth control and the emerging queer networks of the urban North.[51] The popularity of Garvey's masculinist ideology showed that it was not just the Black middle class that was concerned with respectability and traditional gender norms; working-class and immigrant communities also readily subscribed to such values.

Like many other masculinist nationalist movements, notions of racial destiny, gender hierarchy, and sexual comportment were entwined in the ideology of Black nationalism.[52] An important aspect of Garveyism was building strong families to sustain the future of the race, so the duty fell on women to take up maternal and wifely roles. Needless to say, lady lovers' nonreproductive relationships and behaviors were viewed as the antithesis of such an agenda.[53] Journalist John Houghton made this clear in a 1923 article in *Negro World*, where he singled out the ways that "some of the older women of the race" were "doing much to facilitate the plans of the white man that aim at the destruction of the Negro race."[54] Black women who loved women were taking part in behaviors that actively led to the downfall of the race, and further, Houghton suggested that such nefarious behavior was playing into the hands of white supremacists. This line of thinking precluded the possibility that Black lady lovers could ever align with racial uplift, progress, or liberation for African Americans.

In "The Plight of Our Race in Harlem, Brooklyn and New Jersey," Houghton focused on the urban North as a particular site in which these practices occurred, undergirding the argument that the Great Migration helped contribute to the spread of these "immoral practices." He discussed the machinations of lady lovers and their efforts to attract young women instead of the appropriate partner—Black men: "They have a way of discouraging the young girls, and endeavor to fill the places of the men," as "most of them prefer that they die maidens."[55] Here Houghton introduced another sinister trope commonly associated with women loving women: that of the devious, predatory older lesbian.[56] Houghton's reference to young women seduced by older women who nonetheless would still die as "maidens" was similar to the popular Freudian theory of his era that suggested lesbianism was an immature, stunted form of development and that only heterosexual relationships and sexuality permitted a girl to become a woman.[57] Houghton then sensationally emphasized that if these predatory older women seducing younger women were not stopped, they would "aid in" the "extinction" of the race "within a given period of time."[58]

The *Negro World* journalist's suggestion that Black women's desires for other women was a conspiracy spearheaded by white people spoke to another common misconception: that same-sex behavior was not natural to people of the African diaspora but was a European import foisted upon them by white people in a concerted effort to decrease their population.[59] This theory was also noted several years later in the *Pittsburgh Courier* by the Black newspaper's foreign correspondent J. A. Rogers. Discussing queer interracial relations in Africa, Rogers argued that white women in the United States, Europe, and Africa "teach the Negro women Lesbian practices entirely unknown to them before."[60] Rogers suggested that the very act of queer desire between women was not natural to his people and conflated same-sex behavior with a conscious aim to degenerate and weaken the race, which he saw as another type of violence borne out of lesbianism, along with women breaching their hallowed role as mothers.

The masculinist rhetoric of Black nationalism ostracized not only lady lovers but also all Black women who sought to prioritize their livelihoods over motherhood.[61] The murder cases we will turn to now occurred within this larger context in which nonreproductive sex was suspect, even before the trope of the violent lady lover appeared in the context of the urban North. At the same time, as birth control became more accessible and popular for women who had sex with men, reproductive sex was on the wane and sex for pleasure and recreation was becoming more common, which served to make heterosexual women and queer women more similar than different. Concerns over queer Black women's behaviors and their assumed predatory stance toward younger, innocent women now became a visible symptom of the larger changing landscape of urban sexuality in the early twentieth century. As Evelyn Higginbotham argues, "The politics of respectability equated nonconformity with the cause of racial inequality and injustice," and discussions in the Black press on the increasing visibility of Black women who loved women undergird this point.[62] Add to this a type of nonconformity that could potentially undermine the stability of the family and the race, and it became clear that Black lady lovers did indeed constitute a potent new "sex problem."

"WOMAN KILLS WOMAN FOR LOVE OF WOMAN"

Black Newspaper Coverage of Violence between Lady Lovers

In 1922, one of the first newspaper articles to discuss violence occurring within a group of queer African American women appeared in the northern Black press. The *Chicago Defender* ran a short front-page article concerning a "Women Only" party on the South Side that was raided by the police on Thanksgiving Day, when "the piercing screams of a woman had penetrated the street." After Barney Campbell "felt the knife blade" of Verna Scales, they were both placed under arrest and were later fined $100 each, along with the four other women present, whose names and addresses were all printed in the paper.[63] The six police officers on hand stated that there were often complaints registered by the neighbors against this house, "as the women who congregated there were those of an unusual type."[64]

While this particular gathering was broken up because of violence, past complaints against its members may have occurred merely because they were deemed odd, perhaps for their visible gender transgression, public affection, or predilection for socializing without men. In particular, their women-only Thanksgiving gathering pointed to their "unusualness," as such holidays were most often celebrated with biological kin, making their homosocial assembly appear more suspect. The newspaper's choice to include the names and addresses of the women in attendance—a common technique in the Black press when reporting neighborhood events—was potentially damaging to the reputations and livelihoods of the women involved. And by casting them as women of an "unusual type," the article ostracized them from the community, making them appear less sympathetic to the reader. Indeed, printing their names and addresses could have served as a form of community regulation, in which seemingly dangerous elements in the neighborhood were rooted out. Their addresses reveal that almost all of the women in attendance lived within a one-mile radius of each other in the heart of Bronzeville. Several of the party attendees lived on State Street, the central vein of the neighborhood, where masculine women could be seen strolling in men's boots, according to blues singer Gertrude "Ma" Rainey.[65] Indeed, such articles also inadvertently helped readers learn where such "unusual" women lived and socialized.

While the word "lesbian" was not yet used in the Black press to signify same-sex identity for women in 1922, the terminology of "an unusual type" not only highlighted the women's odd behavior but also implied that their whole being was suffused with a form of otherness. The article suggested that similar altercations were common at gatherings of such unconventional women. Yet, read against the grain, the text also revealed that Black women who loved women had created their own networks and were now fashioning their own counterpublics and rituals for major holidays in northern cities like Chicago. Although newspaper coverage of incidents of violence or romance between women had occurred sporadically in past decades, the prior events occurred among isolated same-sex couples and were not situated within larger homosocial groups or spaces such as this 1922 South Side gathering. So, through reporting on such acts of violence, Black newspapers such as the *Chicago Defender* began to document the emerging Black queer networks of the urban North. The appearance of these incidents amid the backdrop of the Jazz Age—when depictions of white and Black lady lovers in popular culture and medical discourse were growing—was met with concern and hostility by the Black press, which served as a mouthpiece for the larger Black community.

In 1926, another violent incident at a gathering of African American women was reported by Black journalists, this time in Columbus Hill, a Black neighborhood on Manhattan's West Side. This case—whose provocative narrative opened this chapter—received more coverage not only because it involved a fatality but also because it occurred during the run of the notorious Broadway play *The Captive*, which received considerable media attention for its discussion of lesbianism. This created an opportunity for Black male journalists to connect the murder in Columbus Hill to the growing discourse on lesbianism in dominant white culture, as according to some theater critics the play had illuminated the issue for the first time to many Americans.[66] *The Captive* was a French import written by Édouard Bourdet that told the story of a young married woman seduced by an older married woman. Both were white, feminine, and upper-class, which gave lesbianism a very different face from the one found in popular sexological literature of the time, which focused on the "primitiveness" of queerness.[67] *The Captive* helped make lesbianism appear more realistic—and therefore more threatening—to the white middle class. Many critics of the play remarked that the production was the first of its kind to broach a rarely mentioned subject.[68] One journalist wrote, "Lesbian love walked out onto a New York stage for the first time last night."[69] Historian Frederick Lewis Allen argued that the play "revealed to thousands of innocents the fact that the world contained such a phenomenon as homosexuality."[70]

As these reviews show, conceptions of modern lesbian identity were crystallizing in public understanding through art and media in the 1920s. Some theater critics tried to educate their audiences by explaining in their reviews of *The Captive* just exactly what a lesbian was. For example, a critic for the entertainment industry publication *Variety* began by noting that the most daring play of the season is *The Captive*. And one of the best written and acted in years. . . . *The Captive* is a homosexual story, and in this instance the abnormal sex attraction is of one woman for another. "Ladies" of this character are commonly referred to as Lesbians. Greenwich Village is full of them, but it is not a matter for household discussion or even mention. There are millions of women, sedate in nature, who never heard of a Lesbian, much less believing that such people exist. And many men, too. . . . It is something new for those who have never heard of the topic and naturally feminine curiosity will be aroused.[71]

As New Yorkers read about the play that brought the subject of lesbianism from the medical books to the Broadway stage, the Black newspaper the *New York Age* published the article that opened this chapter: "Woman Rivals for Affection of Another Woman[,] Battles with Knives, and One Has Head Almost Severed from Body." The article recounted a gin-fueled fight at a women-only rent party in which Reba Stobtoff attempted to decapitate Louise Wright for paying too much attention to a woman known as "Big Ben," whom both women desired.[72] This article put forth a representation of lesbianism that varied from the standard depiction of masculine, aggressive women and their passive, feminine partners. Most notably, "Big Ben," described as a "'man' woman," was not the aggressor but was the object of desire who inspired violence in other women. The article implicitly demonstrated that feminine women were now actively pursuing queer relationships. Such a notion was particularly disconcerting, for it meant that no one could necessarily know who was queer by their visible gender presentation and that masculine "bulldaggers" were not the only type of lady lovers.

The *New York Age* sought to connect this Columbus Hill murder to the plot of *The Captive* in an editorial two weeks later titled "A Rent Party Tragedy." The column began by noting the recent "tragic crime, in which one jealous woman cut the throat of another, because the two were rivals for the affections of a third woman." The editor pointed out that "the whole situation was on a par with the recent Broadway play, imported from Paris, although the underworld tragedy took place on Columbus Hill." That "the story of 'The Captive' should have found its parallel in this locality is a revelation of the fact that the frailties of human nature are much alike, whether in Paris or New York, regardless of complexions."[73] Unlike the discourse of white sexologists who often attempted to distance "civilized"

Europeans from homosexuality by associating it with more "primitive" cultures, here the Black editors of the *New York Age* sought to demonstrate how such "frailties of human nature" occurred among women of European as well as African ancestry. If this new sex problem was wreaking havoc on the Black community, the journalists surmised, at least it was something white women and their families were struggling with as well.

As the editors of the *New York Age* compared the murder of one African American woman by another to a European play in which no one died, they demonstrated the rhetorical violence that the specter of lesbianism conjured at this time. Though *The Captive* did not deal with actual violence, a woman leaving her husband for another woman and a woman killing another woman were perceived as equally tragic events. In the play, lesbianism was represented as a sickness powerful enough to overwhelm a young woman. In the end, after fighting against it, the younger female character surrenders to her desires; the final scene of the play shows her leaving her husband to be with her older female lover. While the Broadway play *The Captive* and the Columbus Hill murder of Louise Wright shared little resemblance, both 1926 New York events represented lesbianism as a potent and dangerous force that women—especially, young, feminine women—were powerless against.

In 1928, another murder involving African American women, this time in Chicago, was reported as motived by romantic jealousy. The front-page *Chicago Defender* headline, "Woman Slain in Queer Love Brawl," ran on the first of December, with the subheading "Bullets Stop Roomer Who Tried to Move." The article recounted the shooting of Mrs. Revonia Kennedy, a boarder in the Bronzeville home of Pearl Anchrum. A photo of Kennedy (fig. 1.1) was printed in the *Defender*, where she appeared stylish with bobbed hair, makeup, and jewelry. The photo's caption noted that Kennedy was shot by Anchrum, "with whom she had been living." But what did it mean for two women to share a home at this time? According to the *Defender*, Kennedy had announced to Anchrum that she would be moving out of her apartment, and in response Anchrum shot Kennedy in the legs while she "sat on a davenport in the dining room." Anchrum denied the charge and offered up a third woman, "Mrs. Azelia Leghorn," as the shooter. Both were arrested, but Kennedy and Leghorn each accused Anchrum of the crime. After Kennedy died from her wounds, the *Defender* noted that "further investigation by the police . . . revealed a strange love

SHOT TO DEATH—Mrs.
Revonia Kennedy, 32 years
old, was shot and killed by
Mrs. Pearl Anchrum, 4158
Prairie Ave., with whom she
had been living.
—Defender Photo.

Figure 1.1. Photograph of Revonia Kennedy.
Chicago Defender, December 1, 1928.

affair between the three women."[74] No further information was given in the press, and the police were never clear about exactly who was embroiled in this romantic relationship. Interestingly, all three of the women involved were married and referenced as "Mrs." No similar titles were used in the articles about other such cases. This suggests that the sexual subjectivities emerging in the urban North at this time were more complex than the binary terms "heterosexual" or "homosexual" can convey, as Black women took part in same-sex relationships despite their legal ties to men.

Census information reveals that Revonia Kennedy was a southern migrant, born Revonia Jones, in Franklin County, Tennessee, in 1897. Her parents, James, a day laborer, and Nora, who raised six children, were born at the end of the Civil War and were both able to read and write.[75] In 1918, at the age of twenty-one, Revonia Jones married Lawrence Kennedy in Chicago.[76] No other information about their marriage is available, nor are there extant divorce records, but Kennedy's death certificate lists her as single.[77] It describes her as fatally shot "by her landlady, Pearl Anchrum," during a quarrel. Anchrum was acquitted of all charges in the shooting of Kennedy, for reasons not stated. Born Pearl Cornell, she was a Missouri native who had married George Anchrum in Chicago in 1922.[78] It is not clear whether she and her husband both lived with Revonia Kennedy at the time of the murder, but by 1930 she was living with him on the South Side.[79]

Though the *Defender* provided no specifics, the newspaper defined the incident between the three women as a "strange love affair." A police statement, though brief, generated the paper's headline, "Woman Slain in Queer Love Brawl." The word "queer" still generally meant "odd" in 1928, though it was gradually becoming a reference to homosexuality. For example, an article that same year in the Black newspaper the *Pittsburgh Courier* reviewed a Los Angeles run of *The Captive*, commenting that "many 'queer' people from all over the world" lived in Los Angeles.[80] At the same time, two other stories in the Black press about "queer love triangles" from 1928 referred to a married man who had a female lover on the side and to a man having an affair with his sister-in-law, respectively. Therefore, by the late 1920s, "queer" events involved a range of departures from heterosexual monogamy, including but not limited to same-sex behaviors.

Also in 1928, the British author Radclyffe Hall's novel *The Well of Loneliness* appeared in American bookstores. Even more influential than *The Captive*, Hall's story centered on elite white women struggling with "abnormal" feelings, focusing on a self-proclaimed masculine "invert." While *The Captive* was written by a man and centered on married men's fears of losing their wives to other women, Radclyffe Hall in many ways fictionalized the story of her own life.[81] A sympathetic portrayal of female queer desire, the novel's short preface was written by sexologist Havelock Ellis, who validated the book's importance as a social, psychological, and cultural intervention. When the novel became the object of an obscenity trial in the United Kingdom and Hall was accused of corrupting minds "open to immoral influence," the publicity only further piqued American curiosity.[82] Not to be outdone, New York State and the United States Customs Service mounted their own obscenity trial of Hall's book, which eventually found the novel acceptable because it lacked sexually explicit passages.[83] Through such publicity and controversy, both *The Captive* and *The Well of Loneliness* increased common knowledge and interest in the topic of lesbianism in the 1920s.

While Radclyffe Hall's characters were privileged British women, her theme of lesbianism attracted the interest of some in New York's Black community. For example, in February 1929, Edgar M. Grey wrote an article on the topic for the Harlem-based *Inter-State Tattler* newspaper in the midst of the *Well of Loneliness* obscenity trial. "Are Women Lovers Harmful?" he asked his readers, while noting that a new book had been published on "the love affairs between two women" without naming the novel in question. The book's author, Grey continued, argued that women "addicted to the habit" of lesbianism are "victims of a condition growing out of certain 'pre-natal' influences over which they have no control." Grey added that he had "no quarrel" with this theory.[84] He then went on to list other experts who also subscribed to similar beliefs, including Sigmund Freud, Havelock Ellis, and Richard von Krafft-Ebing, yet notably while he spoke of "perversion among women" he never used the words "homosexuality" or "lesbianism." Grey demonstrated his cultural capital by citing European thinkers and medical theories but also distanced himself from the topic by expressing concern over the growing problem of "women lovers" in the Black community. His comments are worth quoting at length:

> We do not agree with the author when she attempts to account for
> the practice in *all* the cases of known perversion among women
> by the fact of a general assumption of prenatal circumstances. . . .
> Most of the women who are lady lovers developed the habit, either
> from association with persons who were addicted to the practice, or
> deliberately in search of a substitute for a man. The habit and prac-
> tices were developed either by imitation, or from a desire to explore
> some new sexual region in search of a thrill. In many cases, women
> who have been fooled by men revert to this habit of loving other
> women, in order to salve their feelings, and get even, as it were,
> with the sex of the man who had wronged them.[85]

Here, lesbianism is framed as a choice women make, often as a more positive alternative after negative experiences with men. Havelock Ellis had a similar theory that the women whom men "passed by" chose female partners because they were not attractive enough for normal heterosexual relations.[86] Notably, the idea that lesbianism was a nurturing choice for women had no similar corollary for gay men, further situating lesbian relationships as exercising female agency during a time of changing ideas of gender and sexuality.

Nevertheless, Edgar Grey's argument that it was common for lady lovers to "develop the habit" presented a problem for the Black community. Understanding this, he declared himself ready to expose and discuss this "sex problem": married men must protect their wives and daughters from "this practice," opposing "this class of perverts to the bitter end." After all, the "sex function" was "devised by Nature for the purpose of procreation" so that "the race of mankind should live on." Thus, anything that interfered with procreation "is a matter which society should stamp out." He added that nothing less than the future of mankind was at stake. Grey then turned to the question of how the problem had affected the local Black community: "The most terrible consequences have grown out of women lovers in Harlem. We have seen more than five murders in the year 1928, which grew directly out of this practice between a single woman and a married woman. Men cannot approve of this practice; women cannot approve of this practice; society cannot approve of this practice." Love between women led to murder. No longer was it necessary to summon the decades-old 1892 Memphis murder of Freda Ward by Alice Mitchell to illustrate this; Harlem's Black community was allegedly now a site where such tragedies regularly occurred among "this class of perverts."[87]

———〰〰〰〰———

Edgar Grey's reference to five murders in Harlem was not detailed, but one such 1928 case was well documented in the press. In this year, Harlem began to surpass the Bowery as the site of the most Manhattan murders, which was particularly concerning as the latter downtown district had a long-standing reputation for crime and vice.[88] The *New York Amsterdam News* reported that of the thirty-four homicides occurring in Harlem in the first six months of 1928, half occurred among Black people and half among white people. Of the former, one took place between two women. The paper recounted, "Edna Washington, 25, [was] stabbed to death at 38 West 136th Street on June 19th. Alberta Mitchell, said to have been the dead woman's 'woman lover,' was indicted yesterday by the Grand Jury on a charge of homicide following her alleged confession."[89] Although Grey stated that at least five such murders had occurred in Harlem in 1928 alone, no other similar cases were covered in the Black press that year in New York. Washington's death can be traced at the New York Municipal Archives, as can the trial of Alberta Mitchell, and notably, there is no mention in any of the official records of love between women; only newspapers discussed this angle of the murder.

The case of Alberta Mitchell and Edna Washington was well covered in the Black press not only locally but also in other northeast and midwestern cities. However, the initial coverage of the murder did not suggest that queer desire played any role in the attack. A *New York Age* article first ran with the headline "Woman Stabbed to Death, Man and Woman Held." The story stated that "Mrs. Washington was separated from her husband" and that Alberta Mitchell and Beatrice R. Irvin were both arrested and charged with homicide after "quarrelling over the affections of the man," which resulted in Edna Washington being "stabbed to death with a small dirk."[90] An even shorter article on the murder ran in the newspaper the *Brooklyn Eagle*, which was the only mention of any of these murders in the white press. Again, the text did not mention anything about a relationship or jealousy between women over another woman; the headline "Negress Stabbed to Death" was followed by two sentences about Washington's murder and the questioning of Mitchell and "Rae Irvis," whose name was spelled differently in every article about the case.[91] However, this story was not even provocative enough to warrant front-page coverage; the short article was buried in the back of both newspapers. The murder did not garner front-page headlines until it was revealed that it concerned an all-female love triangle.

One week later, a front-page article in the *New York Amsterdam News* blared the awkward headline "Woman Kills Woman for Love of Woman." The article began, "A death struggle between two women for the love of another woman brought into the spotlight recently a condition, the police say, which is all too prevalent in this community."[92] While this case received scant coverage when it was presumably about a heterosexual couple, once the story became queer, newspapers moralized over what they saw as a growing problem. Washington and her confessed killer, Mitchell, were both in their mid-twenties and lived together at the same address on West 136th Street in Harlem. The article stated that "their object of affection was said to be Beatrice Ray Arvis," who was also in her mid-twenties and living in Harlem. It is not clear whether the roommates were a couple and Washington also desired Arvis, or whether the two were friends who both were involved with or romantically interested in Arvis. Considering that the police were positive that same-sex desire was a key to the case, it is odd that reporters did not give more details. Since Mitchell also accused Arvis of killing Washington, perhaps Washington desired Arvis and Mitchell desired Washington. There is not enough information to make it clear whether Mitchell killed her lover or her rival.

The article also noted that their neighbors "Zena Tate and Emma Barrett, both of 36 West 136th Street, called at the house and learned of the tragedy" and went on to call the police, which suggests that Tate and Barrett may have also been a couple who were part of their social network. When police arrived, "the windows were broken, furniture smashed, dishes dashed to bits and everything" was "in a state of general disorder." The murder and the description of how their home was "completely wrecked by the death struggle" imply both the dangers as well as the impossibilities of queer relationships and homemaking. This case became national news in the Black press; the *Indianapolis Recorder* ran the same story from the *New York Amsterdam News* in early July with the headline "Women Love Woman, One Kills Rival."[93] This suggested that Mitchell and Washington both desired Arvis and that Mitchell killed Washington to remove her competition.

Several months later the case went to trial, and Alberta Mitchell was found guilty of manslaughter. The *New York Amsterdam News* declared that Mitchell would serve time for killing her "'mate' who proved faithless." The article began dramatically by noting that this verdict was "the final chapter in the tale of an eternal triangle—this time one in which the lovers were women" and went on to state that "in a jealous rage because of the abnormal attentions paid by Edna Washington . . . to Beatrice Ray Arvis," Mitchell "buried a knife blade in her 'lover's' neck June 19 and left her cold in a pool of blood."[94] The *Pittsburgh Courier* also covered the outcome with an article blaring the large headline "Woman Gets Manslaughter Verdict in 'Queer Love' Case." The subheadings of the *Courier* article stated, "Sordid Affair Bared" and "Alberta Mitchell Found Guilty of Slaying Girl of Whom She Was Jealous." The *Courier* reporter described Mitchell as "insanely jealous of the attentions paid Beatrice Ray Arvis" by "her friend, Miss Washington."[95] The *New York Amsterdam News* reported that "perverted affection for Edna Washington, 25, who lives with her, is believed to have caused Miss Mitchell to kill her roommate."[96] For the murder of Washington, Mitchell was sentenced to four to eight years in Auburn State Prison for Women in upstate New York.[97]

Notably, most of these articles tell a different story about who loved whom. Did Mitchell kill Washington because she loved her, or because she was jealous of her? Or both? Were they mere roommates, or lovers? The private sphere, long associated with women, could function as a site for homosocial as well as homosexual behavior, and these articles underscore the confusion over the ambiguity of what it meant for two women to share a home in the Jazz Age. The high rents of Harlem and Bronzeville led to the creation of various living situations, from the establishment of boardinghouses to renting rooms out of one's home, that straddled the lines between public and private space. "Opposite sex" guests were often not allowed in boardinghouses as a safety measure against boarders using their rooms for sex work or other illegal activities.[98] However, female boarders could still invite one another over, as laws based on ideologies of respectability often overlooked the possibility of queerness and even created space for it to flourish. And yet at the same time, women-only gatherings on holidays were still deemed "unusual" by police and journalists.

The discrepancies in the various accounts of the Washington murder expose the confusion of reporters and detectives as they came to grips with the newly emerging types of living arrangements and relationships that Black women were now practicing. The differing accounts in the press over who killed whom and why reveal the inscrutability of female romantic relationships and male journalists' inept understandings of how such relationships functioned without the difference of sex. And yet, it is also possible that queer desire was not at the heart of some, or any, of these cases and the journalists simply utilized the growing popular interest in lesbianism, and its implicit connection to violence, to entice their readers and sell newspapers. However, such a hypothesis puts the journalistic integrity of the Black press into question, which is problematic as well. Editors' use of terms such as "mate" and "lover" in quotes shows that journalists did not want to suggest that these relationships paralleled heterosexual relationships, hence the "perverted affection," "insane jealousy," and "jealous rage" of these women that contributed to the violent outcomes of their story. Needless to say, similar stories in the Black press about men who killed their female partners, or vice versa, rarely relied on terminology from sexology that suggested the perpetrators were pathological, though this epistemological leap was usually made when discussing such murders between women.

Through state records such as death certificates and census reports, it is possible to construct more of the details surrounding Edna Washington and Alberta Mitchell. Washington was twenty-four years old when she died, and while one newspaper article referred to her as separated from her husband, she is listed as "widowed" on her death certificate.[99] Both she and Mitchell worked as domestics, which was the most common occupation for Black women in the urban North at this time.[100] According to extant records from the murder trial, Mitchell had only lived at 38 West 136th Street with Edna Washington for five weeks before the murder occurred, while Washington had lived in New York for four years before her death. The 1930 census listed Alberta Mitchell, born in Tennessee, as an inmate at Auburn State Prison for Women in upstate New York, where she worked as a laundress, and also as divorced. So while Mitchell was indeed a southern migrant, Washington may have been one as well, for she was not born in New York either, although it is not possible to ascertain where she was from originally.[101] As the census information and death certificate reveal that both women were married to men at one point, this case further demonstrates that Black women in the urban North who took part in queer relationships also had relationships with men. At the same time, the knowledge of their marriages and the lack of explicit mention in the official reports of the queer aspect of the murder suggest two things: either such discourse was not acceptable in regard to women in official state documentation, or the queer angle of the murder was fictionalized or sensationalized in the Black press in light of the established trope of the "murderous woman lover" to sell newspapers.

~~~~~~~~~~~~~~~~

Taken together, these multiple articles in the Black press demonstrate that the discourse on African American lady lovers and their emerging networks in the urban North primarily depicted such women as violent, jealous criminals capable of homicide. These articles served several purposes: They conflated Black queer women with rhetorical violence against the Black family in a time when decreasing birth rates and the popular Black nationalist movement raised concerns about the future of the race. They further stigmatized southern migrants as unruly and immoral during the Great Migration, as northern racial demographics were shifting. And lastly, they warned the Black community about the increasing visibility and prevalence of this "condition." At the same time, coverage in both the white and Black press of the play *The Captive* and the novel *The Well of Loneliness* demonstrated that not only Black women were now romantically involved with other women. However, these popular 1920s depictions of white lesbians did not feature violence the way articles in the Black press did throughout the decade. Therefore, Black queer women specifically emerged as violent subjects who needed various forms of policing in the Jazz Age.

What these newspaper articles do not reveal is the actual voices of the women involved, who are very rarely quoted. The articles do not describe how the women identified themselves or their relationships, nor do they offer many details about the women's lives outside of the acts of violence that made them newsworthy. Nonetheless, certain facts can be extrapolated from them: Black women gathered and celebrated together in their leisure time without men in New York and Chicago in the 1920s. Increased violence occurred during Prohibition, often due to the unregulated and illicit nature of potent bootleg liquor, which was a likely underlying yet rarely addressed factor in these murders.[102] Women lived together as friends, roommates, and lovers in Harlem and Bronzeville apartments and boardinghouses by the 1920s. Significantly, these articles reveal that Black women who loved women no longer did so in isolation from each other but had begun to form social groups with others who also shared their desires, and this led to increased competition for partners. Above all, these articles show that Black male journalists, the primary authors of these texts, were troubled by the growing queer presence in Black communities of the urban North.

A dearth of similar articles about Black queer men or white women and violence in the interwar era situates these subjects uniquely, suggesting that Black queer women embodied a specific threat in the urban North at this time. The work of sociologists like E. Franklin Frazier underscored this idea. Suffice to say, the majority of African American women who loved women in the 1920s did not enact violence toward their rivals. The following chapters primarily detail the connections and support that Black lady lovers offered each other, yet these newspaper articles provide an important window into how this new type of woman was represented in the Black press. The articles that this chapter has focused on demonstrate that by the late 1920s, there was an oft-utilized trope depicting Black women who loved women as violent and criminal, which did the cultural work of separating such subjects from the realm of the respectable and moral. Yet at the same time, read against the grain, these articles reveal that the Great Migration had brought an influx of women who loved women to the urban North, and these networks of Black lady lovers were crafting new forms of relationships. While the Black press sought to show the impossibility of such a life for women and the irreparable harm their actions could bring about, Black lady lovers kept finding one another, despite the growing social prescriptions against queer behavior.

TWO

The Famous Lady Lovers in the Early Twentieth-Century Black Popular Entertainment Industry

~~~~~~~~~~~~~~~

In 1926, singer Bessie Smith, known as the "Empress of the Blues," was one of the most successful Black performers and recording artists in the United States.[1] While touring regularly through the North and South, she had intimate liaisons with her fellow female performers that she hid from her husband, who served as her manager.[2] At this time, Smith was having an affair with Lillian Simpson, a dancer in her show, and an incident between the two women reveals the larger tensions over the acceptability of lady lovers in the theatrical world, as well as their prevalence. When Simpson refused to kiss Smith backstage in the theater where they were performing, the Empress of the Blues threatened her lover by bragging, "I got twelve women on this show and I can have one every night if I want it!"[3] While this bold statement may not have been completely truthful, it was likely that multiple women on Smith's show were taking part in queer affairs. The touring circuits of the Black popular entertainment industry, which were bolstered by the successful recording careers of women such as Smith, helped to constitute a queer network in one of the few industries offering Black working-class women alternative forms of labor to domestic work.

By 1929, such queer networks were becoming visible to the men who ran the entertainment industry, and they began to rail against the growing presence of lesbianism in the urban North. That year, for example, pioneering Black theater producer and critic Salem Tutt Whitney penned a column for the *New York Amsterdam News* that said that all queer women working in theater should be fired. Whitney declared, "I have been informed that several performers who are now employed will soon be without their jobs because of transgressions they have committed. . . . The edict has gone forth that the Lesbians must go. . . . There can be no reasonable excuse set forth in defense of the Lesbian."[4] Whitney's use of the word "lesbian" to connote women who loved women is especially noteworthy, as this was one of the earliest appearances of the term in the Black press.[5] Performing women were now acting boldly on their queer desires and crafting new relationships that suited their needs. Male theater producers like Whitney found such behaviors "abnormal" and "reprehensible."[6]

This chapter examines the experiences of Black queer performing women in the segregated American entertainment industries of the early twentieth century. The boundary-breaking, overt sexuality of the classic blues women and the emergence of queer interwar urban subcultures and entertainments have been written about extensively.[7] However, rarely has the focus been on the experiences of Black queer women in the entertainment industry and their overall significance in this regard. This chapter looks at how classic blues women and other Black queer performers navigated the industry and created new forms of popular culture. It focuses on the strategies they used to carry out relationships with other women in the industry and to negotiate their queerness on stage and through song. I argue that this expanding set of industries furthered the emergence of Black queer women's networks in two crucial ways: first, through the workplace of the theater, which functioned as a meeting space for performing lady lovers, and second, through their live performances and the dissemination of phonograph records and advertisements that broached queer topics, sometimes subtly and at other times more boldly.

The chapter begins with an examination of touring Black vaudeville troupes and the entrance of Black women into the "race records" industry that took off in 1920 and then looks at the larger place of Black queer women in the theatrical world of the interwar era. The next three sections of the chapter look at the strategies that individual performers used to forge queer connections and navigate and perform their desires: singer Ethel Waters toured with her girlfriend, the dancer Ethel Williams, by her side in the early 1920s. Though Waters's employer, Black Swan Records, sought to represent her as highly desirable to men, the "two Ethels'" relationship was not a secret to many in the industry. I then discuss the queer songs of Gertrude "Ma" Rainey, particularly the lyrics and advertisement of the 1928 record "Prove It on Me Blues," which teased audiences with the possibility of Rainey's desires for women. Then I turn to her younger mentee, Bessie Smith, who pursued relationships on the road with women in her troupe that she hid from her manager-husband. Taken together, this chapter demonstrates how Black queer performing women negotiated their desires and relationships on the road in an era when queerness was still deeply pathologized, despite its increasing visibility in urban culture and prevalence in the entertainment world.

BLACK PERFORMING WOMEN BEFORE THE RECORDED BLUES

In the early 1920s, many Black female performers were "discovered" by the northern, white-run recording industry and became celebrities for a new era. However, most of them had already been performing and touring in Black vaudeville revues for a decade or more. At the turn of the century, southern Black traveling revues were a hybrid of minstrel and vaudeville shows, many of which performed not in theaters but outside under canvas tents. These temporary "tent shows," as they became known, featured singers, comedians, chorus girls, and often female and male impersonators, with many performers taking up multiple roles in any given show.[8] Outside major southern cities, big tent shows could hold huge crowds of up to 5,000 people.

Notably, while white vaudevillians usually performed and toured as solo acts, duets, or quartets, in this era most Black vaudevillians performed in large revues. As most Black theaters were in the Jim Crow South, traveling in large groups created safety in numbers for Black performers; it was also cheaper to travel as a unit.[9] Even though tent shows were temporary spaces, they nonetheless often contained segregated audiences; in 1917, the state of South Carolina went as far as to legally require separate entrances at tent shows for white and Black attendees.[10] In 1914, an African American touring troupe, Alexander Tolliver's Smart Set, began to gain notoriety for its talented artists who combined minstrelsy, blues, and early jazz in their performances. The most important performer to use this show as a springboard to greater fame was singer Gertrude "Ma" Rainey, who first came to prominence in Tolliver's Smart Set along with her then-husband,

William "Pa" Rainey, whom she married as a teenager. Together they were known as the "Assassinators of the Blues."[11] Beginning at the dawn of the twentieth century, Ma Rainey worked with multiple Black-run shows like the Rabbit Foot Minstrels and eventually formed her own troupe to travel through the South.

Traveling vaudeville and minstrel shows brought new musical forms, such as ragtime, blues, and jazz, to Black and white audiences in the South as well as in the North. Women such as Rainey and Bessie Smith became known as performers of the "classic blues," a style grounded in folk blues and the minstrel show tradition that extended back to the nineteenth century.[12] Rainey's style was more "down home" and less sophisticated than Bessie Smith's became by the 1920s; Rainey was often accompanied by a jug band, while Smith preferred backing from performers such as Louis Armstrong who were more associated with urbane polish.[13] The classic blues was a genre sometimes referred to as "vaudeville blues" since singers drew on the stylistic exaggeration, comedic timing, and extravagant costumes and accessories that performers cultivated on the southern vaudeville stage throughout the 1910s.[14] The classic blues allowed white audiences a glimpse into Black culture far less obscured by white expectations and offered Black listeners an important affirmation of their cultural identity in the Jim Crow era.[15]

Popular entertainment by and for African Americans had become more in demand since the turn of the century, yet a vaudeville circuit specifically for Black performers and actors did not emerge until 1921, with the creation of the Theater Owners' Booking Association (TOBA).[16] The emergence of TOBA represented a politicization of Black theater owners and producers as well, since the association was founded to ward off impending disaster to the "colored theatrical industry," which was "threatened by the gross mismanagement and unfair dealings of the booking agents" who controlled the industry.[17] While this association of theater owners did not have Black members only, the others were usually of "decidedly ethnic origins," including Italians and Jews.[18] TOBA shows contained a variety of acts, from dancers and comedians to ventriloquists, and usually featured a headlining female blues singer performing with a large band. Headlining acts that were always popular on the TOBA circuit throughout the 1920s included Ma Rainey—who was known for hawking her own records in the lobby after the show—as well as Bessie Smith, the Whitman Sisters, and husband-and-wife singing comedy team Butterbeans and Susie, among others.[19]

The TOBA circuit was infamous for its poor work conditions: artists performed in run-down theaters that sometimes lacked backstage areas and restrooms, and they were often verbally abused by white theater managers, who paid them as little as possible.[20] All of these inadequacies helped the association earn the nickname "Tough on Black Asses."[21] Blues singer Alberta Hunter refused to play on the southern TOBA circuit and greatly preferred to perform in the North.[22] And when highly successful singers such as Bessie Smith and Ma Rainey, who were more popular in the South than in the North, purchased private tour buses and train cars, this was in part a tactic to avoid the segregated southern transportation system.[23] During a 1922 southern tour, several of singer Ethel Waters's backup musicians abandoned her due to their unwillingness to put up with racist treatment in the South.[24] One of her musicians later recalled, "You went South at the risk of your life. . . . You weren't even treated as a human being."[25] Indeed, Waters recalled that on this tour she performed in a Macon, Georgia, theater where a young Black man's lifeless body had recently been thrown after he was lynched for allegedly talking back to a white man.[26] Bessie Smith's biographer even describes an evening in 1927 North Carolina where she and her troupe had to chase the Ku Klux Klan away from her tent show.[27] While Black women in the entertainment industry could avoid the indignities of domestic service, they still encountered discrimination, poor working conditions, and the threat of racial violence when performing in the South. The commercial success of the classic blues women's recorded songs throughout the 1920s meant they were in greater demand than ever to bring their show on the road—and therefore would be facing such challenges head-on.

By 1905, record players had become common household items, yet throughout the 1910s the white-dominated record industry recorded early blues songs sung only by white women like Marion Harris.[28] W. C. Handy, known as the "Father of the Blues," said that Harris sang blues songs so well that people hearing her records sometimes thought she "was colored."[29] It would not be until 1920 that a blues song sung by an African American woman would be recorded. Although "authentic" blues were associated with southern Black culture, record executives mistakenly assumed there was not a large enough Black audience who owned phonographs to buy such records, nor would white consumers be interesting in purchasing them. This dearth of blues recordings by African

Americans did not change until World War I, when Black participation in the war effort led to an increased racial consciousness and injected more discourse on racial inequities into the national conversation. Thus, in 1916, the *Chicago Defender* launched a campaign to get a Black woman to record popular songs for a major white record label, while simultaneously Black songwriter Perry Bradshaw approached record companies with a similar proposition.[30]

The year 1920 is now regarded as the year when the recorded blues industry exploded, with the groundswell of interest in Black singer and vaudeville performer Mamie Smith's immensely popular Okeh record "Crazy Blues."[31] With this release, the floodgates broke: white male record executives now realized there was indeed a consumer market for "authentic" blues records, and many northern companies hired Black talent scouts to head south and find other female blues singers to sign to their new "race records" labels. And so, beginning in the early 1920s, women such as Ma Rainey, Bessie Smith, Ethel Waters, and Alberta Hunter, all seasoned performers and veterans of the road from years of singing in tent shows, small theaters, and cabarets, went on to become highly successful recording artists. Throughout their fame in the Jazz Age, the classic blues women were singing, recording, and performing queer songs that introduced and interjected Black queer culture into the American consciousness. As these performers navigated queer relationships during their stardom, they helped to craft new subcultures and possibilities for all modern Black women.

BLACK QUEER WOMEN IN THE POPULAR ENTERTAINMENT INDUSTRY

While queer people have long taken solace from a homophobic world in the theater, the role of performance in the lives of Black queer women specifically has rarely come into historical focus.[32] The entertainment industry has played a significant part in the creation of queer networks and communities. As theater scholars have long maintained, this world was a "haven for homosexuality" as well as for the formation of dissident sexual identities.[33] Further, urban show business circles in the interwar era supported a "vast range of lesbian-leaning women."[34] By the 1930s, male journalists such as Black theater critic Ralph Matthews saw lady lovers as an infiltrating queer presence in the Black entertainment industry and wrote regularly about this new social problem. In particular, Matthews was concerned about innocent young southern migrant women being seduced by experienced, hardened, masculine female performers in the big city.[35]

In 1933, Ralph Matthews published an exposé on the "depraved" lives of Black performers in New York, titled "Love Laughs at Life in Harlem" with the subheading "Savage Romances Suffer No Depression as Queer Attachments Keep Show Folks Chuckling. Women Love Women and Men Love Men, and Occasionally the Jig Saw of Sex Gets Mixed." Matthews began by suggesting that "theatrical and night club performers" were "a very peculiar lot." It was their "home life, if you can call it that," that he disapproved of, for while "ordinary folk" were mostly respectable, everything about performers' lives made them different: their "irregular" work hours, their "morals," and especially their love lives.[36] Matthews declared that same-sex romance in Harlem sometimes took on "the aspect of freakishness" yet was "so common" and came in so "many queer forms that Harlem merely winks and passes on[,] accepting them for what they are." Even more disturbing, he continued, was that "the most violent attachments are those between women. Young girls newly inducted into show life may find themselves face to face with the grim and revolutionary problems of being squired with all the artfulness of a male admirer by their dancing partners in the chorus." Matthews depicted "attachments" between women as "violent" without giving any examples, suggesting that the contemporary discourse on murderous lesbian love triangles had influenced him.[37] The figure of the predatory lesbian that Matthews described was threatening, even in chorus girl form, because she usurped a traditional male privilege. Her presence meant that heterosexual men would now have to compete with both women and men for young female companions who were new to the entertainment industry.

Biographies and oral histories of performing women offer a more realistic picture of the contours of the queer networks that ran through the chorus lines of the Black popular entertainment industry. Ruby Walker, Bessie Smith's niece, recounted a story in Smith's biography that suggests some female performers adapted quite easily to queer relationships as they experimented in this new environment where such behavior was common. One of Bessie Smith's lovers in the 1920s, dancer Lillian Simpson, had never been with a woman before she was seduced by Smith, yet soon she was encouraging her friend Ruby Walker to "try it" herself. Simpson suggested that Walker connect with the wife of the musical director of their current show, despite the fact that Ruby only "liked boys."[38] Her story shows that sexuality in the Black entertainment industry was more fluid than the heterosexual/homosexual binary and monogamous marital relations would allow. Such ambiguity made the performance world even more transgressive, with its social codes that threatened the boundaries of respectable and appropriate behavior, yet it also created new opportunities for Black women to take part in relationships that were suited to their specific desires.

While there are few sources that describe live performances by queer blues singers, sexology case studies of some other Black queer masculine performers offer some ideas of what some of these events were like.[39] From 1935 to 1941, the New York–based Committee for the Study of Sex Variants, led by Dr. George Henry, interviewed eighty "sexually maladjusted" men and women and then published the case studies, which were intended for a medical—not a popular—audience. Several of the case studies focused on Black queer performers. The recollections of "Marian J." and "Myrtle K." in the published *Sex Variants* study suggest that white women in the audiences flirted with, touched, and propositioned such performers regularly. When she was younger, the masculine singer Marian J. "was very slender and wore a cowboy costume" and "could hardly get off the stage at times." She explained, "Women are just attracted by my voice. It has an exceptionally heavy quality and a wide range. I've always swayed my audiences by it. Last night a married woman who has been promiscuous with men called me after she had heard me sing. She said that with three weeks at a beautiful place with me she wouldn't be crazy about anyone else. She said she never had a woman before. I told her to forget about it."[40] Similarly, vaudevillian Myrtle K., a noted "tomboy," declared, "I'm pursued more by white women than by colored women. I had to resign from a club because of this." She also admitted, "I never got in trouble about sex except three years ago," when "I was working in the Village and they said I was conducting indecent dancing. The case was dismissed."[41]

These examples show that slumming nights out and seducing Black performers were not the province only of white men but of white women as well. The aggressive reactions of white female audience members to these masculine Black queer performers are also reminiscent of the interracial relationships between girls and women in reformatories and prisons in the early twentieth century. Experiencing desires that transgressed social norms of both race and sexuality was intensely emotional for many women at this time. While interracial queer relationships were not common in this era of racial segregation, liminal spaces like reform schools and performances gave women opportunities to experience such desires.

However, the racial politics of the Jim Crow era emboldened slumming white women to objectify and make a spectacle of Black women, as Prohibition era performances suggest. This makes Gladys Bentley's alleged marriage to a white woman appear even more notable, as such attempts to legitimate queer interracial relationships in this era were quite rare.

As to why the entertainment world was filled with so much queer activity in the first place, performer Maud Russell had her own theory: "Often we girls would share a room because of the cost. Well, many of us had been kind of abused by producers, directors, leading men—if they liked girls. In those days, men only wanted what they wanted, they didn't care about pleasing a girl. And girls needed tenderness, so we had girl friendships, the famous lady lovers, but lesbians weren't well accepted in show business."[42] Russell's reminiscences underscore the fact that affairs between women were common in this milieu, but she also implied that they occurred among women who may have preferred men but turned to the same sex to escape violence and neglect in heterosexual relationships. She even boldly suggested that many powerful men in the industry were queer themselves. Russell also claimed that men's sexual skills were not focused enough on pleasing female partners in this era and that women took a great deal more care with their female lovers than men did. While these may have been romanticized ideas about relationships between women, they nonetheless piqued the curiosity of many female performers. While Russell was interviewed in the 1980s about the interwar era, the recollections of her experiences are nonetheless similar to those of other women of the time.

Similarly, former chorus girl Mabel Hampton also confirmed that the men in the entertainment industry constantly pressured their female co-workers into sexual liaisons. "They'd grab you to go to bed with them," she recalled, and "if you didn't watch yourself, they'd beat the hell outta you."[43] Had Hampton been open to relationships with men, she speculated, she might have found the stage more lucrative. Hampton was a southern migrant from North Carolina who moved to New York as a young woman and found work as a teenager dancing in an all-female company that performed in Coney Island.[44] She met many women there who were also sexually and romantically interested in other women, and she fell "hook, line and sinker" in love with a fellow dancer from Philadelphia. Throughout the 1920s and 1930s, Hampton was able to socialize exclusively with other women, and while working as a performer she "had so many girlfriends it wasn't funny." Hampton also worked in Greenwich Village at the Cherry Lane Theatre, where she socialized with and dated queer white women as well.[45] She performed at the Lafayette Theatre and the Garden of Joy in Harlem in the 1920s, but along with being a chorus girl, she also carried out domestic work for white families to supplement her income. When her biographer asked her why, she replied simply, "Because I like to eat," insinuating that she was not paid well as a chorus girl.[46]

In 1927, Mabel Hampton recalled going to see the lesbian-themed play *The Captive* on Broadway. She "fell in love—not only with *The Captive* but [with] the lady who was the head actress in it." Hampton repeatedly went back to watch Helen Mencken in the role of a young society woman who began an affair with an older married woman. She even found her way backstage to meet Mencken, who asked her why she liked the production. Hampton recalled answering, "Because it seems like a part of my life and what I am and what I hope to be."[47] The theatrical world was where many Black queer women learned they desired women and realized such a life was available to them. Prior to the establishment of explicitly queer bars and venues—which were not available to Black women in many regions until the mid-twentieth century—nightclubs, cabarets, and theaters were important queer meeting spaces.[48] Ethel Waters, who we now turn to, first encountered her partner Ethel Williams when the latter was dancing at the Alhambra Theater in Harlem.[49]

"ETHEL MUST NOT MARRY"

Ethel Waters, Black Swan Records, and Tensions over Racial Uplift

Black performing women who loved women had little choice but to negotiate an industry in which queerness was common yet still looked down upon. The classic blues women were celebrities by the early 1920s, which meant they had to pay attention to how the men who ran the entertainment industry viewed them, as well as to their audiences and fans. Ethel Waters used her sophisticated, urbane image and publicity via the Black press to present herself as desirable to men despite the fact that she brought her girlfriend, dancer Ethel Williams, on her Black Swan tour with her. Waters was one of the first African American women to take the race records industry by storm in the early 1920s, and she reached a celebrity status available to few Black women at this time. Within this industry, Black Swan Records was the most successful Black-owned record company of the era, and Waters was its first breakthrough star, selling enough units to keep the company afloat for several years.[50]

Tall and lithe, Ethel Waters was a talented singer from Philadelphia who nonetheless became famous for singing blues songs about southern migrants in the North who missed life back home, which was a feeling that resonated with many during the Great Migration. So popular was her rendition of "Down Home Blues" that Black Swan sent her on a nation-wide tour to support its record sales. Unbeknownst to many of her fans, the talented dancer who accompanied Waters on tour—and performed a dance number to warm up the crowd before the singer appeared—was her girlfriend, Ethel Williams.[51] Waters and Williams lived together in Harlem at the time, and their relationship was such common knowledge in the Black popular entertainment world that friends referred to them as "the two Ethels."[52] Waters even went as far as to tell a performer friend that she was a lesbian and "the best that ever did it."[53] Mabel Hampton described the two Ethels' relationship as "stormy," recalling, "They used to fight up and down Seventh Avenue" in Harlem. She witnessed this once when Ethel Williams "was after somebody else and Ethel Waters didn't like it." While their managers in the entertainment industry did not approve of such disrespectable behavior, Hampton declared, "Men couldn't do nothing 'cause they were good. . . . They were money makers."[54]

Ethel Waters discussed her friendship with Ethel Williams in her autobiography but did not reveal the intimate nature of their relationship, although she did refer to Williams as a "truly gifted dancer" and a "really stylish girl."[55] When the two women first became close, around 1919, Williams was recovering from an injury and had not been able to work, so Waters suggested she try performing at her cabaret and asked her boss to give Williams a job. Waters, who was making thirty-five dollars a week, asked him to take ten dollars from her weekly pay and give it to Williams along with an additional ten dollars. He responded, "Ethel, you're the damnedest fool I ever heard of . . . but I'll put her on weekends."[56] It is unclear whether this occurred after the two had entered into a relationship or whether the arrangement was part of Waters's courtship of Williams. Whichever the sequence, it worked; soon "the two Ethels" were inseparable.[57] Waters was willing to make economic sacrifices in order to support and perform with the woman she loved. If they were already a couple by this point, they may have been pooling their resources and Waters might not have even suffered financially from cutting her salary.

The short-lived Black Swan Records, the first widely distributed record company owned and operated by African Americans, was launched in 1921 by Harry Pace, a protégé of W. E. B. Du Bois, who had formerly published music with W. C. Handy, the "Father of the Blues."[58] The question of whether Harry Pace was aware of the relationship between "the two Ethels" is difficult to answer for a variety of reasons. Black Swan's commitment to racial uplift through the ideology of respectability contributed to the company's silence regarding the sexuality of its recording artists. Many in the Black middle class saw sexual liberation as hindering the fight for racial justice at this time, despite the loosening of sexual mores associated with the 1920s.[59] At the very least, notions of racial uplift supported the propagation of the race, which queer behavior could not contribute to, and many people of all races saw lesbianism as criminal, immoral, and pathological at this time, if they thought of it at all. Silence on the subject of queerness could therefore imply ignorance of the matter, disinterest, tolerance, or a conscious desire to distance oneself from the topic. However, while Black Swan's president, Harry Pace, remained quiet on the subject of Ethel Waters's relationship with Ethel Williams, he did not have a problem discussing other aspects of her personal life, as long as this would help sell her records. To this end, Black Swan's marketing department crafted an article about Ethel Waters that was published in several Black newspapers but was merely a work of sensationalized fiction.

The article, with the bold headline "Ethel Must Not Marry," stated,

Ethel Waters, star of the Black Swan Troubadours, has signed a unique contract with Harry H. Pace which stipulates that she is not to marry for at least a year, and that during this period she is to devote her time largely to singing for Black Swan Records and appearing with the Troubadours.[60] It was due to numerous offers of marriage, many of her suitors suggesting that she give up her professional life at once for one of domesticity, that Mr. Pace was prompted to take this step.

Some lovesick swains have fallen in love with Miss Waters' picture appearing in the newspapers, while others have been captivated by her voice and personal charm. Although she travels with a maid, it will be necessary for her to employ a private social secretary to attend to her mail if the endearing communications continue on the increase.

While playing recently in Wheeling, W. Va., one promising young physician almost broke up the tour of the Black Swan Troubadours so convincing was his picture of the delights of connubial bliss. When the incident was reported to the New York office Harry

H. Pace lost no time in sending Miss Waters a new contract containing the no-marriage proviso and a salary agreement representing a figure for each night's engagement and each record that most people would be glad to earn in a month, along with a detailed account of his reasons for desiring such an agreement, and the singer promptly signed the papers and returned them to New York. Miss Waters' contract with the Black Swan interests makes her now the highest salaried colored phonograph star in the country.[61]

While it is unlikely that this contract was ever produced, the article showed how Black Swan marketed Waters to Black newspaper readers by presenting her as an object of affection for many "promising" male suitors. It also suggested that, in 1921, a woman who both was married and had a career challenged the pretenses of middle-class respectability, even if she was as successful and popular as Waters. A wife's place was in the home, despite the fact that this expectation was unrealistic for the majority of married Black women in the early twentieth century, as their husbands' wages alone were invariably too meager to make ends meet.[62] As fears of increasing numbers of unmarried women had begun to pose a "lesbian threat" by the 1920s, Waters's single status had to be clarified for her public.[63] Black Swan explained that Waters's desire to please her fans was behind the respectable sacrifice the successful performer made. Of course, in reality, she had no plans at the time to marry any man and was happy with dancer Ethel Williams.

A few months after that December 1921 article was published, another brief article in the *Chicago Defender* stated that "Miss Alberta Hunter, of 4428 Prairie Avenue, entertained last week at dinner in honor of Miss Ethel Waters of the Black Swan Record Company." It was noted that the "other guests present" included "Miss Ethel Williams, a member of Miss Waters' company," and that all in attendance "voted Miss Hunter a charming hostess."[64] Residing at 4428 Prairie Avenue in Chicago's Bronzeville district with blues singer Alberta Hunter was her unmentioned girlfriend, Carrie Mae Ward, who most likely prepared the meal for the dinner party, as Hunter herself did not know how to cook.[65] Hunter was also a recording artist on Black Swan's roster, yet she was not as well promoted on the label as was Ethel Waters—in fact, Hunter's affiliation with the label was not even mentioned in the text, which was most likely written by Black Swan to publicize Waters. The latter was on the road with the Black Swan Troubadours, a band assembled just for the occasion, because Waters was still Black Swan's best-selling recording artist, and the company sought to promote her consistently in print and on tour.[66] While the dinner between the two queer blues singers and their female partners may have been another publicity stunt created by Black Swan, it also demonstrated that Black lady lovers' social networks were growing in the early 1920s, which was sometimes even facilitated by the record companies representing these successful performing women. This brief article further shows the important role that Black lady lovers were playing as culture makers in the Jazz Age.

In the early 1920s there was less national awareness of the idea of lesbianism than there would be even a few years later, when the play *The Captive* and the novel *The Well of Loneliness* increased public visibility of queer women. Ethel Waters and Ethel Williams were therefore able to take advantage of the fact that at this time, their relationship was not yet coded as romantic to the majority of their audiences, despite the rumors that swirled around them at home in Harlem. In 1922, Waters received top billing in a touring revue titled *Oh! Joy!*, and she made sure to secure a part in the production for Williams as well.[67] The two of them created an amusing and memorable entrance for Waters that entailed her girlfriend publicly naming her as her "partner." Waters recounted in her autobiography,

> When I planned my routines for *Oh! Joy!* I wanted to make a different kind of entrance than other well-known record singers were using. Just before my first entrance in *Oh! Joy!* Ethel Williams would go out on the stage.
>
> "Where's that partner of mine?" she'd ask the orchestra leader. "Where's that Ethel Waters? What can be keeping her?" And she'd look all over the stage for me, behind the curtain, in the wings, and, for a laugh, under the rug. She'd mutter, "How can I start our act without that gal?"
>
> After all that build-up I'd come out—in a funny hat and gingham apron that was a gem. I was slim, and when Ethel would ask, "Are you Ethel Waters?" I'd answer, "I ain't Bessie Smith."
>
> Those two lines would wow the audience. Then I'd sing the plaintive and heartbreaking song, "Georgia Blues." . . . Ethel Williams would come out then and dance—and she was always a brilliant performer.[68]

In this act, Ethel Williams referred to Ethel Waters as her partner to emphasize their artistic collaboration, but they were also privately gesturing to their romantic relationship. The format of vaudeville, in which acts of different genres played back-to-back without sharing a connecting theme, was well suited to Waters and Williams's relationship. They were able to tour together without raising suspicion over the status of their relationship since their different art forms fit in with the popular style of entertainment at the time. For those in the audience who did not know they were a couple—which was most likely the majority—this reference to being partners went over their heads yet was still amusing, while those who had heard about their lovers' quarrels on the streets of Harlem may have understood the hidden meaning.[69]

Through their performances, Waters and Williams were able to work together and even hail audience members who also took part in or were sympathetic to queer relationships while not offending those who were not aware of their romance. In this way, queer performers utilized "knowingness," the bond between performer and audience created over the knowledge of double entendres that served as "hidden transcripts" inside the "public transcripts" of their songs and variety skits.[70] The queer blues women engaged long-standing strategies honed by Black performers to communicate with multiple audiences while prioritizing those with whom they felt kinship.[71] Cultural historian Peter Bailey argues that "knowingness" enables performers to "mobilize the latent collective identity of an audience," and audience members' connection to the performer strengthens over their shared competency in decoding hidden meanings.[72] Through such performances, "the two Ethels" delighted in their togetherness on stage, offering an important example of how Black lady lovers found and supported one another as they navigated the entertainment industry.

GERTRUDE "MA" RAINEY AND THE EMERGENCE OF
BLACK QUEER POPULAR CULTURAL PRODUCTIONS

The subtleness with which Ethel Waters alluded to her queerness while performing was not the only available technique for blues women in the Jazz Age. Gertrude "Ma" Rainey's 1928 song "Prove It on Me Blues" and the print advertisement her record company made for it left little to the imagination concerning her status as a lady lover. However, she still preferred to tease her audience regarding her sexuality. Born in Georgia in 1886, Rainey, known as "the Mother of the Blues," began performing in southern minstrel and vaudeville shows as a young teen. She did not record her songs until the white-owned Paramount label "discovered" her in 1923 at the age of thirty-seven, when she had already been performing for close to twenty-five years.[73] By the mid-1920s, she had become a successful recording artist who sold thousands of copies of her records for Paramount. Rainey married men twice, first a fellow performer, William "Pa" Rainey, at age eighteen, and later in life a much younger man, but she was known to enjoy the company of women as well.[74]

Rainey's bisexuality is underscored by the fact that she wrote and recorded multiple songs dealing explicitly with queer issues, such as "Shave 'Em Dry Blues" (1924) and "Sissy Blues" (1926), both of which preceded her most well-known song on the subject, "Prove It on Me Blues." Rainey cowrote "Shave 'Em Dry Blues," which referenced the visibility of mannish women on Chicago's South Side. The song contained the couplets "Going downtown to spread the news / State Street women wearin' brogan shoes" and "There's one thing I can't understand / Some women drivin' State Street just like a man."[75] Notably, referring to a "thing I can't understand" was a common refrain in classic blues songs, which Rainey and Bessie Smith both utilized. For example, in Rainey's "Big Boy Blues" (1927) she sings,

> There's two things I can't understand
> There's two things I can't understand
> Why these married women crazy
> 'bout their back door man
>
> Lord, tie it, big boy, toot it
> Lord, that's my back door man[76]

In this song, the last two lines suggest Rainey takes pleasure in this topic she alleges to not understand, and the meanings are further layered with "back door man" serving as a double entendre for an affair partner as well as for anal sex. Referencing one or two "things I can't understand" became an oft-used blues trope that let a singer name something taboo—that she may have even indulged in—while distancing herself from the topic, allowing the song to be understood by multiple audiences. Rainey did this when she spoke of masculine women wearing men's boots on the South Side streets in "Shave 'Em Dry Blues," and she also went on to present herself as "mannish" in 1928's "Prove It on Me Blues." Along with performers such as Gladys Bentley and Jackie Mabley, Rainey was disseminating new cultural texts of the nattily dressed, masculine Black lady lover in the urban North who came to be known as "the bulldagger."[77]

Ma Rainey also sang a song about losing her man to a "sissy," which was indicative of the increasing queer visibility in urban working-class Black communities at this time; the topic was likewise sung about by gay men like Kokomo Arnold.[78] In 1926's "Sissy Blues," Ma Rainey sang,

I dreamed last night I was far from harm,
Woke up and found my man in a sissy's arms

. . .

Some are young, some are old
My man says sissies got good jelly roll

. . .

My man's got a sissy, his name is Miss Kate
He shook that thing like jelly on a plate

. . .

Now all the people ask me why I'm all alone
A sissy shook that thing and took my man from home[79]

Here, Rainey matter-of-factly introduces the category of "the sissy," a feminine person assigned male at birth who is now competition for women like her. Despite losing her man to Miss Kate with the "good jelly roll," Rainey says nothing negative about this gender-transgressing figure. Indeed, to speak of such everyday matters without judgment was a hallmark of the blues. Songs such as this conveyed new knowledge about gender and sexuality and suggested that while such competition was not welcome, Rainey nonetheless did not take issue with the emergence of "the sissy."

While there are no specific women romantically associated with Rainey, Bessie Smith's niece Ruby Walker alleged that Rainey once attempted to instigate a sexual situation with a group of women from her show in 1926 Chicago, only to have the evening interrupted abruptly.[80]

It seems that Ma had found herself in an embarrassing tangle with the Chicago police. She and a group of young women had been drinking, and they made so much noise that a neighbor summoned the police. The impromptu party was getting intimate, and as bad luck would have it, the law showed up just as everyone began to let their hair down. Pandemonium broke loose as girls madly scrambled for their clothes and ran out the back door, leaving Ma, clutching someone else's dress, to exit last. Ma did not get away, however, for she had a nasty fall down a staircase and practically into the arms of the law. Accused of running an indecent party, she was thrown in jail, where she stayed until Bessie bailed her out the following morning.[81]

This story appears to have informed the marketing of "Prove It on Me Blues," which featured an ad created by Paramount that also included a policeman, echoing the rumor of Rainey's arrest.

Turning to the song itself, first the lyrics should be examined:

Went out last night, had a great big fight
Everything seemed to go on wrong
I looked up, to my surprise
The gal I was with was gone

Where she went, I don't know
I mean to follow everywhere she goes
Folks say I'm crooked, I didn't know where she took it
I want the whole world to know

They said I do it, ain't nobody caught me
Sure got to prove it on me
Went out last night with a crowd of my friends
They must've been women, 'cause I don't like no men

It's true I wear a collar and a tie
Makes the wind blow all the while[82]
'Cause they say I do it, ain't nobody caught me
They sure got to prove it on me

. . .

Wear my clothes just like a fan
Talk to the gals just like any old man
'Cause they say I do it, ain't nobody caught me
Sure got to prove it on me[83]

The line "I want the whole world to know" could be characterized as a type of proto–coming out, as it declares the singer's lack of shame for her desires.[84] And yet, this line is tempered by the couplet "They said I do it, ain't nobody caught me / Sure got to prove it on me," which brings back the ambiguity with a teasing playfulness. While some historical accounts of Rainey suggest that she took advantage of the rumor of her Chicago arrest by writing this song about the topic of queer desire, in the rumor she did indeed get caught, unlike in her song.[85] To write a song in which she got "caught in the act" would not allow for the ambiguity that Rainey favors here, in which she hints at a taboo subject only to dance around the issue of whether she actually took part in queer behavior. The line "Makes the wind blow all the while" referred to the rumors swirling around her, implying that she enjoyed being in the center of them. However, this line replaced the original lyric Rainey wrote, "Likes to watch while the women pass by," which was a much more blatantly queer phrase describing active female desire for other women.

The song "Prove It on Me Blues" is representative of a time when the image of the mannish lesbian, or the "bulldagger," was becoming more visible in American culture, which is further demonstrated by examining the print advertisement that helped promote the song in the Black press. The image ignores the joy Rainey expressed in her song and instead depicts her desires as suspect and deviant. This was likely informed by the discourse in the Black press at the time that represented Black queer women as criminal and violent. As the prior chapter has shown, many of the discussions of lesbianism in Black newspapers in the 1920s referred to "women-only" parties where jealous lovers assaulted their competitors, and such incidents were plastered on the front page with outlandish headlines in order to help sell newspapers.

The ad (fig. 2.1), which ran in the *Chicago Defender* in September 1928, highlighted the tensions at play between Black queer performing women and the entertainment industry, as Paramount Records took the ambiguity over lesbianism in Rainey's song and heightened the controversy by inserting the image of a police officer. Was this done for mere sensationalism or to insert their own negative opinion of lesbian desire? Such melodrama was also common in race records ads; by 1925, the major ads for women's blues songs read like cliffhangers: readers were encouraged to buy a record to discover the outcome of the climactic situations created through text and images in the ads.[86] Paramount Records tended to run its ads exclusively in the *Chicago Defender*, which was read nationally yet still had a solid base in Chicago, where some readers may have understood the connection between the image of the policeman and the rumors of Rainey's arrest in the same city just two years earlier.

The format of this ad was similar to many others that showcased Rainey over the years: an illustrated image of Rainey interacting with other characters was juxtaposed with a few sentences of narrative tailored to fit her latest song. In this case, Rainey was shown wearing a suit jacket and tie, just as she described herself in the song, which was out of the ordinary

Figure 2.1. Paramount Records advertisement for "Prove It on Me Blues." The text reads, "What's all this? Scandal? Maybe so, but you wouldn't have thought it of 'Ma' Rainey. But look at that cop watching her! What does it all mean?" *Chicago Defender*, September 28, 1928.

as she usually dressed quite femininely in promotional photographs and when performing, in gowns, jewels, feathers, and furs. However, since very few images of Rainey have been preserved, and most of them were constructed by the recording industry, there is a possibility that she may have preferred to wear a suit and tie when she was out of the limelight. Freelance illustrators or advertising companies that the record companies hired were usually responsible for such ads, and Black consultants were often brought in by white record companies to make the images and ad copy read "authentically" in hopes that Black audiences would feel that they were being hailed specifically. These ads revealed white anxieties over the increased presence of African Americans in the North, and such a reading corresponds with the image for "Prove It on Me Blues."[87] White reformers saw single Black female southern migrants as a social problem due to their assumed sexual degeneracy, stemming from their race, class, and region and their unmarried or unattached status.[88] This degeneracy could take the form of prostitution, interracial sex, or, by the late 1920s, the newly visible image of the lesbian or mannish woman, who offered yet another option for how single Black women could threaten the social stability of the urban North.

Given this context, what was the *Chicago Defender* reader to make of the text in this ad and the specific reference to the policeman? Not only did he appear in the image, but the text pointed to him to make sure the reader noticed him. While an image of several women loitering on a corner under a streetlamp with an officer in the background usually symbolized prostitution, the appearance of women in masculine attire, such as ties, jackets, and fedoras, was here used instead to signify lesbianism. This choice to insert the figure of the policeman in the ad may have been done to allude to the lesbian orgy rumor from a few years prior; to represent lesbianism as an illicit vice, akin to prostitution; or to merely create sensationalism and build curiosity in the readers in order to stimulate record sales.

Ma Rainey's ability to keep her audience unsure of her sexuality and to never declare her desire for women forthright may have contributed to her popularity. The sexual fluidity and ambiguity of Rainey—married to men, rumored to have had female lovers, and provocatively self-representing as a bulldagger in song—offer many fascinating inroads to understanding constructions of Black women's sexual subjectivity at this time. The record and advertisement for "Prove It on Me Blues" are cultural products that demarcate one of the first representations of Black queer popular culture, and it is particularly notable that such creations came from a woman who was not known beyond mere rumor to have had romantic relationships with women. For women such as Ethel Waters and Bessie Smith, who did take part in queer relationships, such an explicit message did not feel possible or desirable to them. However, as there was no particular female lover who could be "caught in the act" with Rainey, aside from the rumors of her indecent party, she was free to boast and tease her audience, and she brought conceptions of Black queer women's desire and gender transgression further into the public realm as she did so.

ON THE ROAD WITH THE EMPRESS OF THE BLUES

This chapter began with the indomitable Bessie Smith, who never hesitated to take part in same-sex relationships within the Black popular entertainment industry's generally tolerant milieu. Her prodigious talent brought her to an iconic level of celebrity status, particularly among Black southern audiences. Smith's success and fame afforded her the luxury of caring little what others thought of her, yet she still tried to keep her queer liaisons within her circle of friends and colleagues in the entertainment industry. Born in the late 1890s and raised in Chattanooga, Tennessee, Smith began performing with her brother on the city's streets to support themselves after their parents' early death when she was only nine.[89] From 1912 to 1921, Smith traveled extensively throughout the South, singing and dancing for Black and white audiences. In 1918, she was onstage regularly in Atlanta as a male impersonator with dance partner Hazel Green.[90] While such acts were not exclusively associated with queerness at this time, there was a long history of queer women performers who specialized in male impersonation that Smith was likely aware of.[91]

Bessie Smith and Ma Rainey first met on a traveling show they both appeared in, but beyond that there are many different versions of the story told about how they came into each other's lives. The wildest rumor is that the older Rainey kidnapped a young Smith, and gossip about a possible romantic relationship between the two women has flourished over the years. Rainey's biographer Sandra Lieb is unclear on whether Rainey trained Smith as a performer when the two first met, but she argues that the elder's influence is obvious either way.[92] Those who believed the two singers were lovers included Rainey's own guitarist, Sam Chatmon, who told Lieb, "I believe she was courtin' Bessie . . . the way they'd talk. . . . I believe there was something going on wrong." He recalled that if Rainey saw Smith talking to a man, the older woman would "run up" to them and interrupt their conversation because she was jealous.[93] Beyond this, Lieb did not find enough conclusive evidence to pronounce that Rainey and Smith were more than friends. Maud Smith, Bessie Smith's sister-in-law, recalled that Rainey was more of a maternal figure to the younger singer and said the two often laughed over the rumors about how they met when the Smiths visited Rainey at her Georgia home.[94]

After years of performing in traveling tent shows throughout the South, Bessie Smith auditioned for Black Swan Records in the early 1920s. During her test recording, she needed to take a break at one point and reportedly said, "Hold on, let me spit," which so disgusted the company's president, Harry Pace, that he did not offer her a contract.[95] Even if she had not carried out this apparently scandalous and vulgar act in front of Pace, Smith's "unmistakable nitty-grittiness" and "very Black sound" made her an inappropriate choice for Black Swan due to the company's commitment to racial uplift through respectability.[96] Tall, thin Ethel Waters, with her urbane polish and northern background, was a much more palatable choice for Black Swan. Harry Pace could not see how someone as "uncouth" as Smith could assist in his record company's efforts to fight for racial justice, even if she would have no doubt helped it toward its goal of self-sufficiency through economic success.[97] If Black Swan, which was financially successful only for several years before it went out of business, had signed Smith, it is likely that the future of the company would have changed. Instead, she signed exclusively to white-owned Columbia Records in 1923 and went on to sell hundreds of thousands of records for a company that had no problem utilizing blackface minstrelsy imagery to sell blues records. It turned out that the perceived disrespectability of the blues could be disseminated only by white-run record companies that were "indifferent to African American cultural politics" and did not prioritize racial uplift as Black Swan did.[98]

By 1926, Bessie Smith began to pursue relationships with women in her troupe, which she strategically hid from her husband, Jack Gee, whom she had married in 1922. Gee served as her manager and also had affairs with other women himself. Regardless, they were both quite jealous of one another and regularly fought, often violently, over each other's dalliances. For Gee, the money his wife brought in was too lucrative to leave behind, and Smith claimed to love him despite his violence and indiscretions, although they eventually separated in 1930. Once Smith became romantically involved with her fellow female performers, the large troupe of musicians and dancers she toured with learned it was part of their job to keep her queer relationships a secret from both the public in general and her husband in particular.[99]

By 1925, Bessie Smith was successful enough to afford touring the country in her own custom railroad car, which offered her and her troupe more privacy, safety, and dignity in the era of segregated Jim Crow trains.[100] The transient nature of touring and the liminal space of sleeping train cars and boardinghouses, where performers often spent the night, further enabled queer behaviors and relationships for women in the entertainment industry. When traveling through Detroit, Smith and her large revue would often stay at Kate's boardinghouse. Kate's was typical of the small guesthouses adjoining Black vaudeville theaters that catered to traveling entertainers. In the Jim Crow era, these small hotels filled an important need and not just in the South, as African Americans were not always welcomed by northern hotels and guesthouses, either. The amenities at Kate's were minimal: there was no lobby, simply three floors of long, narrow corridors with rows of sparsely furnished rooms.[101] Despite having no frills, these accommodations offered touring revues such as Smith's a safe haven and respite from the road. Indeed, the guesthouses favored by such entertainers had employees who were usually familiar with the queer antics that many of the classic blues women enjoyed.

It had become a tradition on Smith's tours to follow up the final show of an extended engagement with a night of relaxation. Ruby Walker, Bessie Smith's niece, recalled, "We used to put on our nicest pajamas and nightgowns, and go to each other's rooms and show off and drink and have a good time."[102] One particular night, most of the revue ended up in Smith's room on the first floor of Kate's boardinghouse. Marie, a young dancer in the show, wore a pair of bright red pajamas that had been a gift from Smith, and eager to show them off, she performed a few comic steps that amused her friends. Nobody laughed harder than Smith, who called out, "C'mon Marie, show your stuff," encouraging the young woman to escalate her twists and turns. Smith had found her latest romantic interest on her tour, but unfortunately for the new lovers, a few hours later everyone in the building awoke to the sound of screams. Smith's husband, Jack Gee, had made a surprise visit and caught his wife in bed with Marie.[103] Luckily, both women, along with the entire revue, were able to quickly leave Kate's boardinghouse, get on their train car, and leave town without facing any violent repercussions from Smith's husband.

Bessie Smith and her cohort were fashioning a world in which women could enjoy relationships with either sex, where they took part in overlapping queer and straight social worlds and performed their songs to mixed audiences that interpreted the queer blues women's lyrics in different ways depending on their subject position. For example, in the song "Foolish Man Blues," which Bessie Smith wrote in 1927 while she was actively involved with women romantically, she sang,

> Men sure deceitful, they getting worse every day
> Lord, men sure deceitful, they getting worse every day
> Actin' like a bunch of women, they just
> 	gabbing', gabbing', gabbing' away
>
> There's two things got me puzzled, there's
> 	two things I can't understand
> There's two things got me puzzled, there's
> 	two things I can't understand
> That's a mannish actin' woman and a skippin'
> 	twistin' woman actin' man[104]

In this song, Smith describes the subject as a lover of men who is frustrated by their emasculation, while also making visible a queer underworld of gender inversion that was not often alluded to through song. As queer music scholar John Gill notes, "The refrain may have been a mischievous diversion, a hint at her own ambiguous sexuality, or an ironic tease for her audience, who most certainly knew what Smith was talking about."[105] As we have seen with Ma Rainey, it was common in the blues to present a controversial subject and defuse its threat by introducing it with a line about how the singer could not understand it. Audiences and listeners could therefore interpret Bessie Smith's lyrics differently—for those who were concerned by the growing number of sissies and bulldaggers on the streets, "Foolish Man Blues" was sympathetic to their confusion over changing conceptions of gender and sexuality in the urban North.[106] And for those who were part of this world, the song merely served as a knowing wink.

While Bessie Smith's songs generally referred to heterosexual romance, which was likely her own choice as well as that of Columbia Records, as these examples show, occasionally she alluded to queerness or gender transgression in her lyrics, in ways that could both hail her fellow queer audience members through the hidden transcripts of "knowingness" yet would not shock or disgust her less savvy or more conservative listeners. Smith relied on the spaces that touring opened up for queer behavior, from the privacy of boardinghouse rooms to her personal train car, to even the space of the theater itself when just among her troupe members. Yet she also found relationships with men to be important to her life, which led to difficulties negotiating multiple partners. She preferred to keep her queer relationships within the theatrical world, and her touring troupes functioned as meeting spaces for women, married or single, who were interested in other women romantically.

~~~~~~~~~~~~~~~~~~

This chapter has demonstrated how the Black popular entertainment industry served as a meeting place that not only helped queer women build social networks but also functioned economically as an important site of work and livelihood. In this milieu, many performers were sexually fluid and held an aversion to the "domestic" in all of its historical senses for Black women.[107] The classic blues women discussed myriad relationships beyond heteronormative marriage, from queer songs to those about women and men with multiple partners, to some that were about two women coming to an agreement over sharing the same man.[108] However, while queer desire was generally an open secret in the entertainment industry, it was occasionally named as a larger disturbance. Beginning in the late 1920s and into the following decade, the Black press ran sensational articles describing the deviant lives of Harlem performers. Newspaper articles discussed innocent southern migrant women who dreamed of becoming chorus girls falling into the lecherous arms of hardened, masculine performing women. As such articles did reflect the views of many in the Black communities of the urban North, very few women performers outright claimed a queer identity in this era.

Since queer behaviors were usually accepted among those in the theatrical world, if not outside of it, performing women developed strategies to broach this issue in their work. The "famous lady lovers'" labor on the stage and in recording studios produced cultural texts that referenced queerness in layered ways, often naming same-sex behaviors and identities while distancing themselves from them at the same time or referring to them through double entendres that only some would understand. In this way, they could hail audience members and listeners who welcomed such depictions and even identified with them, which helped strengthen and make visible the Black queer networks of the urban North. At the same time, techniques such as Rainey's teasing call to "prove it on me" and Smith's naming of queer identities she claimed not to understand helped affirm their popularity with the majority who still found such concepts immoral, pathological, criminal, or just odd.

Performing women had an exceptional relationship to mobility at this time, which facilitated their queer relationships. Although touring the Jim Crow South could be quite dangerous for African Americans, traveling together en masse brought safety in numbers, and this extraordinary freedom of movement widened women's horizons and exposed them to various regions of the country. These queer performing women were able to create a world not only onstage but also offstage that challenged accepted norms and allowed for behaviors not generally accepted in society. The theater industry and the music industry symbiotically created a system in which classic blues singers regularly toured circuits of Black theaters and theaters open to Black audiences to support their latest records. Within their touring troupes, queer liaisons and networks emerged that sustained performers on long trips away from home. It was not merely the convergence of performers in theaters that was crucial to these growing queer subcultures but the relationships forged in the liminal activity of touring as well.

Performers such as Bessie Smith demonstrate that some married women also took part in relationships with women at this time. She may have taken advantage of her cultural capital by entering into relationships with other women employed in her traveling shows, but her marriage limited her ability to fully enjoy such relationships. Ma Rainey's "Prove It on Me Blues" epitomized the reigning attitude of this era toward lesbianism. Rainey understood that queerness was a topic that could titillate audiences, but she chose to tease them with ambiguity, which was a more provocative and lucrative approach than blatantly admitting to queer relationships. Whereas the white-owned Paramount Records did not mind representing Rainey as a bulldagger in its print ads, Black-owned Black Swan Records tried to draw attention to Ethel Waters's desirability to men while she toured the country with her girlfriend Ethel Williams. Waters and Williams's onstage performance, like the songs of the classic blues women, employed "knowingness" to connect with both queer and straight audiences at the same time. Utilizing these various strategies, the "famous lady lovers" enjoyed exceptional success in the Black popular entertainment industry and helped form the queer networks of the urban North. While it was rare for such successful entertainers to openly claim a queer status, performers like Gladys Bentley who reigned in the Prohibition era milieu of the illicit speakeasy were even bolder in their visibility, as the next chapter will reveal.

THREE

A Freakish Party

~~~~~~~~~~~~~~~~~~~~

Black Lady Lovers, Vice, and Space in the
Prohibition Era Urban North

In 1928, New York City vice commission the Committee of Fourteen hired
a Black male investigator named Raymond Claymes to visit, evaluate, and
document the state of Harlem's nightlife underworld. In the early morning
hours of May 25, Claymes was brought to a "woman's party" in a tenement apartment on West 137th Street, where a married woman, whom he
referred to in his notes as a "madam," was in charge. When he arrived, he
counted fifteen Black women and five men present. All those who were
dancing were couples of the same sex. Claymes noted that some of the
women dancing together were "going through the motions of copulation,"
with "their dresses pulled up to their thighs." He asked the madam what
type of party this was, and he wrote that she replied, "A freakish party,
everybody in here is supposed to be a bulldagger or a c———."[1] He admitted he "was neither" and that his sexual orientation ran "the normal way."
While the madam was unsure whether anyone else present felt similarly,
she encouraged Claymes to approach the women present, nonetheless.

He introduced himself to a female partygoer with the memorable pickup line, "Are you one of these so-called things here or are you a normal, regular girl?" She replied without missing a beat, "Everybody here is either a bulldagger or faggot and I am here."[2] Notably, Claymes then wrote, "After further conversation with her she agreed to commit an act of prostitution for $5, at this place in her room."[3] He then left the premises. This story reveals that in the Prohibition era urban North, Black women were involved in overlapping circles of commercial sex and an emerging queer subculture, where they experienced surveillance that sought to suppress these worlds. Spaces like this "woman's party" helped to further the creation of Black queer social networks, yet they were also connected to an underground economy that flourished in the 1920s and came to the surface in this instance only due to anti-vice organizations seeking to stamp out illegal sex work.

These types of private parties occurred in vice districts that emerged after World War I and grew exponentially during the early Great Migration and Prohibition.[4] Here one could find bootleg alcohol, commercial sex, and nightlife spaces that allowed queer and interracial mingling. Vice districts encompassed Black neighborhoods in most cities, despite the fact that white men dominated most of the illicit industries that took root there.[5] As the 1928 vice report that opened the chapter shows, in such spaces various types of nonreproductive sex, from queer behaviors to sex work, mingled. These overlaps contributed further to the association of emerging Black queer identities with prostitution and the vice-ridden "underworld," which was yet another reason the larger Black community could not accept women who loved women. This chapter argues that the liminal spaces of Prohibition strengthened the social networks of Black lady lovers in the urban North, even though they were situated in vice districts replete with surveillance and policing mechanisms that sought to regulate them. Such oversight took the form of anti-vice organizations like the Committee of Fourteen, as well as the police, nosy neighbors, assorted male "experts," and community leaders. Despite this, Black lady lovers' social worlds flourished as Americans flouted social norms while seeking bootleg liquor and other forbidden pleasures.

During Prohibition, Black neighborhoods in the urban North became increasingly popular destinations for adventurous white "slummers." These curious thrill-seekers were interested in momentarily sampling illicit pleasures such as bootleg liquor, interracial dancing, and same-sex behavior.[6] This constant stream of gazing white tourists in places like

Harlem led writer Langston Hughes to declare the Jazz Age a time when "the Negro was in vogue."[7] This craze for a taste of the "exotic" made African American community leaders even more concerned over the immoral displays and activities that white visitors witnessed in Black districts. White slummers primarily felt comfortable venturing into establishments that featured Black performers for white audiences, such as the famous Cotton Club. But another side of northern Black districts existed where white slummers rarely trod: the world of African American–centered rent parties, speakeasies, and buffet flats. Many of these spaces were created by entrepreneurial women in order to socialize in their own homes, away from the leering gaze of white tourists, as well as to profit off the lucrative Prohibition industry of bootleg alcohol.[8] This chapter will explore these liminal spaces that crossed boundaries of legality and privacy, as some venues were open to the public and other required personal connections to gain access inside residential spaces.

Vivid descriptions of these gathering spaces were preserved by the Committee of Fourteen (COF), which was one of the country's leading private citizen reform associations. New York's City Club and the Anti-Saloon League—both of which played a large role in creating Prohibition laws—founded this Progressive Era group in 1905.[9] Curbing prostitution was the COF's central concern, yet as its investigators sought out illegal sex economies, they came upon queer gatherings and nonnormative gender behaviors, which they described in detail, creating an important archive for historians interested in everyday life among working-class African Americans. At the same time, COF reports were used as evidence to help shut down these spaces in order to end the illegal activities taking place within their walls. Black queer gathering sites were therefore both documented and destroyed through the work of the COF.

Investigator Raymond Claymes's report on a "freakish" "woman's party" raises a number of questions: What were the pleasures and restrictions of Black queer women's social gatherings in residential spaces, and what was the relationship between Black nightlife's illicit sexual economies and ordinary Black women's labor and leisure? These liminal spaces that straddled public and private worlds were crucial sites in the formation of Black queer sexual subjectivities. As this chapter will show, music, dancing, performance, sex, and prostitution, along with the presence of illegal alcohol during Prohibition, all contributed to Black lady lovers' queer worlds in the urban North. Women took advantage of the spaces opened up by Prohibition to socialize and work, yet freedom in such illicit and often temporary venues could be fleeting, which is particularly demonstrated by the story of Mabel Hampton, who will be discussed throughout the chapter.

The creation of the Volstead Act, which inaugurated Prohibition at the start of 1920, was influenced by the work of the COF, and the gathering spaces this chapter focuses on either came into existence or drastically increased in popularity due to this federal ban on alcohol sales. Therefore, a brief overview of the COF and its relationship to Prohibition will first offer historical context for the emergence of different sites of Prohibition leisure—and their surveillance—that will be discussed in more detail. The chapter then explores the unique contours of rent parties, buffet flats, and speakeasies before turning to additional accounts of Black queer women's gatherings found in vice reports and oral histories, followed by a section on the different ways Black queer women were associated with prostitution in this era. I then examine the queer performances of Gladys Bentley in liminal Prohibition spaces before ending with a discussion of how the advent of the Great Depression and the repeal of Prohibition led to a backlash against queer nightlife in the urban North. Taken together, this chapter examines the unique pleasures and dangers that Black lady lovers experienced in the Prohibition era spaces of northern cities.

THE COMMITTEE OF FOURTEEN AND
PROHIBITION ERA VICE SURVEILLANCE

The organization that played the largest role in passing the Volstead Act was the Anti-Saloon League. Founded in 1895, the league was concerned not only with overdependence on alcohol by working-class and immigrant men but also with other nefarious activities associated with saloon culture: sex work, gambling, and the corrupt political machines that often used saloons as central meeting places.[10] The COF was created out of the Anti-Saloon League at the turn of the century in New York over concerns related to the growing presence of sex workers in saloons. Specifically, the COF was formed in response to the 1896 Raines law, which inadvertently allowed New York City saloons to function as brothels.[11] The COF was made up of settlement house workers, temperance advocates, clerics, housing reformers, and businessmen. The committee included well-known progressive reformers like Frances Kellor—an expert on immigrant life with a law degree from Cornell—and was funded by wealthy New Yorkers including Andrew Carnegie. In the 1910s, John D. Rockefeller Jr. became the COF's most important fundraiser.[12] The rise of brothels that became known as

"Raines law hotels" led to the COF's focus on uncovering illegal activities related to sex work, although the committee also understood that commercial sex was a part of city life and could likely never be fully eliminated.[13]

When the Eighteenth Amendment took effect in January 1920 prohibiting the manufacturing, sale, and transportation of alcohol, it was the first constitutional amendment to limit individual rights rather than government actions. This infringement on American behavior played a large role in its eventual repeal in 1933, as the law was wildly unpopular with most citizens. The Volstead Act established the federal Prohibition Bureau to execute the Eighteenth Amendment, but the bureau's agents soon realized the extreme difficulty in enforcing a national alcohol ban. Illegal bootleggers, the rise of the speakeasy, and the willingness of police officials to accept bribes from lawbreaking entrepreneurs made overseeing the ban practically impossible. By the early 1920s, many eastern states, including New York, had basically given up on trying to enforce Prohibition. Prior to Prohibition, the COF had focused its investigations on institutions with alcohol licenses; it was not until after 1920 that it began to investigate private residences and tenements as well.[14] While decreasing the number of houses of prostitution was the COF's central concern, it also attacked the problems presented by new forms of entertainment, as Progressive Era reformers were particularly worried about the harmful effects of vice and popular amusements on urban youth.[15]

While many critics saw the alcohol ban as a massive infringement of personal liberties, there were multiple factions and interests that led to the passing of Prohibition. Most of them shared an underlying belief in promoting morality and sobriety as specifically white, nativist, Protestant cultural values in a time when northern cities were rapidly filling with Catholic and Jewish European immigrants and Black southern migrants. While African American leaders did not agree with such racial associations, some nonetheless saw Prohibition in a positive light. Howard University professor Kelly Miller declared, "The decline of lynching and the abolition of liquor go hand in hand."[16] He and others hoped that decreasing access to alcohol would reduce the number of murderous attacks on innocent African Americans fueled by drunken white violence. Others viewed Prohibition as an opportunity for the Black community to visibly demonstrate respectability through the restraint of temperance.[17]

However, avoiding alcohol was difficult in northern Black districts because they were filled with white-owned speakeasies. These Prohibition era spaces for drinking illegal, "bootleg" alcohol could open, close, and reopen virtually overnight and could appear anywhere from abandoned storefronts to tenement apartments or basements.[18] In 1923, the *New York Age* ran a series of articles titled "Hootch Hell Holes," which noted that Jewish numbers runner and bootlegger Hyman Kassell had a monopoly on Harlem's illicit liquor industry.[19] In the aftermath of successful national campaigns in the 1910s against red-light districts in white neighborhoods, many observers noted that city officials had become lax about increasing crime in Black communities. One 1922 Chicago study claimed that the "protests of colored neighborhoods" against "disorderly houses" and "the painted women in their neighborhood are usually ignored by the police."[20] If officers turned a blind eye to crime and illegal activities in Black districts, there was no reason for such operations to leave.[21] As this shows, the Great Migration, along with Prohibition, created new opportunities for white vice owners and corrupt politicians to hide their illegal activities under "a cover of Blackness" in neighborhoods such as Harlem and Bronzeville.[22]

As speakeasies rapidly multiplied in the 1920s to take advantage of urban dwellers' desires for forbidden alcohol and other vices, prostitution also flourished in these covert spaces. Such venues were particularly important to the livelihoods of Black sex workers, who were less likely to work in upscale settings and often had to ply their trade on the streets.[23] By 1927, the COF found speakeasies to account for 78 percent of all the prostitution violations discovered in its investigations, and it claimed such sites were the "greatest source for the making of new prostitutes."[24] However, while the COF was well aware that Harlem had become a central site for vice and needed further patrolling, the committee had trouble penetrating the district for several reasons. Though the reform organization had long been supported by Fred Moore, the editor of the *New York Age* and former president of the COF's "Colored Auxiliary," finding Black investigators was a constant problem. The organization's white male secretary noted in 1916 that "the colored man has a rather keen sense of racial solidarity" and "objects to acting as a 'stool pigeon' against his own race."[25] Undaunted, the COF occasionally sent white investigators to Harlem but with little success; a 1923 report noted that an agent could not gain any access to buffet flats, which were parties usually hosted by Black women in their apartments with a "buffet" of available illicit activities from which patrons could choose.[26]

Harlem speakeasies were increasingly associated with sex work throughout the 1920s, which brought larger crowds of white slummers into the Black district to visit the more well-known venues. As a result, the COF redoubled its efforts to recruit an African American investigator and hired teacher Raymond Claymes in 1928 to conduct a five-month undercover investigation of Harlem nightlife.[27] Claymes was a Texas native who had studied sociology at Howard University and later attended Yale Divinity School.[28] His COF reports reveal that despite his respectable, middle-class background, he was able to secure the trust of working-class men and women who showed him speakeasies and apartment buffet flats. He filed 130 reports on Harlem spaces, which made up the first in-depth archive of the district's vice activities in a decade.[29] Claymes's reports show that by 1928, Harlem's buffet flats had become even more crucial to the sex work industry than its speakeasies, which was a discovery that surprised white COF investigators, who would not have been able to access that information on their own.[30] After collecting notes on hundreds of similar Harlem establishments, the COF in April 1929 turned Raymond Claymes's evidence over to the police, where it was used to help make over 1,200 arrests, leading to the closing of fifty-nine Prohibition venues.[31] And yet despite such policing, a multitude of similar spaces still remained open to city dwellers for leisure and labor in the Jazz Age.

RENT PARTIES, BUFFET FLATS, AND SPEAKEASIES

The thousands of southern Black migrants who relocated to the urban North in the early twentieth century brought with them the tradition of the rent party. Sociologist Ira De A. Reid explained in 1927 that "it has been the custom of certain portions of the Negro group living in Southern cities to give some form of party when money was needed to supplement the family income." Such parties were particularly necessary for "many families of a low economic status who sought to confine their troubles with a little joy."[32] The New York Age went further, declaring that "the rent party has become a recognized means of meeting the demands of extortionate landlords in Harlem, as well as in other sections, since the era of high rents set in and became a permanent condition."[33] This social gathering was a form of communal support for recently arrived new settlers. In the face of the poor-paying jobs and high rents that made upward mobility in the urban North hard to come by for recent migrants, friends and neighbors banded together and pooled their funds. The rent party was also imbricated in the social fabric of Prohibition, the New York Age explained: "Booze of dubious origin can be secured from the nearest delicatessen, and under its enlivening influence the guests can indulge in the energetic dance movements of the day, until the floor threatens to give way or the neighbors summon the police."[34]

Unfortunately, rent parties could be, and were eventually, taken over by outside forces. A 1938 Works Progress Administration report on Harlem noted that such events, "like any other universally popular diversion, soon fell into the hands of the racketeers. Many small-time pimps and madames who, up to that time, had operated under-cover buffet flats, came out into the open and staged nightly so-called Rent Parties."[35] Similarly, as rent parties became more popular, they also began attracting white slummers from downtown, who thought it "quite the thing" to "chisel" in on Harlem "stomping sessions held ostensibly for the purpose of collecting a kitty to pay off the landlord."[36] Notably, both rent parties and buffet flats were at first usually managed by women, some of whom were former (or current) madams or entertainers. Their knowledge of theatrical circles and the world of commercial sex meant they could easily tap into their networks to bring patrons out for an evening. They were able to secure up-and-coming musical acts, as performers saw buffet flats as ideal spaces to unwind, develop their skills, try out new material, and make decent tips.[37] Musical performances then served as both the main act and as background for dancing between friends, lovers, and sex workers with their clients.[38]

Rent parties were often advertised through calling cards, which could be found "stuck in the grille of apartment house elevators."[39] Sometimes they were also promoted through placing a sign at street level on the building holding the event.[40] The day that Mabel Hampton met Lillian Foster, who became her partner for over forty years, Foster gave her a card for a rent party she was throwing. The two women had met at a bus stop and struck up a conversation, which shows that women also met in public on the street, a setting that has historically been more associated with gay men.[41] Especially considering how such Prohibition events were advertised through small carrying cards, this interaction suggests that this meeting practice between women may have been common. The card Foster presented to Hampton (fig. 3.1) was typical of the genre, which used rhymes and short narratives describing the festivities to entice readers to attend. This one in particular conjured the financial difficulties of the Great Depression as a reason for camaraderie.

Buffet flats were more notorious than rent parties, as they usually offered not only food and bootleg alcohol but also gambling, drugs, commercial sex, and sexual entertainments. Playing blackjack, poker, and other games was a common way to make extra money in one's leisure time at social gatherings. Cannabis, opium, cocaine, and heroin were an increasingly popular part of the milieu of Black entertainment worlds in the 1920s and

Hard times are here, but not stay
So come, sing and dance your blues away, at

A Sunday Matinee

GIVEN BY

L I L L I A N

151 West 130th Street, Room 12.

Sunday, September 25th, 1932

Good Music   Refreshments Served

Figure 3.1. Rent party advertisement given to Mabel Hampton by Lillian Foster on the day they met in 1933. Mabel Hampton Collection, Lesbian Herstory Archives, Brooklyn, NY.

1930s.[42] And drugs were also part of the allure for white slummers in Black districts; *Variety* noted in an article on Harlem that the district between 132nd and 138th Streets on Fifth Avenue was known as "Coke Village," and many of the "white gentry" there were looking for "hop."[43] George Haynes of the National Urban League claimed that buffet flats were merely a combination of gambling parlors and "apartments of prostitution."[44]

Blues singer Bessie Smith's niece Ruby Walker recalled that the buffet flats they visited on tour were welcoming of queer patrons, with a typical flat servicing "nothing but faggots and bulldykers, a real open house." She told Smith's biographer, "Everything went on in that house—tongue baths, you name it. They called them buffet flats because buffet meant everything, everything that was in the life."[45] While not all buffet flats catered to queer clients, the ones that Walker attended while touring in Bessie Smith's entourage were clearly chosen for their acceptance of same-sex activities.[46] While Smith tried not to participate in scandalous behavior out in the open because of her fame, she nonetheless enjoyed watching risqué performances when she visited these spaces. One feature at an infamous Detroit buffet flat particularly captivated Smith: a plump woman performed "an amazing trick with a lighted cigarette, then repeated it in the old-fashioned way with a Coca-Cola bottle." Walker recalled that "she could do all them things with her pussy—a real educated pussy."[47] While rent parties only occasionally featured commercial sex, buffet flats usually did.[48] The "freakish party" witnessed by Raymond Claymes that opened this chapter likely took place at a buffet flat.

While buffet flats were crucial to the Prohibition era, they actually had a longer history: sometimes known as "good-time flats," they evolved out of services created for Pullman train porters. This relatively well-paying position reserved for African American men on Pullman sleeping car trains had emerged with the rise of the transcontinental railroad in the 1860s. Being a Pullman porter had become a respected and sought-after job that was seen as an important entryway into the Black middle class. However, while Pullman porters were crucial to the national transportation system, they were not able to stay in white-only accommodations while on the road.[49] Buffet flats first emerged as hybrid institutions for train porters that borrowed from brothels, whose main service was to "excite, satisfy and make money from male sexual curiosity." But they also shared commonalities with the cabaret culture that arose in the 1910s that gave the new heterosociality of the era a musical backdrop.[50]

Buffet flats became even more popular during Prohibition for making alcohol available for purchase alongside erotic entertainments and live music. While brothels rarely catered to queer women, the space of the buffet flat allowed women to be sexual spectators and, in some settings, take part in flirtations and sexual behavior with other women. The Harlem "woman's party" that opened this chapter and the buffet flats that Bessie Smith and her entourage visited in Detroit reveal that Black queer women took part in and enjoyed such gatherings. While some white slummers discovered this world of buffet flats in Black districts, most parties were underground community spaces for Black locals.[51] Some of the women who threw regular buffet flats in their homes may have received financial backing from others, but the few available accounts suggest that in New York, Chicago, Detroit, and other northern cities, Black women ran the show and made a living off their profits.[52]

While rent parties and buffet flats also featured bootleg liquor during Prohibition, selling and serving alcohol was the primary function of speak-easies, which were mostly white-owned spaces that quickly spread through less-policed Black neighborhoods. There were over 20,000 of them in 1920s New York, and Chicago and Detroit each claimed to be "wetter" than the Big Apple during the supposedly "dry" era from 1920 to 1933.[53] As performer Ada "Bricktop" Smith recalled, "Prohibition made a lot of people *start* drinking, and it didn't make anybody stop."[54] Police increasingly relied on undercover investigations to entrap speakeasy owners, so those who ran them became more secretive and tended to let in only known customers.[55] This clandestine environment made speakeasies even more conducive to queer customers and behaviors because such patrons often wished to remain anonymous. One 1928 COF report noted that investigators had come across "fourteen homo-sexuals of both sexes" in thirteen Harlem speakeasies and nightclubs.[56] Assuming this was only the number of people whom Claymes saw taking part in queer behaviors or transgressive gender expressions, there were likely many more queer patrons present whom he could not identify as such.

Bricktop described her experiences working as a singer in a speakeasy during a Prohibition police raid: "You'd be on the floor singing, a buzzer would sound, and you'd quickly sit down at the table nearest you. The piano top would be closed, the drinks whisked away. When the police came downstairs to look around, all they'd see was some slightly happy people drinking ginger ale or Coca-Cola and talking about the weather. When the police left, things went back to normal. The booze would appear on the tables and the piano player would get busy at the keyboard."[57] While both the possibility and the actuality of a police raid could put a damper on one's evening, some slumming nightlife-goers found such a potential disruption thrilling. Fights and robberies were very common in speakeasies as well; as one Prohibition era musician recalled, bootleg liquor "made the people wild and out of control—they'd fight and shoot and cut and break the place up."[58] A 1930 *Variety* article on the increasing popularity of speakeasies noted, "There is a congenial yet semi-forbidden atmosphere" in such venues that "people seem[ed] to crave." The same article echoed Bricktop's previous observation, commenting that "almost everybody" had "gotten into the habit of drinking rather heavily" in the Prohibition era.[59] This underscored that the aim of Prohibition—curbing drinking through regulating the selling of alcohol—was a spectacular failure. However, socially, Prohibition functioned to connect different types of people who bonded together over their hatred of the Volstead Act and their desire to transgress it, which can be seen in the popularity of liminal spaces like the buffet flat, the rent party, and the speakeasy.

BLACK QUEER WOMEN'S SOCIALIZING IN THE PROHIBITION ERA URBAN NORTH

While public gathering spaces for gay men had emerged by the 1920s, for African American women, private house parties offered the safest environment.[60] Kevin Mumford argues that most Harlem clubs that tolerated queer behavior were "deeply marginalized" as they were located in tenement apartments, while the more visible and accessible a Harlem club became, the more heterosexual its clientele often was.[61] Residential speakeasies and buffet flats were nonetheless quite central to the social life of working-class African Americans during Prohibition, and their secrecy contributed to their survival. Since white people primarily owned the real estate in Black districts at this time, it was common to find Black enterprises, whether buffet flats or beauty salons, in apartments on residential streets.[62] Queer couples still visited mainstream nightclubs and theaters and queer flirtations often occurred there, but these interactions were intentionally subtle and might not have been visible to everyone present. Relationships were negotiated among individuals who were accustomed to socializing in mixed spaces.

When it came to queer patrons attending Harlem speakeasies, Eric Garber argues that "gays were usually forced to hide their preferences," but vice reports tell a different story.[63] For example, after going to the Elks Speakeasy on 2454 Seventh Ave at 1:45 a.m. on May 18, 1928, COF investigator Raymond Claymes wrote, "While visiting here, eight colored women entered, all intoxicated, and ordered drinks which were served to them. They played the automatic Victrola and danced among themselves, doing eccentric dancing, and ballroom dancing, which was very indecent. They patted one another on the buttocks, and went through the motions of copulation."[64] While Claymes did not note who, if anyone else, was in the speakeasy at this time, the Elks was white-owned and both Black and white men and women patronized the venue. This report described what may have been an ordinary scene, in which queer couples could enjoy each other's company out at a local speakeasy, just like any of their neighbors could. That Claymes did not record any men interrupting the female couples might have been significant, as Mabel Hampton recalled that going out in public meant tolerating attention from men who either did not know or care that she liked women. For this reason, she much preferred private parties to spaces like the Elks.[65]

Music was another important element of the speakeasy, generating an atmosphere that enabled women to sensuously engage with one another through dancing. At the Elks, one could "put a nickel in the electric phonograph."[66] By playing music, customers generated additional profits for the venue, which gave the owners another reason to ignore the type of dancing or the makeup of the couples who took to the floor. While patrons could not select their own songs prior to the creation of jukeboxes in the 1930s, Harlem speakeasy phonographs were stacked with popular blues records, and as such music was rarely played on the radio in the 1920s, going out on the town to drink and dance to the blues was further motivation for local queer women to venture to a speakeasy.[67] Claymes noted that the women at the Elks took part in "eccentric dancing," which was a then-popular term referring to a genre of dances like the cakewalk. Vaudeville performers noted for this specialty often performed gymnastically spectacular dances involving high kicks, twirls, and flips. Claymes tried to use detached, scientific language to describe the "ballroom dancing" that went "through the motions of copulation," which was likely a dance called the "slow drag." This popular speakeasy dance done to slow blues songs was very sensual, as partners "would hold onto each other and grind to and fro in one spot all night."[68] The female couples at the Elks were apparently acting no different than straight couples usually did in a speakeasy, and no one aside from Claymes seemed to care. Like the majority of Harlem speakeasies, white proprietors ran the Elks, but unlike in the larger and more established nightclubs, in these illegal spaces Black and queer patrons could seemingly claim a presence.[69]

Since the COF was focused on documenting the commercial sex economy—not specifically queer spaces—it used male investigators to function as potential clients, so any space they could access was a place open to doing business with men. Therefore, Raymond Claymes had no way to enter any actual "women's only parties" that did not also cater to men in search of sex workers. For insights into women's house parties and rent parties, the oral history of Mabel Hampton is again invaluable. In the 1920s, Hampton lived at 120 West 122nd Street in Harlem, where she recalled that her neighbors "were all lesbians; they had four rooms in the basement and they gave parties all the time." Sometimes they would have "pay parties." For these, Mabel and her neighbors brought food, and partygoers contributed cash for a plate of chicken and potato salad. Hampton distinguished between "pay parties" and "rent parties," recalling that "we also went to 'rent parties,' where you go in and pay a couple dollars. You buy your drinks and meet other women and dance and have fun." Rent parties were open to the larger community, while pay parties were just for close friends living in her building. These smaller parties usually entertained up to twelve or fourteen women.[70]

The difficulties that could arise in traveling to these parties influenced Black lady lovers' preference for socializing in private homes. Appearing on the streets or taking public transportation without male escorts and looking like a queer couple—which was often connected to visible gender transgression—could lead to unwanted attention. Hampton recalled of these parties,

> Most of the women wore suits. Very seldom did any of them have slacks [on] . . . because they had to come through the street. Of course, if they were in a car, they wore the slacks. And most of them had short hair. And most of them was good-lookin' women too. The bulldykers would come and bring their women with them. And you weren't supposed to jive with them, you know. They danced up a breeze. They did the Charleston; they did a little bit of everything. They were all colored women. Sometimes we ran into someone who had a white woman with them. But me, I'd venture out with any of them. I just had a ball. . . . I didn't have to go to bars because I would go to women's houses. Like Jackie Mabley would have a big party and all the girls from the show would go—she had all the women there.[71]

This passage ends by highlighting how crucial relationships within the entertainment industry were to Black queer women's social lives. Jackie Mabley was a popular comedian who got her start in vaudeville and then went on to greater success later in life under the name "Moms" Mabley. Her midcentury skits often depicted an elderly woman obsessed with younger men. However, it was well-known within the theatrical world that Mabley was a "bulldyker" who favored wearing men's suits offstage. One 1930s theatrical reviewer referred to her style as "the inimitable-mannish-Mabley-manner."[72] As a successful performer and party host, she played an important role in sustaining local queer networks and introducing women like Mabel Hampton to friends and potential lovers in the Prohibition era.

QUEER AFRICAN AMERICAN WOMEN AND
SEX WORK IN THE PROHIBITION ERA

While this chapter's opening story suggests that some of the patrons at the "freakish" "woman's party" investigated by the Committee of Fourteen may have also been sex workers, Raymond Claymes's other reports also describe queer women out on the town with friends and partners. It is probable that any space investigated by the COF included the presence of sex workers, because knowledge of queer women's spaces without commercial sex would not have been available to male vice agents, as discussed in the last section. And as prostitution usually paid more than domestic work, which was the most common form of labor for Black women in the early Great Migration, sex work was an option for women regardless of sexual orientation.[73] Yet this common association between the "underworlds" of prostitution and queerness further contributed to negative ideas around lesbianism.

The commercialization of sex was on the rise during Prohibition, and speakeasies and buffet flats were often filled with women available for sex in exchange for payment. In the early twentieth century, sexualized performances in buffet flats were often billed as "sex circuses," which functioned as a prelude to the performers and their clients changing locations to a backroom or nearby boardinghouse for sex. One New York theatrical tabloid reported on a Harlem buffet flat featuring a performance that "Sappho in her most daring moments never imagined," involving "little yellow girls, little black girls," and "little white girls" who were "all writhing around together on the dark blue velvet carpet under the white glare of the spotlight." Notably, the journalist also described "the high peel of laughter" during the performance coming from the audience, which revealed the presence of women watching this spectacle alongside men.[74] This suggests that sex circuses in Harlem at this time were not merely for the male gaze but attracted women as well. The feminine laughter may have signified the women's discomfort or embarrassment in witnessing such a performance, or perhaps it was a reaction to the unexpected feelings generated by the scene itself.

As in any performance, the proclivities of the actors onstage did not necessarily resemble their desires offstage. Nonetheless, an account given by a young sex worker in New Orleans who took part in sex circuses with a female colleague was likely not exceptional: "Neither one of us was afraid to do them things the johns liked. . . . We came on with everything we could think of, includin' the dyke act," and "We got to like it so much" that "we'd lot of times do it when we was by ourselves."[75] This quote suggests that some sex workers learned about queer behaviors on the job in order to please male clients and then incorporated them into their private lives as well. These queer performances, permitted within the illicit Prohibition era search for "new thrills," were also opportunities to transmit sexual knowledge about queer acts and desires.

As increasing numbers of women took part in sex work during Prohibition, Black women became even more suspect to authorities. This led some working-class women who claimed they would never take part in commercial sex to nonetheless be framed and arrested for doing so.[76] Young unmarried Black women were often assumed to be sex workers by the police both for their single status and because they lived in neighborhoods associated with vice.[77] In the eyes of reformers, anti-vice committees, judges, and religious authorities, Black urban life was intimately tied to commercialized vice. This was, again, in part because Black migrants were forced to live in or adjacent to red-light districts due both to segregation and to long-standing racial ideologies that imbued African Americans with lesser morals and values than white people.[78] Working-class Black women who took part in commercial sex during Prohibition usually did so because they had few other avenues to support themselves. And at the same time, other women who were not sex workers were viewed as capable of such work and were even arrested under false pretenses.

Unmarried Black women and women who lived together were especially vulnerable to charges of prostitution. In 1924, for example, when Mabel Hampton was twenty-two years old, she was imprisoned at New York State Reformatory for Women at Bedford for three years under false charges for solicitation.[79] Hampton was a southern migrant and made a living alternatively as a performer and a domestic worker. She had been involved in romantic relationships with women since she was seventeen.[80] According to her, on the night of her arrest, she and a female friend were waiting for their male dates, "who promised to take them to a cabaret." The family she worked for was currently out of the country, and the two women were waiting to be picked up at the family's home. When their dates arrived, policemen raided her employer's home, arresting Hampton and her female friend.[81] She explained to the prison parole board that she had never been a sex worker and had been seeing her male suitor for a month, noting that he "wanted to marry her." She eventually realized that her date worked as a "stool pigeon"—or a police accomplice—and had arranged her arrest.[82]

Notably, when recounting this arrest many years later to Joan Nestle, the founder of the Lesbian Herstory Archives, Hampton added, "I hadn't been with a man no time."[83] Perhaps Hampton chose to strategically present herself as heterosexual to the prison authorities, allowing them to believe that she was romantically involved with the man who had come to take her and her female friend to a cabaret. Concurrently, it is possible that

Hampton may have been taking part in a type of sex work known as "treating," to complement her wages as a domestic worker and a chorus girl. The practice of treating involved working-class women exchanging sexual favors with male companions—possibly but not necessarily including sexual intercourse—for an evening out on the town.[84] It was not uncommon for Black women working as domestics to take part in some type of sex work in order to make more money.[85] However, perhaps Hampton did not want to reveal this to Nestle, who was specifically interested in historical narratives concerning lesbian identity.

Hampton served thirteen months of her sentence at New York State Reformatory for Women at Bedford but was released early after promising under oath that she would not return to New York City and "its bad influences." However, when Hampton began attending social events in Manhattan again, a nosy neighbor reported her activities to authorities and she was forced to return to prison and complete her full sentence.[86] While some historians have argued that privacy existed in Harlem tenement apartments in part because of "the willingness of those not bound by familial ties to look the other way," this example shows that neighbors also sought to regulate the suspect behavior of those in their immediate surroundings as well.[87]

Mabel Hampton's false arrest under solicitation charges was not an isolated incident, as this was a common practice in 1920s New York. This situation casts light both on the corruption of the police force during Prohibition and on the threat that single Black migrant women posed to northern cities.[88] The *New York Age* ran multiple articles and editorials the same year Hampton was arrested about the "notorious" Charles Dancey, a "stool pigeon and police 'pimp,'" who had framed "innocent and unsuspecting girls and women" so that "certain rookies, and ambitious, but conscienceless officers, might make 'records.'"[89] The articles blatantly alerted readers, in all capital letters, that "ALL WOMEN AND GIRLS ARE WARNED AGAINST PERMITTING DANCEY OR ANY OF HIS ASSOCIATES INVEIGLING INTO COMPROMISING SITUATIONS THAT WILL PROBABLY LEAD TO THEIR UNDOING."[90] False arrests were sought by the police to meet quotas, which burdened innocent women with unfounded criminal records that could rarely be expunged. In the eyes of the court, many Black women were guilty until proven innocent, as they were assumed by white juries to be naturally drawn to crime and deviance.[91]

The problem did not end with the arrest of Charles Dancey; later in 1930, the *New York Age* ran a lengthy editorial titled "Framing Women in

Harlem." An inquiry had recently been conducted by the Appellate Division of the New York Supreme Court into the corruption of the state's lower courts, which found "a sordid system of vicious oppression, which made as its prey defenseless women, regardless of the fact whether they were guilty of crime or not." The editors noted, "Many of the judges refused to believe that women could be framed in such manner by the police and the stool pigeons." They then discussed the earlier case of Charles Dancey, describing his technique for targeting innocent women in Harlem: "The stool pigeon would seek entrance to some apartment occupied by one woman or more, on some specious excuse, and soon after the police would follow and arrest the inmates on the charge of keeping a disorderly house or plain prostitution."[92] Both single women and women who lived with other women were sought out by male police informants, which shows the overlapping ways that Black queer women, single women, and sex workers were conflated and deemed suspect for their lack of heteronormative living arrangements in the Prohibition era.

Single women living in apartments or boardinghouses often had to work to maintain the appearance of respectability that their unmarried status could bring into question, as the case of Charles Dancey shows. In addition, heterosexuality was usually presumed during this era by anyone not appearing to transgress gender norms. While lesbian identity was becoming more visible, two feminine young women living together in an urban setting were still more likely to raise suspicions of sex work rather than queerness. This happened to a couple named Olivia Walton and Margaret Mason, who lived together in New York from 1926 to 1928. The women attempted to pass as heterosexual by claiming to be married to two men with whom they also lived. However, their neighbors thought they were sex workers and the men their pimps. One neighbor claimed to have seen Walton "indulging in normal and abnormal sexual acts," and others were said to be aware of the women's relationship.[93] Women known to be queer could now also be conceived of as sex workers; both types of deviance were compatible forms of "outlaw" identity.[94] Indeed, for social workers by the early twentieth century, homosexuality, promiscuity, and prostitution all fell under the umbrella category of "sex delinquency."[95]

Similarly, middle-class Black critics often referred to queer women and sex workers in the same breath when discussing the social problems of the urban North. George Schuyler, a columnist for the Black socialist periodical the *Messenger*, noted in a long 1923 screed on "the underworld" that "there are certain distinct types among the folks the farthest down: the prostitute, the pimp who lives off her earnings, [and] the sexual perverts," all of whom "feed upon the social organism" and "infest the places of recreation, amusement and refreshment, both proletarian and bourgeois." Schuyler then argued, "Homosexual practices and heterosexual perversions are almost universal amongst the folks farthest down." Then turning specifically to women, Schuyler observed, "The female pervert who takes the aggressive role in homosexual practices affects and exaggerates the mannerisms of the masculine; bass voice, mannish walk, etc. Often they are maintained by a prostitute. They boast of their ability 'to take any woman away from her man.' A pimp generally becomes uneasy when one of these 'bulls' engages his girl in conversation. The female homosexual pervert strives for the companionship of young, unsophisticated girls."[96]

Here, journalist George Schuyler seemed to rely on nineteenth-century sexological categories that identified only "a female pervert" as masculine, or inverted, while her assumedly feminine partner, whether a sex worker or, paradoxically, a "young, unsophisticated girl," was not labeled as such. Later in the article, Schuyler commented that there were disproportionate numbers of African Americans in the underworld because they were paid less than white people while being forced to pay higher rents, and further, more Black women than men lived in urban areas.[97] These skewed ratios were often attributed to the fact that while Black men had difficulties finding factory work in cities, Black women had little problem finding domestic work. While disproportionate populations of the sexes in the urban North had been commented on in earlier decades by experts such as Kelly Miller, before the 1920s this fact was not explicitly tied to concerns over women's queer relationships as it was now.[98]

Black theatrical producer and columnist Salem Tutt Whitney critiqued the troublesome visibility of lesbians and sex workers in Harlem and imbued his plays with ideologies of Black middle-class respectability. As mentioned in the last chapter's opening, Whitney penned a 1929 article declaring that lesbians should be kicked out of the entertainment industry. That same year, his musical *Deep Harlem*, went from being performed uptown at the Lafayette Theatre to a brief stint on Broadway. According to a white *Variety* critic, the play featured "all the dusky Harlem types" that one encountered on Seventh Avenue, including "Brown skin prosties, nances, [and] lesbians."[99] The critic assured readers that these lurid characters were included in the performance only "for comedy effects, while the better classes inhabiting [Harlem] are also worked in."[100] In one of his *New York Amsterdam News* theatrical columns, Whitney listed the cast of characters of the musical, which included "The Lesbian," "The Lesbian's Pal," and "The Sissy."[101] While Whitney did not approve of queer behavior, particularly in the entertainment industry, he acknowledged that queer men and women had established a visible presence in Harlem by the end of the 1920s.[102]

Similarly, Willie "The Lion" Smith, a popular pianist in the early twentieth century, wrote an autobiography offering details of the daily life and social networks of the New York music underworld, strongly linking vice, queer sexuality, and music and entertainment. While working at a club in Newark, New Jersey, in the 1910s, Smith "got a real bad crush" on a "delicate beauty" named Maude, whom "all the Newark pimps" were trying to get "in their stables." While attempting to court her, he discovered she was queer, which was "quite a shock" because he believed he had never met such a woman before. After this realization, he "left her alone and let the pimps battle over her to their heart's content."[103] Later in his memoir Smith remarked that "history gets made in the night clubs and cafes, anyplace where alcohol is present. It is there that one runs into all kinds—nags, fags, lesbians, pimps and hustlers."[104] Lesbians were now stock characters in urban nightlife and vice districts, often mentioned in the same breath as their outlaw sisters, sex workers.

In the early twentieth century, similar assumptions aligning prostitution and queer sociality emerged. A 1921 report carried out by sociologist Howard Woolston for the Bureau of Social Hygiene, *Prostitution in the United States*, discussed women who had "entered the life" of prostitution, or had even "grown up in the life."[105] But not long after, the phrase "in the life" also came to mean either "queer" or participating in Black queer social life. According to Joseph Beam, editor of the groundbreaking book *In the Life: A Black Gay Anthology*, "in the life" was a phrase "used to describe 'street life' (the lifestyle of pimps, prostitutes, hustlers, and drug dealers)" and was "also the phrase used to describe the 'gay life' (the lives of Black homosexual men and women). Street life and gay life, at times, embrace and entwine, yet at other times, are precise opposites."[106] Just as Black lady lovers could be found in all walks of life, so too did some of them take part in the underground sex economy that thrived during Prohibition.

THE SPECTACLE OF GLADYS BENTLEY'S PROHIBITION PERFORMANCES

As we have seen, live music and performance were important elements to Black queer women's socializing in the Prohibition era. One of the most popular and notorious performers to emerge from this milieu was Gladys Bentley. She fashioned her own identity in 1920s Harlem after a childhood in Philadelphia, where she was taunted by her fellow schoolchildren for being fat and unfeminine. And worse, her parents tried to have her lesbianism cured by doctors, so she ran away from home to New York City at age sixteen.[107] In Harlem's burgeoning queer entertainment world, she was able to turn these past liabilities into something new and powerful: "the tough-talking, masculine acting, cross-dressing, and sexually worldly bulldagger."[108] Unlike many other popular Harlem artists at this time who hinted at their same-sex desires or acted on them but rarely discussed them, Bentley was always open about her love of women and, as previously mentioned, went as far as to have a public wedding ceremony with her partner, a white female singer.

Bentley's deep alto voice complemented her masculine appearance, and she quickly began to garner a reputation at local clubs for remaking popular songs with titillating double entendres. Bentley first became well known for singing "naughty" versions of popular songs, such as a take on the popular Broadway tunes "Sweet Georgia Brown" and "My Alice Blue Gown" that turned them into an ode to the joys of anal sex. As one of the only known examples of Bentley's unrecorded songs from her live performances, the lyrics deserved to be shared:

And he said, "Dearie, please turn around"
And he shoved that big thing up my brown.
He tore it. I bored it. Lord, how I adored it.
My Sweet Little Alice Blue Gown.[109]

According to one of her biographers, after Bentley encouraged her audience to sing along with her on such songs, "it was just a matter of time before the house got raided."[110] The illicit themes of her music fit right in with the atmosphere of Prohibition. Such queer and "robust salacious songs" performed in speakeasies bolstered the risky atmosphere in which bootleg liquor was served.[111] At the same time, more mainstream clubs that remained lawful and did not serve alcohol had to rely on talented and mesmerizing performers such as Bentley to attract audiences in the first place.

As white newspaper nightlife columnists like Louis Sobol began to regularly attend and report on her performances, Bentley's popularity with slumming audiences increased. She became a feature at Harlem clubs like Connie's Inn and the Ubangi Club, which were known for their talented

Figure 3.2. A 1933 "A Night-Club Map of Harlem," featuring Gladys' Clam House. E. Simms Campbell, Library of Congress Control Number 2016585261.

Black entertainers and starkly white audiences, although she had to tone down her more risqué lyrics there. She soon became so popular at Harry Hansberry's Clam House that in the late 1920s and early 1930s it was renamed Gladys' Clam House in her honor, as shown in figure 3.2.[112] Some of these clubs allowed light-skinned Black patrons, but others did not, much to Harlem locals' chagrin. Bentley nonetheless performed in men's clothing and flirted with female audience members, taking advantage of the curiosity people had about her modern new persona: the confident, swaggering bulldagger. As her biographer noted, "She seemed to thrive on the fact that her odd habits" were "the subject of much tongue wagging."[113]

Notably, while Bentley's appearance was explicitly queer, her recorded songs usually played with queer and feminist themes within heterosexual narratives. One of her records, "Worried Blues," was concerned with the poor ways that men treated women, prefiguring the coming feminist critiques of domestic violence and unequal heterosexual relationships.[114] This song repeated the confrontational question, "What makes you men folk treat us women like you do?" Another of her recorded songs, "How Much Can I Stand?," posed the provocative question, "Who the devil heard of an angel that gets beat up every night?"[115] While her records—which were not nearly as popular as those of the women discussed in the previous chapter—stayed within parameters of the heteronormative, in her live performances she had more freedom to make queer behaviors and desires visible.

A 1933 review of Bentley's show details a common plot device of hers. W. E. Thomas, journalist for the *Baltimore Afro-American*, described the scene: "A fat Black woman dressed in shirtwaist and skirt, with her hair plastered back on her head, sang wicked blues in a deep contralto voice. She bemoaned her girlfriend who had deserted her for another woman. While she sang she went from table to table, scanning the faces of the female patrons as though she expected to find said girl-friend there. Much to the delight of the audience, every once in a while she'd feign recognition only to find disappointment upon closer inspection."[116] This performance took place in Greenwich Village, where the audience would have mostly been white, so Bentley—who married a white woman herself—was likely flirting primarily with white female audience members.[117] While interracial queer relationships were not unheard of at the time, they were more the exception than the norm in the Jim Crow era.

Writer Langston Hughes described Bentley as "a large, dark, masculine lady, whose feet pounded the floor while her fingers pounded the keyboard—a perfect piece of African sculpture, animated by her own rhythm." She had "an amazing exhibition of musical energy" and would perform all night long with "scarcely a break between the notes, sliding from one song to another, with a powerful continuous underbeat of jungle rhythm."[118] Hughes notably portrayed Bentley here with the language of "primitivism," a popular interwar concept used especially in conjunction with the growing interest in music and art influenced by the "Negro vogue" and white slumming. Hughes had employed such language when it was the province of the avant-garde before the 1920s, and he also asserted an open pride in the supposed "primitive" qualities of his race.[119] In a time when many educated African Americans looked on figures like Bentley and Bessie Smith with disdain, Hughes embraced them as authentic. The names of Harlem clubs that attracted the biggest white crowds of the era—the Cotton Club, the Ubangi Club—smacked of this same primitivism, which was supposed to appeal to white people looking to escape their busy, modern lives with a trip to somewhere free and wild, if only for a night. As one 1925 New York guidebook noted, one of the pastimes of white New Yorkers was "to observe the antics of members of its enormous negro population . . . their unfailing sense of rhythm, their vocal quality, something primitive, animal-like and graceful in their movements."[120]

This idea of race essentialism was also held by wealthy white Harlem Renaissance benefactors like Carl Van Vechten and Nancy Cunard, who embraced African cultures as pure, exotic, and spiritual.[121] Black folk culture, including the blues, was especially appealing to them. Taking a vested interest in Black culture during the Jim Crow era marked these white supporters at the time as socially liberal, yet in retrospect it is clear that this admiration was a doubled-edged sword, as white patrons of African American art also objectified and denigrated Black artists.[122] Similarly, slumming in Black neighborhoods enabled white and heterosexual people to take part in cross-racial and taboo sexual behaviors, yet at the same time it solidified their privilege and power over Black locals and performers.[123]

Gladys Bentley became so popular during Prohibition that by the early 1930s she headed down to midtown clubs from Harlem, where her toned-down but still raunchy performances were soon discovered not only by journalists but by the police as well. One reporter in 1934 referred to Bentley as a victim of New Deal "reform" under the auspices of Mayor LaGuardia's new efforts to "clean up" New York entertainments.[124] She had been appearing at the King's Terrace on West Fifty-Second Street, where complaints made over her "dirty songs" led to her dismissal from the venue, and soon after that the police padlocked the establishment's doors.[125] Bentley not only had performed with a troupe of feminine male dancers but was said to have been responsible for "the filthiest offering of the evening" when she went through the audience during her show and "at each table she stopped to sing one or more verses of a seemingly endless song in which every word known to vulgar profanity is used."[126] The popularity of Gladys Bentley in the Prohibition era opened opportunities to move her act from Harlem to Midtown, but her shows were not acceptable for non-slumming, white middle-class audiences. New Deal programs in the 1930s sought to reform the social problems of the Great Depression, but the search for more wholesome urban entertainments and a new government commitment to cleaning up dirty acts did not bode well for Bentley's titillating performances.

While Gladys Bentley was a subaltern figure in society, during Prohibition she brought life on the margins to the center of the world. As someone who represented "the other" in multiple ways, from her race to her gender presentation and size, she attracted audiences who may have viewed her as a spectacle, but the success she experienced gave her power as well. Bentley made unabashed lesbianism more visible in the decade in which the concept truly came into the national consciousness. Her risqué performances helped cultivate the audacious and transgressive attitudes that women who did not need men could afford to enact. But as the country entered into the Great Depression, entertainment opportunities for Black performers began to shrink, and critics of queer artists like Bentley became increasingly harsh.

THE GREAT DEPRESSION AND THE END OF PROHIBITION IN THE URBAN NORTH

Black journalist George Schuyler wryly declared decades after the fact that "the Depression did not have the impact on the Negroes that it had on whites," because African Americans had been in a "Depression the whole time."[127] Indeed, economic disparities had already burdened Black northern urban districts in the 1920s with high rents, low wages, and poor housing conditions, straining residents for years prior to the stock market crash.[128] In fact, the *Chicago Defender* sounded an alarm in January 1929, months before the October crash, when it announced that firms had been discharging employees for months, "many of whom have been faithful workers at these places for years."[129] The Urban League also noted that "race workers" were being replaced "by workers of other races," leading the *Defender* for the first time to tell its southern readers to stay in the South and dispense with plans to migrate North.[130] During the Depression, most African Americans in the urban North got by on a measly "subsistence budget" with little opportunity to save for the future or splurge on "culture."[131] The white slumming crowds also dwindled, as they too had less disposable income for such adventures.

As economic relief came to some Americans in the form of New Deal legislation, domestic workers and farmworkers, two occupations held by the majority of working-class African Americans, were not included in some of the new programs such as the Social Security Act.[132] White southern Democrats saw to it that these significant New Deal reforms would primarily benefit and bring upward mobility to members of the white working class and help them access the middle class. Southern Democrats did not want African Americans to make such a climb; they wanted them instead to remain a worker class that those of the white middle class could utilize through domestic service, farm help, and custodial work to maintain their status. At the same time, many new programs putting Americans back to work were available only to men, such as the Civilian Conservation Corps. Taken together, excluding African Americans and women from some of the New Deal programs sent the explicit message that the government did not see Black women as essential to economic recovery and the implicit suggestion that they were not full citizens worthy of assistance during a difficult time for the entire nation.[133]

While Prohibition had played an important role in increasing the visibility of queer urban identities, the Great Depression helped precipitate a revolt against gay life in the 1930s. This was connected to both the new crisis in gender arrangements, as "emasculated" men lost their jobs and status as household providers, and the 1933 repeal of Prohibition, which was replaced by new restrictions on queer nightlife spaces in many cities.[134] Since authorities believed speakeasies had "eroded the boundaries between respectability and criminality," the repeal of Prohibition ushered in an era of increased surveillance and control of the sexuality of nightlife patrons.[135] This occurred in part because by the early 1930s as the Depression dragged on, a general revulsion had set in against the material "excesses" of Prohibition. As more struggling Americans came to believe that such hedonism should not be tolerated during an economic downturn, a campaign against the visibility of the gay world was launched in New York and cities throughout the nation.[136]

Following Prohibition's repeal came new state laws to control the consumption of liquor and to regulate the spaces where it was consumed, which was used to police the presence of queerness. As Lisa McGirr argues, the expansion of state authority that Prohibition had initiated did not disappear with repeal but rather "lurched forward in new directions."[137] Repeal gave each state the right to regulate their alcohol sales, so in New York, the State Liquor Authority became the exclusive authority to license the sale of liquor and was the final arbiter of which venues were legitimate and worthy of a liquor license. Those venues seeking to serve alcohol were required to not "suffer or permit such premises to become disorderly."[138] While "disorderly" was not explicitly defined, the State Liquor Authority took this term to imply that the presence of queer patrons, sex workers, gamblers, and other "undesirables" made a venue disorderly. This meant that proprietors who openly welcomed such patrons in their establishments would risk losing their liquor license.[139] In the two and a half decades following repeal, the State Liquor Authority would go on to close hundreds of bars that "welcomed, tolerated, or simply failed to notice" the patronage of queer men and women.[140] However, this may have affected Black lady lovers less than others, for while they gathered in the liminal spaces opened up by Prohibition, as we have seen, they often preferred to socialize in their own homes. Although Prohibition's repeal brought most of the illicit venues of the era to an end, Black queer women had never been able to fully rely on commercial venues to provide them with a safe and welcoming environment in which to socialize.

Soon after the 1929 stock market crash, some popular theaters were no longer able to afford expensive, elaborate stage shows, so they shut down or became movie theaters.[141] Yet, despite the economic crisis, queer performances continued in places like Harlem, emerging from now defunct speakeasies into more legitimate clubs. However, Black lady lovers performing in these venues received more negative critiques in the Black press than ever before. In 1934, Gladys Bentley starred in a new show at the Lafayette Theatre, one of the biggest Black theaters in Harlem, where she performed with a "pansy chorus." The New York Age's theater critic, Vere Johns, described Bentley as "a large and ungainly woman" who "cuts her hair" short and "dresses in tuxedos."[142] While she had appeared in smaller venues in Harlem for the past five years and had become the talk of the town, Johns had somehow never come across her before this performance, suggesting he did not frequent the cabarets and speakeasies of Harlem but only the respectable theatrical venues. Or perhaps the critic was familiar with her but did not concede this point since he did not want to be associated with her. Bentley, whose chorus line of six male "pansy" dancers referred her to as a "gorgeous man," disgusted Johns. He wrote that if the members of her chorus line were "put into dresses," they "would be indistinguishable from chorines." The critic admitted that he "could not enjoy their part of the show as [he] had a burning desire to rush out and get an ambulance backed up against the stage door to take them all to Bellevue for the alienists to work on."[143]

Several weeks later, Johns took note in his column again of Bentley and her troupe, which he reported "gave first class portrayals of sex perversion, and I have it on the printed word of the dramatic editor of the Amsterdam News that theirs was no play-acting, but the real thing. Be that as it may, the effect on me was a feeling akin to that of seeing some hideous deformed cripple, and a case for an expert alienist only. Persons who can find humorous entertainment in such things, I must regretfully place in the category of morons and moral imbeciles."[144] While the most well-known medical authority on homosexuality in this era was Sigmund Freud, who argued that the majority of individuals who desired the same sex did not need or want medical treatment, the notion that queer people were mentally ill prevailed for much of the twentieth century. Vere Johns's extreme reaction to the gender transgression he witnessed on the stage suggested that he not only was concerned with the acceptability of such performances but feared they might disrupt the notion that high-minded theater was art, which for him was constantly in the service of racial uplift.

As this example shows, in the post-Prohibition era, Black queer performance emerged from basement speakeasies into the legitimate theaters of Black districts, and cultural critics frequently reacted in horror. The Great Depression heralded a more conservative moment as the transgressive gender expressions enjoyed onstage during the "anything goes" Jazz Age were now met with a backlash. This waning tolerance for gender transgression during the economic downturn was coupled with the desire to "clean up" entertainment in the era of New Deal reform. Another example of the growing demonization of lady lovers in the 1930s can be found in a short series of fictionalized articles by Ralph Matthews of the *Baltimore Afro-American*. His stories argued that the Black entertainment world was full of masculine female predators who leeched on to innocent newcomers and lured them into an underworld of perversion.[145] This narrative detailed a young chorus girl named Ruby who had recently arrived in Harlem from rural North Carolina, hoping to make it big in show business. Soon she was being courted by a "handsome" female performer named Pert Fleason, who tells Ruby, "You seem so frail, so weak, all alone in New York. You need someone to protect you. Someone to care for you and love you. Won't you let me take you under my wing? We could mean so much to each other."[146] In part 2 of the story, Pert brings the oblivious Ruby to a women-only club in Harlem, where she finally realizes the magnitude of the situation. As Ruby closely looked at the women in the club, "their charm vanished. The finely chiseled chins became long and pointed. . . . Shapely arms, exposed by evening gowns . . . became hairy, and smiling white teeth in even rows, jutted out from the corner of the curled lips like—yes, that's what they were—fangs! She was in a den of she-wolves, and Pert—God curse her soul—had led her there."[147] Soon Ruby was safely back in the arms of a male suitor, declaring, "I made my escape just in time and I'm never going through the woods again without my big, strong woodchopper."[148]

In these stories, Ralph Matthews represents lady lovers in the entertainment industry as violent, animalistic, deceitful, and willing to bribe and manipulate women in order to take sexual advantage of them. His protagonist, Ruby, is at first lured in by their glamour but eventually comes to her senses and makes the correct heteronormative choice of a male partner for protection. The figure of the predatory lesbian that Matthews describes was threatening because heterosexual men now had to compete with women as well as men when attempting to seduce women in the entertainment industry. Such women were now usurping men's roles by signifying their sexual agency and desire, upsetting traditional gender roles in which women were passive and only men were active—or lovers of women.

Other sensational stories about aggressive women overstepping their privileges abounded in the Black press during the Great Depression. *New York Age* columnist Marcus Wright denounced the "sophisticated ladies and their boyish bobs" who strolled down Seventh Avenue in Harlem "serving death warrants on all women lovers." He warned the "fellows" to "keep their eyes open and watch their women. If you don't you might lose Susie."[149] Even worse, a 1934 front-page article in the Black newspaper the *Philadelphia Tribune* called attention to the prevalence of queer women in vice districts who sought to seduce high school girls at local rent parties and "watch[ed] their every move" when they left for school in the morning. Such women, who "ruin[ed]" girls, often appeared normal and self-respecting yet were actually "sex perverts" who "arrange for orgies with persons of their own sex."[150] A 1936 article in the *Baltimore Afro-American* cited statistics that 400,000 male and female inverts lived in the United States, and while this was an "amazing total," what was even worse was that the country also held "almost five million" perverts, whom the newspaper defined as "people who might be normal but are corrupted by inverts."[151]

Taken together, these examples show that throughout the Great Depression, concerns about the visibility of Black lady lovers were growing more prevalent. Such women threatened decent society and sought to bring "normal" girls and women down to their depths. Usurping the male privilege of sexual access to women, lady lovers were especially unsettling in an era of precarious financial stability, when men's social and economic power as heads of household was emphatically being called in question. While Black queer women's identities and social networks became more visible than ever during Prohibition, a backlash to the loosening of sexual mores and gender roles in the Jazz Age arrived swiftly in the 1930s during the Great Depression.

~~~~~~~~~~~~~~

This chapter has described a variety of spaces found in Prohibition era northern cities, from speakeasies to rent parties and buffet flats, where Black women who loved women socialized and worked. Such gathering sites were backdrops for experimenting with a variety of queer behaviors and identities, which resulted in making these concepts more visible to mainstream America.[152] These spaces stimulated the emergence of Black queer networks. However, they were also renowned for their lack of respectability due to their geographic proximity and connection to illicit urban underworlds.

Buffet flats, where queer behaviors and commercial sex mixed, had begun to flourish prior to Prohibition and became even more popular during this era as locals sought to distance themselves from the racial voyeurism of white "slummers" and as Black neighborhoods became vice districts. Rent parties were historically connected to the economic circumstances of segregation and racial inequality and arose as a communal solution to high rent prices. These parties were "recommended to newly arrived single gals as the place to go get acquainted," and women such as Mabel Hampton often met their partners through such gatherings.[153] Prohibition also created new entrepreneurial opportunities for Black women, which was very important during an era when men ran most commercial recreations.[154] Queer women—particularly entertainers—threw these parties and frequented speakeasies and buffet flats. Speakeasies were most often white-run spaces, yet many earned reputations as welcoming to queer African Americans. Here, women who wished to go out on the town could congregate, drink, and dance in an illicit setting that accepted a range of "deviant" activities, from queer dancing to playing sexual songs and showcasing queer performances. These Prohibition era spaces helped Black lady lovers sustain their queer networks within a larger, northern urban Black community.

Aside from queerness, the other most visible illicit sexuality in these spaces was commercial sex, as the chapter's opening story reveals. Lesbianism and prostitution have historically been conflated due to nonreproductive sexuality's association with criminality. Racialized stereotypes about Black women's immorality and licentiousness, coupled with economic inequalities that have affected Black women's lack of employment opportunities and their proximity to vice districts, have further historically connected Black women to sex work. Due to these reasons and others, some Black lady lovers in the urban North were erotic performers and sex workers in Prohibition spaces. Yet at the same time, many women who did not work in these fields were assumed to do so by corrupt white policemen looking to meet their quotas and by neighbors who saw single Black women as suspect.

While the Prohibition era's permissive air helped usher in a period of increasing visibility for queer behaviors and identities, the onset of the Great Depression and the following repeal of the Volstead Act caused a backlash that further demonized queer women for rejecting traditional maternal femininity and appropriating male privileges. Further, lady lovers' implicit association with the underworld contributed to their demonization by race leaders and others concerned with the social ills that the world of vice brought into the Black community. Despite all of this, during Prohibition, women were able to experiment with new identities and relationships in liminal spaces, and while the cultural institutions of the era may not have withstood the Depression, the social networks that had emerged could continue to be maintained. From women-only house parties to female couples dancing the slow drag in speakeasies, Black lady lovers carved their own worlds out of segregated cities that sought to suppress them.

FOUR

Intimate Friends and Bosom Companions

Middle-Class Black Lady Lovers
Crafting Queer Kinship Networks

In August 1927, fifty-two-year-old writer, activist, and lady lover Alice Dunbar-Nelson went to see singer Ethel Waters perform in the musical *Africana* on Broadway. She wrote afterward in her diary that she enjoyed the show chiefly because of Waters, who was "loveable." Her friend Geraldyn Dismond, a newspaper gossip columnist, introduced the two women backstage, and Dunbar-Nelson wrote that Waters "was lovely to meet" and declared she "would like to know her."[1] While the world of the classic blues singers and that of Black "high society" women might appear separate, in the Jazz Age, performers like Ethel Waters and Alberta Hunter socialized with writer Dorothy West, dramatic actress Edna Thomas, and heiress A'Lelia Walker. West first made a name for herself as one of the youngest of the Harlem Renaissance era writers, and in the 1930s she had relationships with several women, eventually living with writer Marian Minus, with whom she coedited an important literary journal. More interested in motherhood than in being a wife, West sought marriage with multiple queer male writer friends, from Langston Hughes to Bruce Nugent and Countee Cullen, all for the purpose of having a child with one of them—a dream she never realized.

Dorothy West's close family friend, actress Edna Thomas, also had an unusual domestic arrangement.[2] By the late 1930s she lived in Harlem with her husband, Lloyd Thomas, along with her lover, the white British aristocrat Olivia Wyndham. The Thomases' home was an extension of their community, and other friends would regularly stay with them as well, including Dorothy West and her cousin, who lived there for a time. To explain the arrangement, Edna Thomas would tell friends—even those also known for their queer liaisons—that Wyndham was merely "a house guest" who "helped with expenses."[3] During the Great Depression, economic reasons for their domestic intimacy could be highlighted over romantic ones, particularly for a relationship so unconventional as to combine non-monogamy, bisexuality, and love across the color line in the Jim Crow era.

This chapter will examine the unconventional relationships that middle-class Black lady lovers took part in during the interwar era, from open and hidden love triangles between women, their husbands, and female lovers, to marriages of convenience between women and gay men, as well as arrangements in which two women made a home and a life together, which had once been considered innocent but was now becoming rather suspect. Through enacting relationships outside the accepted heterosexual nuclear family, these respected lady lovers helped forge modern new ideas of gender, sexuality, and kinship. This chapter also excavates sources revealing some of these women's thoughts on their queer desires, given that there are more documents available to access their "inner worlds" than there are for working-class historical subjects, ranging from diaries, correspondence, and sexology case studies. These sources chart the depths of their desires for other women, regrets for affairs that could not be, sadness for lack of opportunities to have families of their own, and dreams of the Black queer communities they hoped to establish.

Black lady lovers of different class backgrounds often shared similar strategies for negotiating their queer desires, which is not surprising considering that most women kept their same-sex attractions under wraps in this era. Further, successful creative Black women often traversed different social classes throughout their lifetimes. African American social class at this time was complex; as Sterling A. Brown pointed out in a 1932 issue of the Black periodical *Opportunity*, the Black middle class differed in many respects from its white counterpart. He argued that the African American "elite" was generally "only one remove—even our 'ritziest' only one and a half removes—from our masses."[4] Alice Dunbar-Nelson's diary offers examples of this. While she had a reputation for being "distinctly aristocratic," she detailed having to sell her jewelry at a pawn shop to pay her water bill before attending a women's club function at a "palatial" estate.[5] Further revealing the complexity of social class for Black women at this time, writer Dorothy West grew up among the wealthiest of African American families in Boston. This was due to her father's success in the fruit industry, but he himself had been born into slavery. However, similar to West's good friend Alberta Hunter, the blues singer, who grew up as the daughter of a domestic worker employed in a brothel, West never acknowledged her female lovers in public, and both "frequently boasted" about relationships with men.[6] Both women enjoyed the company of gay men and "gave similarly evasive answers when asked why they never married."[7] Even women who did make a life and home with another woman, like Howard University's first dean of women, Lucy Diggs Slowe, did not refer to them as romantic partners in public, or even in letters—at least not in correspondence that has survived.

This chapter documents these influential women's experiences to demonstrate the lengths that Black lady lovers would go to in order to have the relationships they desired, even though they knew that queerness was not accepted in "high society." The women who will be centrally discussed in this chapter—Alice Dunbar-Nelson, Dorothy West, Edna Thomas, A'Lelia Walker, and Lucy Diggs Slowe—created alternative forms of kinship to counter the heteronormative nuclear family model through their own domestic arrangements as well as through the Black queer gathering spaces and cultural texts they created. They met in literary salons, worked to uplift their communities through clubs and organizing, created art, and played a central role in the Harlem Renaissance and in Black women's higher education.

While the interwar era saw the growing visibility of queer identities and independent, modern women, the emerging sentiment of race pride hailed as the New Negro era had a distinctively masculinist tenor. This is most visible in the story of Lucy Diggs Slowe, who sought to help Black female students at Howard University succeed while leading a privately queer life off campus. To do so she took part in "dissemblance," which was a common survival strategy for Black women in a society that potentially viewed them as immoral merely for their race and sex.[8] Hazel Carby notes that "the link between Black women and illicit sexuality during the antebellum years had powerful ideological consequences for the next hundred and fifty years."[9] Well into the post-slavery years, there was still a mentality on the part of white people that Black women could not be raped because they were inherently licentious, immoral, and sexually available to white as well as Black men.[10] Darlene Clark Hine argues that this historical legacy greatly contributed to this notion of "dissemblance," under which "the behaviors and attitudes of Black women . . . created the appearance of openness and disclosure but actually shielded the truth of their inner lives and selves from their oppressors."[11]

The concept of dissemblance is often associated with the Black women's club movement, which emerged at the end of the nineteenth century in part to combat the prevalent white perception of Black women as hypersexual, as well as to uplift the race. The pressure to appear chaste contributed to the silence of many clubwomen who loved the same sex and enjoyed flirtations and affairs with other women. Women such as Alice Dunbar-Nelson took part in queer relationships while understanding the strategic significance of deploying respectability. Her diary is important for many reasons, not least because it gives glimpses of stories and rumors about the queer liaisons that Black married clubwomen from around the country seemingly enjoyed in the early twentieth century. Indeed, for some of these professional women in positions of leadership, private queer behaviors and respectability were not irreconcilable.

RESPECTABILITY AND QUEER DESIRE IN THE LIFE OF ALICE DUNBAR-NELSON

Alice Dunbar-Nelson is a particularly important figure in African American women's history because her diary was only the second one written by a Black woman to ever be published.[12] Born Alice Ruth Moore in 1875 New Orleans, her father was a merchant marine and her mother was a seamstress. She attended public school and graduated from Straight University in 1892 and then began teaching and played a prominent role in the musical and literary society of Black and Creole New Orleans. She came north in 1896 for further academic opportunities and started teaching in New York the following year, eventually completing an English thesis at Cornell University. She married the influential poet Paul Laurence Dunbar in 1898 and they made a home in Washington, DC, but the marriage did not last long and they separated in 1902. Her biographer suggests this might have been related to her love of women, as her husband shared a "vile story" about her with their social circle, which was the final straw for her in their relationship. However, he had also physically and mentally abused her since before they wed, which appeared to be the larger problem.[13] Her negative experiences with Dunbar may have further led her to seek out relationships with women, in hopes of encountering less of the violence she had endured with a male partner; still, there may have been multiple reasons she ended the marriage, for later in her life she had no issue with actively loving both women and men.

After the separation from her first husband, Alice Moore Dunbar then moved to Wilmington, Delaware, which became her home for the next three decades. She first served as head of the English department at Howard High School for over a decade and was also active in multiple social movements, including women's suffrage and anti-lynching, and in Black women's clubs. She also published stories, articles, and poems.[14] Dunbar married journalist Robert Nelson in 1916, but her diary reveals that throughout her life, she had close, intimate relationships with women as well as men. One woman in particular who gave her emotional sustenance and encouragement after her divorce was Edwina B. Kruse, the founding principal of Howard High School.[15] A letter from Dunbar-Nelson to Kruse in 1907 exclaimed, "I want you to know dear, that every thought of my life is for you, every throb of my heart is yours and yours alone. I just can not ever let any one else have you."[16] Dunbar-Nelson went as far as to write a lengthy unpublished novel based on Kruse's life, titled "This Lofty Oak," which demonstrated the strength of their bond.[17]

Dunbar-Nelson, like many college-educated African Americans of her generation, had a complex relationship to social class. Even educated, "middle-class," professional Black women like her still had firsthand knowledge of working-class life, as the earlier pawn shop anecdote suggests. Her biographer notes that she had "the breeding, education, culture, looks, and manners of the 'higher classes' (and thought of herself in this way)" but lacked the money "to back it up."[18] At the same time, despite her refined comportment, she went to Harlem dives and cabarets, enjoyed bootleg whiskey, played the numbers, and indulged in what she called a "low taste" for underworld films.[19] However, Dunbar-Nelson's appreciation of Prohibition era culture did not extend to flaunting the details of her queer affairs, as she still believed it was absolutely essential that they remain hidden.[20] Not only was she in her mid-forties as the 1920s began, with her ideas about sexuality and decorum cemented in an earlier era, but she also lived in Delaware, which, unlike Harlem, had a lower tolerance for scandalous Jazz Age hijinks.[21]

For such reasons, Alice Dunbar-Nelson enjoyed visits to Harlem, and her diary offers a few peeks into the queer Prohibition era world she experienced there. During one 1928 trip, she went to the Cotton Club, which she wrote "does not welcome 'us.'" Notably, Dunbar-Nelson was so light-skinned that she often passed as white, which granted her entrance to venues that welcomed only white patrons.[22] Afterward she went to a speakeasy called the "Mexico," which she referred to as "one of those Low-downers, with plenty of local color, a bar, good beer, and good food, quite reasonable."[23] Dunbar-Nelson also visited A'Lelia Walker's infamous Harlem salon, the Dark Tower, on this trip. She stopped in "for a salad and a cup of coffee" and noted in her diary, "Anne Dingle and Eunice Hunton Carter very much together."[24] Both prominent women in their communities, Dingle was a schoolteacher and "social leader" according to the *Chicago Defender*, while Carter was a Smith College graduate who in 1935 would become New York's first African American assistant district attorney.[25] The two women were both married to men when Dunbar-Nelson bumped into them, and if her assumption was correct, they showed that more middle-class Black women were embarking on queer relationships or affairs alongside traditional marriage and family. Interestingly, after mentioning this couple, Dunbar-Nelson began referring in her diary to a man she thought might be gay as a "male Ann[e] Dingle" in a disparaging tone.[26] Considering her own desires for women, this revealed the conflict she experienced over feelings that she knew were not socially acceptable outside of spaces like the Dark Tower.

However, this tension was not unique to Alice Dunbar-Nelson's life, as there were other married Black women in her sphere who carried on queer affairs while married to men. Dunbar-Nelson traveled in circles among other Black women who "defied respectability through exploration of the erotic" and understood that "moving within the boundaries of respectability meant balancing discretion with desire."[27] In another 1928 diary entry, she mentioned a visit from clubwoman "Mrs. Narka Lee-Rayford," who appeared to be of interest to Dunbar-Nelson, as she noted that they "wanted to make whoopee," yet later she seemed disappointed to find her in a "heavy flirtation" with another clubwoman, Mrs. Lethia Fleming. Both women were leaders of the Federation of Colored Women's Clubs and attending a convention, and their public display of affection left Dunbar-Nelson with her "nose sadly out of joint." She wrote that her husband, Robert Nelson, who came home just as Lee-Rayford left, "was cross, of course," when she showed "any interest in any male or female."[28] Despite her desire for female partners and apparent lack of interest in monogamy, her marriage provided the "cocoon of respectability" so crucial to middle-class African American women, who were vulnerable to criticism and censure concerning their behavior and who sought to avoid the scandal, humiliation, and loss of social and financial status that any accusations of immorality could bring.[29]

The most significant ongoing relationship with a woman that Alice Dunbar-Nelson detailed in her diary was with journalist Fay Jackson Robinson, who founded the first Black intellectual weekly newspaper.[30] They were both married to men, and their attraction was intellectual as well as physical, extending to world affairs through the lens of journalism.[31] While few details are mentioned in her diary, it is clear the two had a special connection, but given their circumstances as married women and the social constraints of the era, a future between them was not deemed possible. Still, Dunbar-Nelson recorded a "perfect day" spent with Robinson and friends in San Francisco in March 1930. They explored the city's "cliffs and hills," went out to the ocean, looked at art by Rodin at the Legion of Honor, and later enjoyed abalone steaks at the States restaurant downtown, after which Robinson spent the night with Dunbar-Nelson at her nearby hotel.[32] The next day she wrote that she put up their "queer folding bed" and said goodbye to her "lovely new-found California friends," especially "Fay-Fay, Little Blue Pidgeon with Velvet Eyes."[33] Then she wrote a sonnet about Robinson that began with the intriguing line, "I had not thought to ope that secret room."[34] Considering Dunbar-Nelson had likely had relationships with women before, such as with Edwina Kruse, it is not clear what she meant by this, but it does suggest taboo desire or emotional vulnerability. Perhaps she had not experienced such longing as Robinson stirred in her in many years and was trying to remain true to her husband.

However, despite their "perfect day" together, it soon appeared that Fay Jackson Robinson was involved with another mutual friend, artist Helene Ricks London, and to complicate matters, both women were romantically interested in Dunbar-Nelson. On March 29, 1930, she wrote in her diary,

Letter from Helene. It *was* pretty raw. But enclosed a mutilated
scrap of a letter from Fay to her, showing that Fay had made certain

promises to Helene about me—not to get friendly, I judge. God it hurt! I must have dropped Helene's envelope and all in my blind rage. [Her husband] Bobbo got it, read it—he *will* read my things, diary and all—God, he *puffformed*. Called Helene and Fay horrible names. I don't know how I assumed an air of nonchalance and cool indifference—which threw him off. Inwardly I raged—at Fay's deceit, at Helene's asininity—hurting of me with Fay's letter, at Bobbo's meddlesomeness and coarseness. It nearly wrecked me. Got through somehow. . . .
Went to market with Bobbo. Came back and deliberately tried to get drunk—and played poker. Succeeded in getting drunk. Maudlin tears and satisfied Bobbo. Tears of rage and pent-up emotion.[35]

This diary entry allows a rare glimpse into how Black lady lovers negotiated their marriages while pursuing women at the same time. Dunbar-Nelson's husband read her mail, revealing the queer love triangle his wife was involved in, which clearly hurt him. She performed emotional distance from the women to ease his concerns and sought to "satisfy" her husband, despite feeling like she wanted to "commit murder" because her "little blue dream of loveliness should end thus."[36] The diary reveals that working to maintain healthy, agreeable relationships with her husband as well as with the women she desired led to jealousy, mistrust, and anger. The next month she sent a sonnet to Fay Jackson Robinson beginning with "I knew I'd suffer if I let love come," which suggested how she felt about their relationship, and perhaps about all the relationships with women she attempted to initiate while married to a man.[37] The heterosexual nuclear family unit clearly did not offer Dunbar-Nelson what she wanted, but other options did not seem truly available either.

A few months later, in June 1930, Dunbar-Nelson noted in her diary that Fay Jackson Robinson had left her husband, which looked "like a hell of a mess." She went on to write, "Privately, I think they were both after [a woman named] Tesse and [her husband] John won," again revealing the complicated love triangles that the married women in her milieu found themselves in, as they sought to create relationships that satisfied all of their needs.[38] Despite ending things poorly with Robinson, a year after their special San Francisco date, Dunbar-Nelson wrote, "Anniversary of My One Perfect Day. . . . And still we cannot meet again."[39] Disappointment and longing permeate her diary, showing the complexity that Black lady lovers encountered in navigating social convention and their desire for female companionship alongside their expected marriages to men. Her diary also reveals the ubiquity of queer flirtations and liaisons carried out by women in her social circles, many of whom were also involved in leadership positions and doing crucial "race work" in the interwar era. While they kept their queer relationships hidden, some Black women who were focused on racial uplift through respectability still found relationships with women compatible with their way of life. Yet even women a generation younger than Alice Dunbar-Nelson, like Dorothy West, had difficulty straddling these worlds.

DOROTHY WEST

A "Reserved Bostonian" Fostering Black Queer Literary Networks

While Dorothy West is a well-known figure in the field of African American women's literature, as an integral member of the queer Harlem Renaissance she has been invisible and left out of significant works on the topic.[40] Best known for her 1947 novel *The Living Is Easy*, West wrote and published many short stories in the Black press and anthologies at a young age and went on to write sketches for the New Deal agency the Works Progress Administration during the Great Depression as well. In the interwar period, West had relationships with several women and would live with writer Marian Minus for many years, with whom she coedited a literary journal. A Boston native whose identity was always tied to her birth city, Dorothy West moved to New York in 1926 at age nineteen with her cousin Helene Johnson, a poet, after they both won literary awards from *Opportunity* magazine, the National Urban League's periodical. West actually tied with Zora Neale Hurston for her short story prize, which the two women shared. The older Hurston magnanimously introduced newcomer West to Wallace Thurman and "his avant-garde coterie," and soon the young writer found herself in a circle of artistic, intellectual bohemians that crossed lines of race, gender, class, and sexuality. Within this world, Black women in particular helped one another secure job opportunities, and as women in the arts, they depended on each other for advancement and encouragement and even emotional and sexual relationships.[41]

Dorothy West met actress Edna Thomas through her mother, Rachel West, and Thomas helped the younger woman get one of her first acting jobs as an extra in a 1927 production of *Porgy*, which influenced the later popular opera *Porgy and Bess* by George Gershwin.[42] Gay Harlem Renaissance mainstay Richard Bruce Nugent appeared in the production with

West, and the two of them became close—so close that he was the first of several queer men whom she asked to help her have a child.[43] Nugent had recently written and published the first poem by a Black man on the topic of queer love in the short-lived Harlem Renaissance journal *FIRE!!*, which was started by Zora Neale Hurston, Langston Hughes, and some of their colleagues to "burn up" the older and more conservative approaches to African American literature of the past.[44] A 1928 letter from Nugent to West revealed their mutual affection, which she hoped to parlay into something more serious. Nugent opened his letter to her, "Much love and many kisses. Even more. Golden leaves against a flame striped blue. And amethyst cliffs rearing from a night drunk sea. Everything beautiful."[45] Nugent wrote in a florid style that now reads as "campy," yet at the time it intrigued and drew West further in.

Some two years later, while Dorothy West was still enthralled by Bruce Nugent, her cousin Helene Johnson wrote her saying, "I think you ought to marry whoever you want no matter what he is like, if you love him. When you have your little baby," Johnson went on, "you can do as you like about separation, but my little Darthy would make such a beautiful mother. The older we get, the less illusions we have, and as far as abnormality goes, I don't think that's important at all." Johnson saw West's potential marriage as primarily a way to secure the child she knew her cousin and close friend wanted, claiming, "Once you had your baby, you'd have your whole future free and ready for your career."[46] Perhaps West was strategically choosing queer men as partners in order to have a marriage of convenience in which both partners would be free to see the same sex while maintaining a veneer of heterosexual respectability. Coming from a conservative Boston background, she likely looked down on either having a child out of wedlock or getting a divorce, preferring instead to marry a man whose knowledge of her queer affairs would not destroy their union. A few weeks after receiving the letter from her cousin, West wrote to her friend the writer Countee Cullen, "I loved Bruce and perhaps I still do. . . . I did want our lives to mean something together, and, of course, to me that meant a baby. That's all I've ever really wanted, and Bruce seemed so strong, and I liked his fine mind."[47] Later in life, West—who never did marry or have children—said in an interview that while she had always wanted to be a mother, she did not "want to get married and have to nurse a man," because the "man becomes the woman's child."[48] She was busy with her writing and tending to her literary community and did not want to spend her life's energies doting on a husband who would likely be threatened by her ambition.

At the same time, Dorothy West was attracted to men and sought equal relationships with them, in particular with Countee Cullen, who often took her to Harlem drag balls and had affairs with men himself.[49] In one 1931 letter to him, West wrote, "Dear Baby, of course I'll wait two years if you want me to. . . . I don't mind a bit being poor. I sort of wanted us to climb holding on to each other. But, my darling, you are cautious, and that I can't change, and perhaps I don't want to."[50] This suggested a naïveté on West's part, as Cullen had already briefly married W. E. B. Du Bois's daughter, Yolande, in 1928 but then left her the following year in Paris and went off to London with his best friend and possible lover, Harold Jackman, known as one of the "handsomest men in Harlem."[51] Cullen enjoyed West's company and her writing and responded, "I like you too much to want to hurt you even ever so slightly in no matter how remote a future. You and I have never had a real heart-to-heart talk about those things which must figure very greatly in our lives if we are to have the supreme relationship to one another; and I am fearful lest you are more sanguine about your knowledge of certain things, and your ability to bear them than you are actually equipped to do so."[52] Here Cullen seemed to speak evasively of his desires for men and how West would handle this aspect of his life if they were to marry. She also pondered whether or not marriage was something she wanted as a woman, despite the supposedly more equal relationships that the new 1920s notion of "companionate marriage" had brought about; in the same 1931 letter to Cullen, she wondered if "perhaps marriage is a dull business for women," suggesting a feminist sensibility.[53]

In 1932 at age twenty-five, West took part in what appears to have been her first queer relationship, with Mildred Jones, a graphic artist and recent graduate of the Hampton Institute. The two were roommates in the Soviet Union, where they traveled along with twenty other young African Americans to make a film titled *Black and White*. The film's producers, from the Meschrabpom Film Corporation of Moscow, had proposed to create "a realistic portrayal of Negro life in [Jim Crow] America," but their purported narrative was so inaccurate that the film was never finished.[54] Writer Langston Hughes, who was the most well-known figure in the group, referred to Jones and West with the couple-like descriptor "Mil and Dorothy" in a 1932 letter to his agent. However, while they were all in the Soviet Union, West had feelings simultaneously for Jones as well as for Hughes. She wrote to him after they had gone their separate ways, "I wanted terribly to see Mil and you, and I did not know whom I wanted to see most." West's first romantic experience with a woman may have made her anxious and bolstered her desires for a more conventionally accepted relationship, as she declared to Hughes, "I never stopped loving you, not for one moment, and after my first feeling for M[ildred] had passed, my love for you grew steadily and sturdily."[55] West then also asked Hughes to provide her with a baby and promised she wanted nothing more from him, but her desired arrangement never took place.[56]

Dorothy West rarely mentioned her female lovers in interviews and never alluded to anything beyond friendship with women. Despite her attempts to keep her queer partnerships hidden, those close to her nonetheless claimed they "always knew." As childhood friend Joyce Rickson recalled, "We called them queer then. But she wasn't queer in the sense that 'ooo' you know, it was just the way it was. . . . And we always knew that [she and partner Marian Minus] were together, and it didn't make any difference to us, it was just the way things were."[57] West sought to present herself as "well-behaved from the cradle to the grave," which was expected of a proper Bostonian, but the female lovers she chose tended to be more unconventional than she.[58] Mildred Jones had a witty line she used when propositioned by men she was not interested in: "Sorry, I'm looking for the same thing you are."[59] West's later long-term love, Marian Minus, was more active in radical Black circles than she and "dressed mannishly," never trying to hide her lesbianism. However, it was still not obvious to her friend and collaborator the author Richard Wright, who fell in love with Minus and was later shocked to learn of her sexual identity.[60]

Dorothy West most likely met Marian Minus through mutual friends in the early 1930s. Minus was living with her mother, Laura Whitener Minus, who was born in South Carolina. When Marian was a small child, her parents left the South for Ohio when her father, Claude Wellington Minus, was a professor at Wilberforce University.[61] In 1934, during the Great Depression, West was living in Harlem with a friend and working as a Home Relief investigator while editing her new literary publication, *Challenge*. Marian Minus was then a college student at Fisk University in Nashville who visited New York on school breaks, staying with her mother on West 117th Street.[62] After completing her bachelor's degree in sociology at Fisk, Minus attended the University of Chicago for graduate school, although she never finished her advanced degree in social anthropology.[63] While in Chicago in 1936, she met Richard Wright and became a member of the South Side Writers Group, which consisted of twenty Black authors interested in social issues.[64] By 1937, West had moved in with Minus and her mother in Harlem. The couple would go on to live together for a decade in New York and then on Martha's Vineyard.

In 1937 they began coediting *New Challenge* together (formerly known as *Challenge*), which became an influential, if short-lived, Black literary journal, along with associate editor Richard Wright, who would go on to great fame after publishing the novel *Native Son* in 1940.[65] Other Black queer writers and thinkers like Alain Locke, Pauli Murray, and Mae Cowdery published in *New Challenge*, making the journal an important text documenting the Black queer literary world of the 1930s. Despite their differences, West and Minus connected on an intellectual and political level. Both of them were nostalgic for the zeitgeist-like feeling of the Harlem Renaissance era. In a letter sent to West while Minus was still an undergraduate at Fisk University, the sociology major told the writer, "It only makes me sad that so few [writers from the 1920s] are keeping on. That's what I like about you. You're like someone with a precious torch who knows the value of its light and shields its flame from the shifting and shiftless winds."[66] The journal that the couple edited together received critical praise. The *Atlanta Daily World* announced that the *New Challenge* quickly "won acclaim as the most important and significant Negro literary journal of the decade."[67]

The creation of *New Challenge* shows that lady lovers were on the front lines of forging Black intellectual culture in the 1930s. Helping to generate Black queer literary communities had been a goal of West's for many years. She wrote to Countee Cullen in 1933, "It has long been my dream to preside over a small salon. . . . There is so much I want for my friends. . . . I have in mind an experiment. . . . [Guests] will love my friends because they love me . . . and since there is no deception in my world, they will gradually learn and accept."[68] West brought this concept to life through her literary journal, edited with her partner Marian Minus, and in so doing helped Black lady lovers become more central to the intellectual currents of the interwar era. No doubt one of the women who gave her the courage to do so was actress Edna Thomas, a friend of West's mother who had a rather unusual domestic living arrangement in Harlem.

THE TRIO

Edna Thomas, Lloyd Thomas, and Olivia Wyndham

In 1928, Dorothy West, in need of a place to stay, found herself temporarily living with actress Edna Thomas and her husband, theater manager Lloyd

Thomas.[69] West referred to Thomas as "Aunt Edna" and "Tommy" when she wrote letters to her mother, revealing the close kinship between the two.[70] After Edna Thomas helped West get her first acting role in *Porgy*, the show brought them to London, where Thomas and the other women in the cast kept an eye out for her, as she was quite young at the time.[71] The older actress was beloved in the New York performance world, and her long theater career inspired the young Dorothy West.[72] Thomas appeared in many popular shows in the 1920s and 1930s, from *Porgy and Bess* to *Lulu Belle*, and later went on to work in film as well, securing a small role in *A Streetcar Named Desire*.

When Edna Thomas first left her hometown of Boston for New York, she worked as a social secretary for Madam C. J. Walker, the famous Black hair-care entrepreneur and the first female self-made millionaire.[73] While employed by Walker she met her future husband, Lloyd Thomas, who worked as the manager of Walker's Harlem hair salon.[74] It was not until Madam Walker's death in 1919 that Thomas entered into the theater world, when she was in need of a new form of income to support herself and her husband.[75] Before she became a professional performer, Edna Thomas had frequently participated in amateur theatricals and fundraisers, and her talent for singing spirituals was well known. During a 1918 benefit performance, she came to the attention of the Lafayette Players, the first major African American "legitimate" theater company.[76] The Lafayette Theatre, the troupe's home, was the premiere Black theater in Harlem, and its director, Lester Walton, tried to convince Thomas to join the group. Thomas was in a "family 'spat'" with her husband at the time, and since Lloyd was "entirely repulsed" by the idea of her becoming a professional actress, she signed up with the Lafayette Players in part to get "even" with him, although she still sought his permission to do so, which he eventually granted.[77]

News of Edna Thomas joining the Lafayette Players made headlines, as she was "well known socially in New York, Boston, and several other cities."[78] The *New York Age* noted not only that several theater managers "made her flattering inducements to go on the stage" but that "she ha[d] won several prizes in beauty contests and [wa]s regarded as one of the race's most beautiful women."[79] By 1921, Thomas had her first starring role in a play, and the *New York Age* declared, "Her performance is living up to the expectations of her many friends and admirers" who predicted that "her efforts before the footlights would be crowned with success."[80] It was rare for a woman already considered part of "Negro society" to enter into the theater world, which was often associated with disrespectable be-havior, as we have seen. But Thomas nonetheless made the transition, in part because the Lafayette Players represented the "high culture" of drama and tragedy and not the bawdy dives of the Prohibition era.

Fifteen years later, Thomas had made such a large impact on the the-ater world that her peers, such as writer Nella Larsen, referred to her as "the greatest Negro actress living."[81] Perhaps due to her artistic success, she felt comfortable creating an unorthodox domestic situation, as by now Thomas made a home in Harlem with her husband, Lloyd, as well as with her female lover, Olivia Wyndham. Her paramour was a white British woman born into an aristocratic, artistic family; Wyndham had been a popular figure in the overlapping 1920s London queer world and the circle of bohemians known as the Bright Young Things.[82] Few women were known to take part in long-term interracial queer relationships at this time, making the Thomas-Wyndham partnership notable.

Firsthand details of their relationship are unusually plentiful, as in the mid-1930s both women were interviewed under pseudonyms for a sexology study by the New York–based Committee for the Study of Sex Variants led by Dr. George Henry.[83] Their case studies were first published in 1941 in the book *Sex Variants: A Study of Homosexual Patterns*. From 1935 to 1941, members of the committee interviewed eighty "sexually mal-adjusted" men and women and then published their case studies, which were intended for a medical, not a popular, audience. The committee's aim was to study "those who express affection and passion in a manner unfamiliar to the majority" in order to achieve "progress in the prevention as well as in the treatment of sexual maladjustment."[84] The individuals who took part in this study were introduced to the doctors by a volunteer who used the pseudonym "Miss Jan Gay," a journalist and novelist in the Greenwich Village "lesbian scene of the 1920s and 30s" who made contact with and interviewed prospective subjects.[85] It is not known whether the participants were paid for their interviews, were aware of the aim of the study, or would have agreed that "sexual variation" should be prevented or treated, which implied that queer desire was not healthy.[86]

Edna Thomas's lover, Olivia Wyndham (anonymized as "Pamela K."), began her interview for the study by proclaiming, "From a background of the tradition, refinement, and luxury of a picture-book English castle to residence in a middle-class negro apartment house in Harlem suggests a metamorphosis which is inexplicable to my American friends."[87] Here, Wyndham implies that the intense segregation and racial inequality in the United States was the reason her new friends found her migration so odd. After years of relationships with both men and women in England, as well as in France during World War I, Wyndham "came to the United States and promptly fell very much in love with" Edna Thomas, noting she was "twelve years older [than Wyndham] and married, but had ceased having relations with her husband." From the first afternoon they met, Wyndham pursued Thomas "unremittingly," which the latter's case study verifies. Edna Thomas recalled that she "yielded" to Wyndham after avoiding her because she believed "white women [we]re unfaithful." However, Wyndham continued to pursue Thomas "to the point of annoyance" until eventually Thomas "had the most exciting sexual experience" of her life with her; five years later, at the time of her interview, she admitted that their relationship "afford[ed] a tenderness" she had never known before, despite her lengthy marriage to Lloyd Thomas.[88]

Edna Thomas came from a background very different from that of her British lover, stating in her interview (anonymized as "Pearl M.") that she was "the illegitimate daughter of a 12-year-old mulatto nurse maid" from Virginia. She did not know her father, but he was said to be "one of those southern gentlemen who ha[d] no scruples against making concubines of their servant girls."[89] This all-too-common southern scenario further underscored Thomas's noted difficulty in trusting white women like Olivia Wyndham, considering her white biological father's violence toward her young mother and abandonment of his family. Thomas insisted that she turned to a queer relationship only because her husband ignored her sexually and romantically by "going around with younger women," but she had no regrets and her five years thus far with Wyndham had been "rich and important," not to mention that she claimed they "always ha[d] orgasms together."[90] The two women lived together for the rest of their lives, with Lloyd Thomas "intermittently present."[91] However, to maintain appearances, Thomas would tell straight and queer friends alike that Wyndham was merely "a house guest" who "helped with expenses."[92] While some sources suggest Lloyd Thomas preferred men himself, Thomas did not mention this in her case study, but she did note that when they first met, "his indifference fascinated" her.[93]

By the late 1930s, the Black press had picked up word of the trio's unique relationship and ran several articles about how the aristocratic Wyndham had given up her elite British life to live with an African American couple in Harlem, which clearly turned a few heads and sold some newspapers as well. In 1938, a *New York Amsterdam News* headline blared,

"Rich British Woman Forsook Own People to Reside in Harlem." The article stated that Wyndham "shared a four-room studio apartment with Lloyd Thomas and his actress wife, Edna," which suggested that the trio were rather cozy together. Similarly, Edna Thomas was referred to as her "intimate friend," and the author noted that at Wyndham's country home in Connecticut, "Olivia is visited each week-end by Edna and at times by Lloyd," further detailing the close relationship between the two women.[94] Wyndham was described as "English to the core" with a preference for "mannish clothes" and "smoking from a very long [cigarette] holder." She "like[d] to see Edna act," after which "she and Edna usually return[ed] home together."[95] While the articles in the Black press do not explicitly refer to Thomas and Wyndham as more than friends, by the late 1930s, lesbianism was becoming a more well-known concept, and readers could draw their own conclusions about their unconventional living situation. At the same time, the larger context of the still-ongoing Great Depression explained why taking in a "house guest" and charging that person additional rent would be economically beneficial for a Black couple, despite their good standing in Harlem society. Through creating such unconventional living arrangements, Edna Thomas helped make queer forms of kinship more visible in Black "high society," which in turn opened up the realm of possibilities for other young Black women with aspirations beyond the heteronormative nuclear family.

GEORGETTE HARVEY

A Brief Investigation

While multiple historians have noted that George Henry's *Sex Variants* contains case studies of Edna Thomas and Olivia Wyndham, there are other interviews with Black queer performers in this sexological study who have yet to be identified.[96] One of these case studies seems quite likely to be that of actress Georgette Harvey, a friend of Edna Thomas's who also performed in *Porgy* with Dorothy West. She went on to appear in popular productions such as *Mamba's Daughters* and even came close to being selected for the role of "Mammy" in *Gone with the Wind*, which eventually went to Hattie McDaniel.[97] The physical and narrative descriptions in the *Sex Variants* case study of a "Marian J." and Georgette Harvey are so similar that it seems quite likely they are the same individual, especially when one takes into account the fact that Harvey's friend Edna Thomas was also interviewed and that Harvey likely knew Jan Gay, who helped recruit subjects for the sexology study.

Harvey was a large, masculine woman from St. Louis who came to New York in 1900 at age eighteen to begin her career in theater and went on to spend over a decade performing in Russia at the beginning of the twentieth century. She was friends with Bruce Nugent, who wrote a short biography of her while he worked for the Federal Writers' Project in the late 1930s. Nugent referred to Harvey's "coffee-brown complexion" and "deep—very deep—contralto voice," noting that while she started off singing in church, she soon "went bad" and sought a life on the stage, which caused much "consternation" to her "fairly respectable family."[98] In New York, she created a vaudeville troupe of young women, the Creole Belles, whom she took to Europe and "ruled with an iron and autocratic hand." Nugent suggestively wrote that Harvey "husbanded her girls, their energies, and their talents in more ways than one." Eventually, she brought her troupe to Russia, where they stayed for sixteen years, as she "took full advantage of the exciting strangeness which her color and that of her troupe afforded." There, Harvey, "with her florid gestures and generous physique, her stentorian tones and blustering personality, easily became the focal point of any scene."[99] Her troupe eventually came home after the Russian Revolution but not before a stint in Japan. Harvey's part in 1927's *Porgy* then brought her back to the American spotlight, and later she went on to a featured role in Gershwin's *Porgy and Bess* and even made some minor films.

Georgette Harvey and Edna Thomas were close friends with white theater manager Cheryl Crawford, who was also queer and had "a peculiar habit of opening doors for younger women."[100] Crawford played a big role in bringing both *Porgy* and later *Porgy and Bess* to the stage and in giving parts to her many queer actress friends. In 1935, when *Porgy and Bess* was a current Broadway hit, Harvey threw a party for the director, Robert Mamoulian, where she served as the "director of ceremonies." Guests included George Gershwin and Ethel Waters, among many other celebrities. Notably, one of the attendees was "Miss Jan Gay," the woman who played a large role in securing queer New Yorkers as subjects for sexology studies in the 1920s and 1930s.[101] Her attendance at this event, which likely shows she knew Harvey, offers further evidence that this case study in *Sex Variants* was of the actress.

The subject given the pseudonym "Marian J." was described as a "large, middle-aged mulatto woman" who had been a professional entertainer for four decades, two of which were spent in Europe. The doctor who performed her case study noted, "Her deep voice had such great power and beauty that her hearers [we]re carried away by it."[102] Just as Bruce Nugent described Harvey, "Marian J." began singing in church and entered into show business at age eighteen. She began performing in Europe soon after and spent twelve years in Russia, but after the revolution she "lost everything" and went to Japan, where she stayed for two years before coming back to the United States at age thirty-seven. Marian J.'s interview ended with her declaring, "Homosexuality leaves you with a lonely life. I wanted to have children and I regretted very much that I haven't any. It isn't a thing to be happy about. Socially you are ostracized." At the same time, she pointed out, "There are as many married women mixed up in it as there are single. It's prevalent all over the world."[103] This underscored her personal knowledge as a performing woman who had the unique opportunity to travel at length internationally. Clearly there was at this time a tension between the growing prevalence of queer women's identities and communities around the world and the social threat that they represented, as women who did not need men as partners. While Harvey was able to travel and was successful financially, she nonetheless experienced social exclusion due to her love of women, which was likely exacerbated by her masculine gender presentation. While she was part of an interracial network of queer professional performers, her lack of children—and perhaps lack of long-term partners as well—led Harvey to view her identity in negative terms. To be perceived as a visibly queer Black woman in the early twentieth century, regardless of one's class position, meant that life was constantly challenging.

A'LELIA WALKER

The Joy Goddess of 1920s Harlem

This social ostracization Georgette Harvey pointed to is one of the reasons it is difficult to discern whether some well-known women from this era had romantic relationships with other women. In the case of A'Lelia Walker, it was not until her death that it became clear to many that Mayme White, her female roommate and "employee," was likely more akin to a spouse. Walker, the heiress daughter of millionaire hair-care entrepreneur Madam C. J. Walker, played a significant role in supporting the queer networks of 1920s Harlem. Her parties and salons served as spaces in which platonic, economic, and romantic relationships between white downtowners and Black artists were kindled and same-sex flirtations were welcome. So infamous were her social gatherings that Langston Hughes declared Walker "the joy-goddess of Harlem."[104] A'Lelia Walker had multiple past marriages to men and was not only said to always have "a circle of handsome women attending her" but was also noted for being "especially fond of homosexuals."[105]

Before her early death at forty-six in 1931, A'Lelia Walker appears to have had a significant relationship with her "secretary-companion," Mayme White, the daughter of George Henry White, a politician and attorney from North Carolina.[106] By 1926, White was making regular overnight trips from Philadelphia to visit Walker in New York, and after the stock market crash of 1929, White moved into Walker's Harlem home permanently.[107] Akin to Edna Thomas and Olivia Wyndham's situation, the financial challenges wrought by the Great Depression created opportunities for Walker and White to live together for reasons understood to be financial—not romantic. And since Walker employed White, their constant companionship was not suspect but rather viewed as work-related. Society columns in the Black press also discussed the activities of the two women in tandem. A 1930 *Baltimore Afro-American* column on New York's "social whirl" noted that Walker and White had "changed their day" for welcoming guests to Wednesdays instead of Thursdays.[108] A column from a few weeks later noted that while A'Lelia Walker had headed to New Haven for the Harvard–Yale football game, Mayme White "remained in town so she could be near the hotspots."[109] By mentioning these bits of social news together, the two women's closeness and domestic intimacy was insinuated.

Regardless of whether A'Lelia Walker's love of women can be "proved," she most definitely played an important role in establishing queer-friendly spaces and supporting queer writers during the Harlem Renaissance. Her creation of a membership-only salon in her home in 1927 known as the Dark Tower furthered her vision of crafting a hub for Harlem's artists and intellectuals. One of the first articles in the Black press to mention Walker's new "Harlem Artists' Rendezvous" noted that those "invited to register as members can bring their friends and enjoy an evening of real informal human association" where "people may sing, dance, play cards, read or simply converse." The large room used for the gatherings was "beautifully decorated and lettered with quotations" from the poetry of Countee Cullen—whose work the salon was named after—and Langston Hughes. At the Dark Tower, one reviewer declared, "the honored member or the fortunate guest finds pleasure and freedom, culture and refinement, beautifully combined in every arrangement and in the conduct of the whole affair."[110]

Pleasure and freedom were celebrated in a most liberating fashion at some of Walker's gatherings, as Harlem performer Mabel Hampton recalled.[111] She reportedly attended a party thrown by A'Lelia Walker where all the guests were naked and relaxing on pillows in a large room without any other furniture. They were served food and drinks by naked women, and Walker herself wore only shorts. Hampton said the couples present were made up of "men and women, women and women, and men and men" and that such parties happened regularly in the 1920s, "but you couldn't get in unless you knew somebody." Hampton herself was told, "Whatever you see, don't repeat it" when she entered Walker's party.[112] The privacy around the events the heiress hosted served to protect her guests in an era before wider social acceptance of queer sexuality and gave them a safe place to be themselves.

The Dark Tower salon lasted for less than a year, but A'Lelia Walker nonetheless had cemented her reputation as "the great Harlem party giver" whose soirees were "as crowded as the New York subway" at rush hour.[113] When Walker died in 1931, Langston Hughes declared that her funeral marked "the end of the gay times of the New Negro era in Harlem."[114] Her death brought to the surface more hints that her relationship with her "secretary-companion," Mayme White, may have had a romantic component. At the very least, the two women were intimate friends, which, coupled with Walker's reputation as a lover of "homosexuals," suggests the relationship may have been more than platonic. Consider the fact that Mayme White was with Walker the night she died; the two women were sharing a guest room while visiting their friend Mae Fain for her birthday in New Jersey. Walker had high blood pressure, which ran in her family, and she suffered a cerebral hemorrhage, just as her mother had. The Black press declared that she died from a stroke brought on by a "too elaborate dinner" of lobster, champagne, and chocolate cake.[115]

More than 11,000 mourners and onlookers came out to pay their respects to Walker, while 1,000 attended her invitation-only funeral, demonstrating her vast popularity in Harlem. Walker was laid out in her casket in an elaborate gown, wearing a silver and amber ring that Mayme White had given her. Her "closest companion" also sat in the front row along with Walker's relatives.[116] Both of these details suggest a romantic element, but White went on to sue Walker's estate for four years of back wages when she found that she was left out of her will. This detail creates more ambiguity around their relationship: Was she left out of the will because she was *not* a spouse-like figure, or because naming her would have made her visibly appear to be such a partner, which had to be avoided? A gossip column in the *Pittsburgh Courier* stated that the "testimony will be plenty hot if all the details are revealed," leading readers to wonder about the contours of their relationship.[117] The week the lawsuit was filed, the *Chicago Defender* noted, "Fashionable New York, and in fact, all of Harlem discussed anew the interesting character of Miss White and her still more interesting association with the late Mme. Walker."[118] Again, it was hinted that there was something unusual or salacious about the nature of the women's partnership. After the second week of the hearing, when it seemed likely that White would be awarded the funds she sought, the *Chicago Defender* declared, "There is a general sigh of relief in the socialite sections" as well as "a few blushes and not a few regrets," further raising the specter of an intimate relationship between the two women.[119]

As the richest Black woman in New York during the "anything goes" Prohibition era who surrounded herself with queer men and women, A'Lelia Walker was in a position to be able to employ the woman she loved. It is not clear which started first, their professional or romantic relationship, but regardless, those who followed the society pages in the Black press knew the two women lived together and of their comings and goings. Walker and White appear to be another example of the "open secret" of queer relationships in this milieu, where same-sex couples were generally treated as married heterosexual couples but did not display affection publicly or refer to the romantic aspect of their companionship. In this way they were akin to the Boston marriages of the nineteenth century, but through Walker's actions, like opening the Dark Tower salon, she also helped create modern Black queer gathering spaces and networks.[120]

LUCY DIGGS SLOWE

Howard University's First Dean of Women

Outside of bohemian New York in more conservative Washington, DC, educator Lucy Diggs Slowe made a home with her partner, playwright and teacher Mary Burrill.[121] In 1922, Slowe became the first dean of women at Howard University, responsible for overseeing the female students' life on campus. She lived two miles from her work with Burrill in a beautiful house on Kearny Street, where they regularly welcomed female Howard students and entertained friends and guests. She relied extensively on a homosocial network of Black female activists and educators for emotional and political support while also working to instill feminist ideologies into Howard and its female students.

This made her a threat to the male administrators of the university who valued traditional gender norms, bolstered by the masculinist spirit of the New Negro era.[122] Slowe dealt with constant pushback from the president of Howard, who resisted her attempts to offer female students more opportunities and eventually told Slowe to move from her off-campus home into a women's dorm. Slowe's story highlights how feminism and lesbianism were seen as overlapping threats by both Black and white male authorities in the early twentieth century who hewed to traditional gender roles and respectability in their fight to uplift Black students. Slowe and Burrill's relationship also reveals how, despite the growing awareness of lesbian identity by the late 1930s, some Black professional women nonetheless preferred to identify with older, less sexualized conceptions of female relationships, like romantic friendships and Boston marriages.

Despite the fact that Slowe and Burrill had a close relationship for twenty-five years, there is very little extant evidence that suggests it was explicitly sexual or romantic, but what is clear is that they were intimate friends, roommates, and life partners, and those close to them knew this and accepted it. Due to the necessity of appearing respectable in this era, Slowe and the women in her educated social circles worked hard to present themselves as upstanding and moral. She and Burrill met in 1912 when they were both English teachers, and they began living together in 1918.[123] When writing to Slowe, friends always sent their regards to "Miss Burrill," and Slowe often referred to the two women's shared home.[124] As both were already in their mid- to late thirties by the time the 1920s' more modern notions of sexuality began to creep into the national consciousness, earlier Victorian notions of sex and gender permeated their upbringings.

This meant that their early twentieth-century relationship bore more similarities to the earlier Boston marriages of the late nineteenth century than those of the Jazz Age, when bisexuality, if not lesbianism, became more common among bohemians and society elites. Slowe's biographers refer to historian Carroll Smith-Rosenberg's idea of two women living in "emotional proximity" to each other to describe their relationship.[125] While Smith-Rosenberg's work on romantic friendships between young women focuses on the nineteenth century, this concept still helps explain why Slowe and Burrill were accepted as a couple by their communities, for it may have been the lack of overt romantic affection between them that made people comfortable with their relationship. They seemingly benefited from the ambiguity of two unmarried women living together, which may not have been afforded to two men at this time.[126] While many other white educated women of Slowe's generation, who grew up in the Progressive Era, dedicated their lives to their careers and to creating more opportunities for women instead of focusing on marriage and motherhood, Slowe and Burrill are one of the few known long-term African American female couples of their generation. As Black women seeking to serve as moral and intellectual exemplars for future generations of female students, they were conscious of presenting as respectable and as morally upright as possible to assuage any semblance of impropriety.

When Lucy Diggs Slowe agreed to the new position of "Dean of Women" at her alma mater, Howard University, in 1922, she did so only on the agreement that she would not be made to live on campus. One point of her written job negotiations stipulated, "It is agreed that the suite of rooms now used by the Acting Dean of Women be placed at my disposal, but that I shall not be required to live on the campus."[127] This was significant for multiple reasons: she was in a relationship with Mary Burrill, which she did not want to make more visible by living on campus, but regardless of her relationship status, she wanted to have her own autonomy, which was a lesson she sought to instill in the female students of Howard as well.[128] Within a year, Slowe bought her home for her and Burrill, where entertaining students became a common activity. She created multiple annual events for Howard women on campus and had regular meetings with female faculty. However, beginning in 1925, male authorities at Howard sought to move Slowe onto the campus to better "protect" the young women of Howard.[129] While she managed to stay at her Kearny Street home with Burrill until her death, in 1933 the Howard University Board of Trustees informed her that she would have to move on campus to better oversee the female students' activities. In response, Slowe wrote a letter to the white board president, Abraham Flexner:

> Upon what I believed to be a bona fide agreement, . . . I bought a
> home situated on a lot 100 by 150 feet, with six large maple trees on
> it. I have planted 50 rose bushes and put in a rock garden with many
> different kinds of flowers in it. I have made numerous improvements
> to the house to make it more suitable for entertaining students.

Every year groups of students meet with me around my open fire or under the trees on the lawn for conferences on various subjects. Some of my most effective work has been done around my fireside away from all that suggests college routine and official authority. The students have found my home a retreat from college life, and have always come to it with fresh enthusiasm. Our graduates write me that they consider the hours spent at this retreat among the happiest at college.[130]

This letter shows how Slowe, as Howard's dean of women, helped young Black women become intellectuals and interlocutors by introducing them to "the life of the mind" and actively cultivating a community at a time when few in higher education took them and their futures seriously. By centering the enrichment of Howard's female students and not passively accepting the decisions of the male-dominated board of trustees, Slowe pushed back against a New Negro ethos that emphasized Black masculinism, for which she was punished by some of her colleagues.[131] She created the "New Howard Woman" for her students to emulate, in a time when the New Negro ideal upheld Black men while the New Woman was depicted as white.[132] Notably, considering that Slowe and Burrill had lived together for years at this point, her partner's absence from the letter focused on their home is intriguing—if they were "just friends," would she have brought her up, or was even that considered too odd by the 1930s? The explicit lack of mention of Burrill, who was likely present at some of the student gatherings, coupled with how often she was mentioned in letters to and from close friends, further suggests their relationship was more than one of just platonic best friends and roommates. The conversations debating whether Slowe should live off campus danced around the issue of whom she shared her home with, and the reason always given for her needed move was to supervise the female students. This double standard offended Slowe, as the dean of men was not being asked to make a similar sacrifice. Slowe was regularly frustrated by how an administration with progressive views on racial issues could still hold such conservative positions on gender issues, such as upholding a policy that forbade female professors who got married from continuing to teach at the university.[133]

At the same time that Slowe was being told to move out of the home that she owned, a female physician who had been employed at Howard to care for the health of female students was let go due to alleged financial reasons. Upset over this, a group of female students sent board president

Abraham Flexner a petition calling to reinstate their doctor. Clearly frustrated by this student activism, Flexner wrote to Slowe and insinuated that "something is certainly wrong in the relationship between you and them" because the female Howard students took "such silly steps" as to petition him "without conference with" Slowe. He then used this incident as an example of "evidence of the importance of you being on their grounds," despite the fact that only one-fourth of Howard's female students lived on campus while the majority lived at home with their families in the DC area.[134] Slowe responded, "May I say that there is the most wholesome relationship between the women of the University and the Dean of Women."[135] This exchange is one of the more obvious examples of how queer subtexts could not rise completely to the surface but were still present and were seen as beyond the pale in such a setting as Howard University, which was focused on Black uplift via respectability.

Upon her unexpected death in 1937 at age fifty-two due to complications from high blood pressure, the vast influence of Lucy Diggs Slowe can be gleaned from the fact that 365 people and organizations sent flowers and letters to pay their respects.[136] From the outpouring of sympathy Mary Burrill received, it appeared that most friends knew of the intimate relationship between the two women. What is not clear is whether they were viewed as a married couple or as close, sisterlike friends, for the language of friendship and sisterhood dominated the sympathy letters sent to Burrill. But then, it was not common in 1930s middle-class society— especially in conservative Washington, DC—to use terms such as partner, lover, girlfriend, or wife when referring to two women. One of the most moving letters sent to Slowe's grieving partner was from their friend Mollie T. Barrien, who wrote, "My dear Miss Burrill, I was deeply shocked to learn of the death of your dear friend. My heart aches for you, for I know you two loved each other as only sisters could. I know your life will be sad and lonely without her sweet companionship, but I pray that God will give you strength to endure the separation, knowing that when God wills it, you two will be together once more never to be separated again."[137] Barrien understood the exceptional bond between these two women, yet still viewed it in a platonic light, or at least used words that conveyed their connection as such, despite their closeness. Others referred to the two women's "intimate" connection as "constant friend[s]" and "close companion[s]."[138] It was obvious in the couple's community that each was the most significant person in the other's life and that Slowe's death would affect Burrill like no other.

Regardless of whether people thought their relationship was romantic or platonic, it was clear that these two women made a life and a home together and were devoted partners. It seems that Lucy Diggs Slowe's status, achievements, and leadership were extraordinary enough that her unconventional relationship was apparently accepted or overlooked by the communities that she enriched. No male relative or paramour was in the picture or ever mentioned, and more and more people understood what this meant by the late 1930s, as popular and medical texts on lesbianism continued to proliferate throughout the decade.[139]

Mary Burrill spoke up for Slowe after her death, when she responded to a sympathy letter from Howard University's trustees by telling them they had taken Slowe for granted during her time at the institution. Burrill went as far as to turn her letter to the board of trustees of Howard into a press release, which she apparently sent to media outlets.[140] She wrote that the university "might have become a great experimental ground for the education of Negro women," but Slowe was "handicapped" by an administration that gave her only $200 a year for programs for 1,000 women. Burrill also decried the low salary Slowe was paid, despite her attempts to rectify it over the years, knowing that her male colleagues were receiving raises that she was not given. Burrill closed her letter with the strong statement, "Howard University had in its midst in the person of Lucy D. Slowe a great woman but its President and Board of trustees could not see it."[141] Burrill's advocacy for her partner shows the lengths she went to support her, even in death. She played a central role in organizing Slowe's memorial, in removing her personal effects from the university, and in creating an archive of her papers that would eventually be donated to Howard University.[142] Slowe left half of her house to Burrill in her will, which decreed that her companion was a joint tenant in the home who had the right to stay there. She still lived there in 1940 with her niece and two young grandnephews.[143] The year after Slowe's death, a friend noted that Burrill kept her "picture on her piano and beside it a silver vase," always filled with fresh flowers, usually carnations.[144]

As two professional Black women with successful careers making a home together in Washington, DC, Slowe and Burrill inspired a generation of Howard students. Slowe's personal life and achievements in higher education fashioned a terrain on which new possibilities for African American women's lives could take root.[145] She not only encouraged her students to look for more than a husband in college, but she also served as such a role model herself. Black lady lovers like Lucy Diggs Slowe created opportunities for young Black women at Howard to become connected to the world of culture and ideas. As a woman who shared her life with another woman, she never had the opportunity to be economically supported by a man. Yet at the same time she knew that, regardless of marriage to a man, most Black women would have to work as well, due to the low wages and discrimination Black men faced. Lucy Diggs Slowe is an important example of how Black lady lovers' unconventional life choices positioned them as leaders, showing Black women of all sexualities how to live an independent life outside of the heteronormative domestic sphere. Black lady lovers' bold choices to live autonomously allowed them to open new avenues to the next generation of Black women. At the same time, Slowe was able to go so far professionally and socially by maintaining a seemingly desexualized relationship with a woman, and the ambiguity over what type of relationship they shared distanced her from impropriety, which was a requirement for a pioneering educator of female college students at the most highly regarded historically Black college in the nation.

The women discussed in this chapter supported each other emotionally, socially, romantically, and economically in a time when relationships between women were becoming more visible but were still not tolerated or accepted in respectable society. Despite not taking on the expected role of wife and mother, the women examined here all created familial forms that suited their needs while playing important roles in their communities. Dorothy West sought to create queer kinship ties with Black gay men in order to have a child while pursuing relationships with women as well, eventually settling down with partner Marian Minus. While some women in this milieu did not want to be tied down with children, others, like West and Georgette Harvey, regretted not being able to become mothers. At the same time, Harvey had the unusual opportunity to bring young Black chorus girls around the world for many years, taking the ultimate advantage of the entertainment world's mobility. West, Minus, and A'Lelia Walker helped to birth Black queer literary communities through creating a journal and a salon, the latter of which was rumored to also be the site of sexually charged, private gatherings as well. After several marriages to men, Walker was able to make a home with a woman she also employed, Mayme White. Edna Thomas, Walker's close friend, also experimented with new forms of queer relationships, living with both her husband and her female lover in a Harlem apartment that served as a guest home to West and many others.

Educator Lucy Diggs Slowe, as the first dean of women at Howard University, also lived with her female partner, playwright and teacher Mary Burrill, for many years. Her unorthodox living arrangement and feminist values positioned her as a threat to the male leaders of Howard, who sought to instill more traditional gender norms in their students. Slowe and Alice Dunbar-Nelson demonstrate how middle-class Black women strategically took part in queer relationships while still remaining respected and valued members of society. By not drawing attention to their female partners or referring to themselves with the modern terminology of sexual identities, they were able to take part in queer relationships that remained hidden in plain sight, or were perhaps deemed open secrets to some.

As we also see from the examples of Edna Thomas and Olivia Wyndham and A'Lelia Walker and Mayme White, the economic precarity caused by the Great Depression presented opportunities for women to move in together and share homes without making such arrangements appear suspect. Just as the contexts of the Great Migration and Prohibition opened up new spaces in northern cities for Black lady lovers to meet, the Great Depression further created an environment in which women's intimate relationships could serve multiple needs. Black middle-class women who loved women in the interwar era were at the forefront of crafting unconventional relationships and queer communities that would serve as models for future generations of women.

CONCLUSION

If, as our opening story showed, Black women choosing female partners was hailed as a new "sex problem" on the horizon in 1920 Chicago, the interwar era saw this issue expand across northern cities and even nationwide.[1] In 1933, a Black newspaper columnist in Los Angeles declared that "Lesbians" were being caught "disgustingly caressing" on Hollywood film sets. The next year he opined, "Down with Lysistrata, queen of Lesbia! (Humph, they're more plentiful every day in this man's town)."[2] However, what was deemed a problem to some merely represented the opportunity for a new type of modern life to others. As this book has shown, Black queer women in northern cities created networks and geographies of sociality and pleasure in the early twentieth century. They found one another on the streets and in cabarets, rent parties, speakeasies, literary salons, universities, and social and political organizations. The privacy that could be found in the Prohibition era urban North created unprecedented opportunities for queer flirtations and behaviors. Black lady lovers in the interwar era created networks and spaces that centered their desires and aspirations. They worked together and supported one another economically, emotionally, and romantically.

Lady lovers particularly converged in the Black entertainment industry, where thousands of women toured on vaudeville circuits singing and dancing, traveling by segregated train and boardinghouses, and connecting with other women in a generally queer-tolerant environment. By having relationships with women they performed with on the road, they took advantage of the liminal, transitory state of touring to enact behaviors still not socially sanctioned. At the same time, the Black and white male theatrical managers and producers who controlled their careers spoke

135

negatively of lady lovers. Some, like Salem Tutt Whitney, even actively sought to eliminate them from the industry. Despite this, performing women created some of the first cultural texts to make visible Black queer desire and gender transgression, from Ma Rainey's record "Prove It on Me Blues" to Gladys Bentley's outrageous songs and flirtations with her female audience members. Women like Rainey and Bentley changed the cultural landscape by creating bold musical assertions of their right to pleasure and self-ownership in the Jim Crow era, when racialized bodies were patrolled and regulated in the North as well as in the South and were marked as deviant in the general white imagination. As blues singers and performers, Black lady lovers changed the music industry by showing how popular Black female singers could be and brought people together through their songs about the hardships and pleasures of everyday life.

Black women in the interwar era had unprecedented access to mobility and travel, which allowed them to exercise their agency and make a life with other women, often far away from their families of origin. From the Thanksgiving gathering of only women of an "unusual type" to Mabel Hampton's house parties, A'Lelia Walker's Dark Tower salon, and Lucy Diggs Slowe and Mary Burrill's parties for female Howard students at their shared home, Black lady lovers in the interwar era created networks and spaces that centered their desires and aspirations. And through their visions and actions, they helped normalize women's relationships in an era when queer women's increasing visibility was leading to further pushback against homosexuality.

At the same time, this book has shown that not all married lady lovers felt the need to leave their husbands to act on their queer desires. Their ability to craft new forms of relationships beyond monogamous, heterosexual marriage is one of their central contributions to changing norms of gender and sexuality in the early twentieth century. One case study in Dr. George Henry's *Sex Variants* revealed that by the 1930s, some Black queer women could even speak without a trace of shame about their sexual desires. The pseudonym "Susan N." was given to a feminine, biracial woman of twenty-six who worked in the theater world. While she exclusively dated women, she often socialized with gay men for safety and comfort and was contemplating marrying one to make their "social position more secure." Susan recalled that by the time she was fifteen, she "was attracted to women and . . . was conscious of them as possible lovers," such as her mother's cousin, who was a queer showgirl. When she was twenty, Susan's mother accused her of being in love with a girl, and she admitted this was true. She was then forced to leave home, so she went to live with her great-aunt, but when the aunt later learned of Susan's sexuality, she too was unsupportive. Susan then moved in with her current girlfriend, and for the first time she felt emotionally stable and content with her "new way of life." Regarding men, Susan said, "I'm not afraid of a man but I have no desire and I see no reason why I should waste my time doing things I don't care about." She then declared, "If I were born again I would like to be just as I am. I'm perfectly satisfied being a girl and being as I am. I never have had any regrets."[3]

Instead of suffering through unwanted but socially expected relationships with men, Susan bravely sought the relationships with women she desired, despite the fact that her family did not support her. In doing so, Susan helped create this possible way of life for other women, as she positioned herself as a sexual subject who was not ashamed of her desires. And as a woman of color, who was expected to hew to the politics of respectability and practice dissemblance when it came to topics like sexuality, her stance was particularly transgressive. Looking toward her future, Susan was excited by the possibility of marrying a gay male friend and having a child. She could imagine a family made up of a queer woman and man who made a home and a life together, who were parents but also had their own sexual and romantic partners. In envisioning such a future, Susan and her artistic and theatrical circles, like those of Edna Thomas and Dorothy West, created modern new forms of kinship beyond the heteronormative nuclear family. Aware that the larger society looked down upon and discriminated against queer women, Susan hoped to hold on publicly to the privileges and opportunities bestowed on heterosexual families while still maintaining same-sex relationships in private.

Popular performers like blues singer Bessie Smith also married men while continuing to have relationships with women. Smith wanted to experience motherhood as well, even though those around her did not exactly view her as the maternal type. This was due to her reputation for heavy drinking and occasional violent outbursts, not to mention a successful career that demanded constant travel. Smith's interest in having children also surprised some since the topic was rarely discussed in women's classic blues songs, suggesting that the "cult of motherhood" was not as relevant or accessible to the lives of successful performers as it was to the average woman.[4] Regardless, Bessie Smith unofficially adopted a six-year-old son at the height of her fame in 1926.[5] Jack Gee Jr., nicknamed "Snooks," was the biological son of one of her chorus girls, a single mother who had been having a hard time making ends meet before Jack was born. While Smith claimed the adoption was official, her biographer points out that the process was not performed through the proper channels but was just a mutual agreement between the two women.[6] This further shows how queer blues women like Smith created alternative kinship structures to suit their desires, despite their lack of validity in the eyes of the state.

Similarly, multiple Black lady lovers held marriage ceremonies in the 1920s and 1930s that were also not viewed as "official" or bestowing any legal rights or privileges but were still meaningful to the couples and their loved ones. Most famously, Gladys Bentley married her white female partner in a civil service that took place in Atlantic City, and true to form, she wore a tuxedo for the occasion.[7] Mabel Hampton also attended a wedding for two Black women in their Harlem home in 1938. Their friends were married by a reverend who was known to be gay himself and specialized in marrying queer couples. The bride wore a white dress with a veil, and her groom—as Hampton referred to her—wore white pants. Hampton noted that the groom was so masculine that she passed as a man at city hall, where they went to take a blood test, and during the ceremony the groom was referred to as "man" and "husband."[8] Black queer couples strategically navigated the rules in place through gender transgression, falsification of information, and the help of queer religious authorities to celebrate their relationships and demonstrate they were as important as any heterosexual marriage.

At the same time, Black lady lovers also interacted with the state when they were policed, primarily under the guise of a growing "sex problem" and even more so under suspicion of sex work, which anti-vice organizations and the state saw as a greater social threat than lesbianism. As we have seen, Mabel Hampton had to serve three years in New York State Reformatory for Women at Bedford after being framed for prostitution, a common practice by which policemen and male informers took advantage of single, working-class Black women in cities. Some lady lovers also took part in sex work to make a living, as the underground economy grew during Prohibition and legal work became more difficult to find during the Great Depression, especially since Black women were often the "last hired and first fired."[9] And as acts of violence increased in the eras of bootleg alcohol and economic downturn, depictions of murderous lady lovers began to appear in the Black press, which were also among the first articles to discuss the topic of lesbianism in papers like the *Chicago Defender* and the *New York Amsterdam News*. Such depictions further conflated Black lady lovers with the underworld and made them appear even more disrespectable.

This work has also shown that long before a distinctly gendered, "butch/stud–fem(me)" culture arose in the midcentury, Black queer gender-nonconforming women who took pride in their masculinity were visible in settings from turn-of the-century prisons and reformatories to Prohibition era theater performances.[10] Post–World War II working-class lesbian bar culture did not appear fully formed out of thin air but emerged as part of a new generation of queer gathering spaces that were coming from a lineage of Prohibition and Great Depression era speakeasies, rent parties, and buffet flats that welcomed and sometimes even centered lady lovers. Indeed, Elizabeth Lapovsky Kennedy and Madeline Davis surmise that the Harlem Renaissance was formative for working-class lesbian culture nationwide.[11] The social networks of Black lady lovers who cared for one another, helped each other find work, spent holidays together, and inspired one another to create cultural productions and gatherings created a foundation from which future communities and identities could develop.

In the postwar era, it would become more common for two women to live together as a couple, and the gender roles of working-class couples were expected to conform to the postwar model of one masculine and one feminine partner. While such gender roles were also common among Black female couples before the 1940s and 1950s, there was not the same expectation to hew to such guidelines before the identity categories of butch, stud, and fem(me) emerged in the postwar era. As many interwar examples show—from the masculine Gladys Bentley and her flirtations with white feminine women (and marriage to one of them), to Mabel Hampton's recollection that "the bulldykers would come and bring their women with them" to the "all-women parties" she attended—visible gender differences were common then too.[12] While words like "bulldagger" and "mannish" existed to describe masculine women, there was no term akin to "fem(me)" to describe feminine women who loved women in the interwar era. The solidification of butch/stud and fem(me) as a social norm in the queer world shows both a growth of the social networks that created a large enough population to be described by such terms and perhaps a growing social pressure to conform to a certain type of relationship within that world. There may have been more freedom to love women across gender roles in the interwar era, which created more opportunities and acceptance for relationships between feminine women and women married to men.

Similarly, the jealous violence that often accompanied postwar lesbian bar life was not a new phenomenon but also occurred among interwar lady lovers, as this book has shown. Experiencing little to no societal and familial support and enduring multiple forms of discrimination as Black women who loved women, they occasionally took out their frustrations on one another. A common assessment of post–World War II working-class lesbian bar culture is that, considering the visible violence and jealousy displayed between women, it was not feminist or political.[13] Such a critique could also be leveled at the interwar world detailed here, but this ignores the many forms of oppression that Black lady lovers dealt with at this time, from segregation and lack of work opportunities to judgment from family, community, and places of worship and criminalization and surveillance by the state. Homosexuality was pathologized and seen as immoral and deviant in the interwar era; it was threatening in its growing visibility. Black women, already deemed hypersexual by a white supremacist society, were seen as always already sexually deviant, even before broaching the stigmatized issue of queerness. Considering all the challenges such subaltern subjects navigated, the violent behavior discussed in chapter 1 reflects this lack of care and support. Yet despite these challenges and also because of them, women sacrificed for one another, helped each other gain work and housing, looked out for each other when touring on the road, and shared affectionate moments in the liminal spaces of Prohibition. And some were courageous enough to make a life and a home together in an unsupportive society, uplifting each other in life and—as the story of Lucy Diggs Slowe and Mary Burrill shows—even in death.

By centering the experiences of Black lady lovers in the interwar era urban North, a different perspective emerges on multiple historical issues. In the Great Migration, not only were Black southern migrant women specifically seen as threatening to the social order of the North, but lady lovers and the acts of violence that brought them into the Black press were represented as the worst of the newly forming southern migrant communities. At the same time, Black queer women played important roles as leaders in fields like music, literature, and higher education throughout this era. Black queer southern migrants and performers became celebrities who captured the nation and crafted songs that spoke of migrants' lives. Black lady lovers' networks and creations enriched American culture in the 1920s against the background of the Great Migration. And during Prohibition, Black lady lovers carved out important spaces in this lawbreaking era for women to meet one another, from speakeasies to buffet flats, rent parties, and private parties. As the Great Depression began, many queer women often felt more resistance to their unconventional way of life, as a cultural backlash to the excesses and transgressions of Prohibition took hold. Despite this, Black lady lovers continued to privately honor their desires by nurturing their queer relationships and networks amid the pleasures and hardships of city life.

ACKNOWLEDGMENTS

My journey to write this book began, unbeknownst to me at the time, during my unforgettable undergraduate education at Hampshire College. During my first semester there, I discovered the work of Eric Garber, who opened my eyes to the world of queer Prohibition era Harlem, in a class co-taught by E. Frances White and Margaret Cerullo. I first listened to the records of Bessie Smith and Ma Rainey in the campus library, and the lyrics about their unabashed desires educated me as much as anything I read in my gender studies and cultural studies classes. I also met lifelong friends Rumeli Snyder, Morgan Daniels, and Kat Case at Hampshire, whom I can't imagine not knowing.

I then spent a memorable decade in San Francisco, which ended with the Humanities MA program at San Francisco State University, where Cristina Ruotolo introduced me to the historical study of popular music and exciting scholarship, like Angela Davis's *Blues Legacies and Black Feminism*, that has been so influential on my work. My foray into queer historical scholarship began in Carel Bertram's class on cultural memory, which I am so grateful for all these years later. Saul Steier, Mary Scott, and Laura Garcia-Moreno at SFSU also supported me throughout my journey to find my path as a scholar, and Barbara Loomis not only led me to the study of women's history but guided me into the world of doctoral programs as I decided to pursue a PhD.

This book began at the University of Michigan, where I was lucky to have mentors like Jay Cook and Gina Morantz-Sanchez. Jay equipped me with the tools to shift from a cultural studies scholar to a cultural historian and urged me to think bigger and to engage with the messiness and complexity of the past. Gina always encouraged me to articulate a more lucid analysis of my historical subjects and helped me contextualize my work through the rich historiography of women's history. I was also privileged to work with Gayle Rubin and Sherie Randolph, who helped me complicate common historical narratives about gender and sexuality and introduced me to the historiography of African American women's history while pushing me to further engage with race and power in all their complexity.

Many other people and institutions at the University of Michigan helped me bring this book into existence: Howard Brick, John Carson, Matthew Countryman, Deirdre de la Cruz, Aimee Germain, Nadine Hubbs, Deborah Keller-Cohen, Mary Kelley, Kathleen King, Matt Lassiter, Adela Pinch, Hannah Rosen, Sidonie Smith, Scott Spector, Valerie Traub, and Elizabeth Wingrove, among others. I was well supported in my time at Michigan through the Rackham Graduate School, the Institute for Research on Women and Gender, and the Institute for the Humanities. Friends and colleagues at Michigan who gave me feedback and sustained me while working on this project include Danielle Abrams, Emma Amador, Jacki Antonovich, Tiffany Ball, Mira Bellwether, Rabia Belt, Chelsea Del Rio, Scott DeOrio, Paul Farber, Kara French, Aston Gonzalez, David B. Green, Lauren Gutterman, Maria Hadjipolycarpou, Sarah Hamilton, Trevor Hoppe, Donia Jarrar, Randa Jarrar, Jennifer Johnson, Jina B. Kim, Nora Krinitsky, Kim Kunoff, Kris Kurzawa, Sara Lampert, Katie Lennard, Annah MacKenzie, Austin McCoy, Rostom Mesli, Candace Moore, Patrick Parker, Carla Pfeffer, Holly Rapp, Mejdulene Shomali, LaKisha Simmons, Ronit Stahl, Marie Stango, Wendy Sung, Jacques Vest, and Brian Whitener.

Many archives and several archive-based fellowships also supported this project. An African American History and Culture Fellowship from Emory University's Stuart A. Rose Manuscript, Archives, and Rare Book Library allowed me to spend two weeks in Atlanta while I worked on my prospectus. Serving as a Martin Duberman Visiting Scholar for the summer of 2011 was my gateway to spending two fabulous years researching and writing in New York City, so I thank the New York Public Library for this enriching opportunity. This project fundamentally shifted after a wonderful month of research in the summer of 2012 in Chicago, where I served as a Black Metropolis Research Consortium Short-Term Fellow. I offer gratitude to numerous archivists and librarians at Emory; the Manuscripts and Archives Division of the New York Public Library; the Lincoln Center Performing Arts branch of the New York Public Library; the Schomburg Center for Research in Black Culture; Special Collections at the University of Chicago; the Chicago History Museum; the Center for Black Music Research at Columbia College; the Chicago Public Library; the Southern

Folklife Collection at the University of North Carolina at Chapel Hill; the David M. Rubenstein Rare Book and Manuscript Library at Duke University; the Rare Book and Manuscript Library at Columbia University; the Beinecke Rare Book and Manuscript Library at Yale University; the New York Municipal Archives; the Lesbian Herstory Archives; the GLBT Historical Society in San Francisco; the Bentley Historical Library at the University of Michigan; and the Moorland-Spingarn Research Center at Howard University. Thanks go to Catherine Conner, Katie Kretzmann, Vagina Jenkins, Michelle Morgan, and everyone else who gave me a place to stay during my archival visits.

This project has also been strengthened through feedback received at conferences from many people, including Paul Amar, Davarian Baldwin, Simon Balto, Daphne Brooks, Catherine Conner, Jennifer Evans, Anne Gray Fischer, Dayo Gore, Chad Heap, Cheryl Hicks, Heather Love, Leisa Meyer, Kevin Murphy, and Einav Rabinovitch-Fox. I am most grateful for the mentorship and support of Nan Enstad, whose scholarship has served as an important model to me. I have also been lucky to be part of a community of so many fabulous queer historians who have helped this book come to fruition, such as Julio Capó, Alix Genter, Eric Gonzaba, Christina Hanhardt, Emily Hobson, Kwame Holmes, David Hutchinson, Jennifer D. Jones, Aaron Lecklider, Amanda Littauer, Jen Manion, LaShonda Mims, David Minto, Anthony Mora, Kevin Quin, Don Romesburg, Dan Royles, Hugh Ryan, Emily Skidmore, and Stephen Vider, among others.

Many thanks go to Case Western Reserve University, where I was honored to serve as an African American Studies Postdoctoral Fellow under the mentorship of Rhonda Y. Williams, who gave me important feedback on my manuscript. I was thrilled to bring Kevin Mumford to campus during my year at Case, who offered intellectual support and inspiration as a scholar; my own work is indebted to him, and I thank him for his mentorship ever since. I was also privileged to meet John D'Emilio during my year at Case, whose work has been so pivotal to my own, and I thank him for his continued encouragement. Jonathan Sadowsky and Kenneth Ledford in Case's history department were also welcoming and offered mentorship and feedback during my year in Cleveland. I also appreciate being ushered into the local queer community there by Rachel Kacenjar and Suzanna Massey.

I am grateful for Kalamazoo College's Women, Gender, and Sexuality program and the Arcus Center for Social Justice Leadership, where I served as a Mellon Postdoctoral Teaching Fellow. My colleagues Taylor Petrey,

Lisa Brock, Charlene Boyer Lewis, Janelle Werner, and Ryan Fong were so welcoming and gave me a great launching pad for my project. I also appreciate my fellow postdocs Melanie Garcia Sympson and Matt Newman, as well as everyone else I spent time with in Kalamazoo, especially Davison Sarai Artemis.

At the University of Memphis, my work has been supported by the College of Arts and Sciences, the Marcus Orr Center for the Humanities, and the history department. I am lucky to have so many supportive colleagues, like Beverly Bond, Karen Bradley, Guiomar Duenas-Vargas, Christine Eisel, Aram Goudsouzian, Chrystal Goudsouzian, Ben Graham, Brian Kwoba, Selina Makana, Scott Marler, Susan O'Donovan, Suzanne Onstine, Caroline Peyton, Catherine Phipps, Sarah Potter, Amanda Lee Savage, Kathy Lou Schultz, Steve Stein, Beverly Tsacoyianis, Dan Unowsky, and Lyn Wright. I am also very grateful to Peggy Caffrey for the time she spent reading earlier drafts of my manuscript.

Completing a book while living alone during a pandemic has been no small feat. Zoom writing groups have been central to my sanity and productivity over the last few years, and I thank Anne Balay, Tiffany Ball, Sarah Dees, Scott DeOrio, Basak Durgan, Jennifer Johnson, Amanda Littauer, Don Rodrigues, and everyone else who kept me on track while cultivating community in a particularly difficult time. Other friends in Memphis I am very thankful for include Ari Eisenberg, Charles Hughes, Coe Lapossy, Paola Cavallari, and Joy Fairfield. Yo Clark and Aileen Herald have both played a crucial role in my well-being over the last few years, and I appreciate them and their work so much. And while Susannah Bartlow is no longer in Memphis, her friendship has sustained me in a major way over the last handful of years; I'm so glad we met here.

Chapter 1 of this book is based on an article published in the *Journal of African American History*, and I am grateful to the University of Chicago Press for allowing me to reprint the material and thank V. P. Franklin, Cheryl Hicks, Kali Gross, and LaShawn Harris at *JAAH*. At the University of North Carolina Press, I have been lucky to work with Mark Simpson-Vos, Dominique J. Moore, Andreina Fernandez, Mary Kelley, and Martha Jones, who, along with my readers, have helped shape and hone my project over the last few years. I am so thankful for their patience, persistence, and attention to detail and for believing in me and this book. And many thanks go to Valerie Burton and Julie Bush for their guidance and thoroughness in bringing this book into physical existence.

I am also grateful to my family, which encompasses both biological and platonic forms of kinship. Thanks and love go to my dad for instilling in me a passion for the arts and literature from such a young age and for his continued support. I know my mom would be proud to see this book come into the world. She told me that when she found out she was going to have a daughter, she was so glad because she knew I could be anything I wanted. Queer historian was probably not what she had in mind, but I think she would have gone along for the ride. Love and thanks go to David, Diana, Gayle, Zac, Courtney, Genevieve, and Myles, who make the holidays warm and bright, even if we don't get to see each other as much as we'd like. While professor life has given my life much meaning, I truly left my heart in San Francisco before this whole thing started. Living there in the 1990s and first years of the 2000s sent me down this path, thanks to my former bandmates Jessy and Jessie, who were even more obsessed with cool historical ladies than I was. Aaron, Brontez, Dia, Eli, Elizabeth, Heather Renée, Jameson, Joey, Kat, Melissa, Riley, and so many other folks I don't get to see enough—you'll always be my queer family.

Lastly, I offer humble gratitude to the incredible, indomitable women who came long before me whom I have had the honor of writing about—I can only hope to do justice to their groundbreaking lives.

NOTES

ABBREVIATIONS

COFR   Committee of Fourteen Records, Manuscripts and Archives
       Division, New York Public Library, New York City
LDSP   Lucy Diggs Slowe Papers, Moorland-Spingarn Research
       Center, Howard University, Washington, DC
MHC   Mabel Hampton Collection, Lesbian Herstory Archives, Brooklyn, NY

INTRODUCTION

1. "Have We a New Sex Problem Here?," *Chicago Whip*, November 27, 1920, 1.

2. Secondary sources examining the importance of the Great Migration include Grossman, *Land of Hope*; Marks, *Farewell—We're Good and Gone*; Trotter, *Great Migration in Historical Perspective*; Griffin, *"Who Set You Flowin'?"*; K. Phillips, *Alabama North*; Hahn, *Nation under Our Feet*; Baldwin, *Chicago's New Negroes*; and Wilkerson, *Warmth of Other Suns*.

3. E. Franklin Frazier, "Chicago: A Cross-Section of Negro Life," *Opportunity*, March 1929, 70; Frazier, *Negro Family in the United States*, 272; US Bureau of the Census, *Negro Population*, 152.

4. Frazier, *Negro Family in the United States*, 272; US Bureau of the Census, *Negro Population*, 152.

5. On "old settlers" and "new settlers" see Grossman, *Land of Hope*, 8; and Baldwin, *Chicago's New Negroes*, 9.

6. On the politics of respectability, see Higginbotham, *Righteous Discontent*; Gaines, *Uplifting the Race*; Wolcott, *Remaking Respectability*; and Cooper, *Beyond Respectability*.

7. Recent books such as performance studies scholar E. Patrick Johnson's *Black. Queer. Southern. Women* and literary scholar and historian Saidiya Hartman's *Wayward Lives, Beautiful Experiments* explore somewhat similar topics: oral histories of contemporary Black southern lesbians and "the revolution of Black intimate life" in the early twentieth century, respectively. Other books such as Treva Lindsey's *Colored No More* and Cheryl Hicks's *Talk to You Like a Woman* have brought sustained attention to the experiences of Black women who loved women in the interwar era. While there are

now historical monographs on Black gay men's history, such as Kevin Mumford's *Not Straight, Not White*, there is less scholarship focused on modern Black queer women's history. New scholarship that addresses and overlaps with this book's subjects includes Green, *Love, Activism, and the Respectable Life of Alice Dunbar-Nelson*; Greenidge, *Grimkes*; and M. Scott, *TOBA Time*.

8. I have found one similar murder case involving white queer women in the 1920s and none involving Black gay men. Regarding Black press coverage of queer men, the most common portrayals of gay men were regular reports on the popular drag balls that happened annually in Black districts in the urban North. While journalists sometimes made fun of the gay men and "female impersonators" at these events, they were rarely represented as criminal.

9. See, for example, John Houghton, "The Plight of Our Race in Harlem, Brooklyn and New Jersey," *Negro World*, April 21, 1923, 8.

10. M. Mitchell, *Righteous Propagation*, 235; Summers, *Manliness and Its Discontents*, 91; Blain, *Set the World on Fire*, 12.

11. "Race records" was the category used to denote record companies' subsidiary labels created to sell blues, spirituals, sermons, and novelty records to African American audiences. The term arose in the early 1920s and was eventually replaced by the category "rhythm and blues" in the 1940s. See Suisman, *Selling Sounds*; and K. Miller, *Segregating Sound*.

12. A. Davis, *Blues Legacies and Black Feminism*.

13. Albertson, *Bessie*.

14. As audiences understood and delighted in these titillating performances in illicit spaces, they constituted a counterpublic—similar to a subculture—through their acknowledged tension with the larger public, both the larger Black community and the dominant white culture. See Warner, *Publics and Counterpublics*, 56.

15. A. Davis, *Blues Legacies and Black Feminisms*; J. Brown, *Babylon Girls*.

16. D'Emilio and Freedman, *Intimate Matters*, 240–41.

17. Marcus Wright, "The Talk of the Town," *New York Age*, August 18, 1934; Gertrude "Ma" Rainey, "Shave 'Em Dry," 1924, Paramount Records 12222-A.

18. Ralph Matthews, "Women in Pants—Old Stuff Say Our Girls," *Baltimore Afro-American*, March 18, 1933.

19. Hull, introduction to *Give Us Each Day*, 22.

20. See, for example, Smith-Rosenberg, "Female World of Love and Ritual."

21. "Dr. A. C. Powell Scores Pulp Evils," *New York Age*, November 16, 1929.

22. Powell, *Against the Tide*, 210.

23. "Dr. Powell's Crusade against Abnormal Vice Is Approved," *New York Age*, November 23, 1929.

24. "Dr. Powell's Crusade against Abnormal Vice Is Approved"; "Dr. A. C. Powell Scores Pulp Evils."

25. Powell, *Against the Tide*, 216.

26. Hicks, *Talk with You Like a Woman*.

27. Chauncey, *Gay New York*; Mumford, *Interzones*.

28. Mumford, *Interzones*, 35.

29. Chicago Commission on Race Relations, *Negro in Chicago*, 202; Muhammad, *Condemnation of Blackness*, 226.

30. Nan Alamilla Boyd uses the term "wide open" to define a city or district where illicit activities can take place free of legal repercussion, such as gold rush–era San Francisco. See Boyd, *Wide-Open Town*, 2.

31. Blair, *I've Got to Make My Livin'*, 175.

32. Hughes, *Big Sea*, 244; Mabel Hampton, interview by Joan Nestle, "Mabel Hampton, Undated (Tape 1)," MHC, http://herstories.prattinfoschool.nyc/omeka/items/show/95.

33. Chauncey, *Gay New York*; Mumford, *Interzones*; Thorpe, "'House Where Queers Go'"; Heap, *Slumming*.

34. Vogel, *Scene of Harlem Cabaret*, 56.

35. Garber, "Gladys Bentley," 58.

36. Jungle Alley was the nickname for a block of 133rd Street in Harlem populated by clubs patronized by white slumming audiences.

37. W. E. B. Du Bois, "Harlem," *The Crisis*, September 1927, 240.

38. Hine, "Rape and the Inner Lives of Black Women"; Hammonds, "Toward a Genealogy of Black Female Sexuality"; K. Brown, *Good Wives*; Morgan, *Laboring Women*; Camp, *Closer to Freedom*.

39. Ellis, *Sexual Inversion*; Chauncey, "From Sexual Inversion to Homosexuality."

40. Newton, "Mythic Mannish Lesbian."

41. Lisa Duggan coined the phrase "lesbian love murder" to refer to a specific trope that emerged in the 1890s in which a masculine woman killed her feminine object of desire when the latter left the former for a male partner. While women rarely identified as "lesbians" in this era, Duggan argues that these cases helped formulate the concept of modern lesbian identity. See Duggan, *Sapphic Slashers*.

42. Gilman, *Difference and Pathology*, 89; Hart, *Fatal Women*, 4; Somerville, *Queering the Color Line*, 27.

43. Somerville, *Queering the Color Line*, 133.

44. Ellis, *Sexual Inversion*, 124.

45. Carter, "Normality, Whiteness, Authorship," 160. It is also important to point out that alongside these troublesome associations, sexology case studies could also validate the feelings of queer readers and bring about the realization that they were not alone in their experiences. See Oosterhuis, "Richard von Krafft-Ebing's 'Step-Children of Nature.'"

46. Muhammad, *Condemnation of Blackness*, 59–60.

47. Muhammad, *Condemnation of Blackness*, 4.

48. Rafter, *Partial Justice*, 141; US Bureau of the Census, "Summary of the Population of the United States,"11.

49. Faderman, *Odd Girls and Twilight Lovers*, 72. These would later morph into the more commonly known "butch/femme" identities or roles by midcentury.

50. Otis, "Perversion Not Commonly Noted," 113.

51. Hicks, *Talk with You Like a Woman*, 225.

52. Potter, "'Undesirable Relations,'" 408; R. Alexander, *Girl Problem*.

53. Hicks, *Talk with You Like a Woman*, 230–32.

54. Wolcott, *Remaking Respectability*; M. Mitchell, *Righteous Propagation*; Summers, *Manliness and Its Discontents*; Chapman, *Prove It on Me*; Blain, *Set the World on Fire*.

55. Hunter, *To 'Joy My Freedom*, 166.

56. "Too Familiar," *Chicago Whip*, September 9, 1922.

57. Gordon, *Woman's Body, Woman's Right*; Chesler, *Woman of Valor*; May, *Barren in the Promised Land*; Simmons, *Making Marriage Modern*; Celello, *Making Marriage Work*.

58. Smith-Rosenberg, "Female World of Love and Ritual"; Faderman, *Surpassing the Love of Men*; Hansen, "'No Kisses Is Like Youres.'"

59. Simmons, "Companionate Marriage and the Lesbian Threat"; Faderman, *Odd Girls and Twilight Lovers*. "Companionate marriage" was a new modern conception of heterosexual marriage in which both partners were considered equal companions and both their emotional and sexual needs were to be tended to, not just the husband's.

60. Stevenson, "Distress and Discord in Virginia Slave Families"; J. Jones, *Labor of Love*, 58; Simmons, *Making Marriage Modern*; Williams, *Help Me to Find My People*.

61. Lindquis, *Black Social Science*, 180.

62. Chauncey, *Gay New York*, 365–68.

63. Richardson, "No More Secrets, No More Lies," 66.

64. Hull, "Researching Alice Dunbar-Nelson," 17.

65. Hine, "Rape and the Inner Lives of Black Women," 912.

66. Scholarship on the intellectual life of the women in chapter 4 includes Hull, *Color, Sex, and Poetry*; Mitchell and Davis, *Literary Sisters*; Miller and Pruitt-Logan, *Faithful to the Task at Hand*; Lindsey, *Colored No More*; Green, *Love, Activism, and the Respectable Life of Alice Dunbar-Nelson*; and Beauboeuf-Lafontant, *To Live More Abundantly*.

67. Cooper, *Beyond Respectability*, 9; Green, *Love, Activism, and the Respectable Life of Alice Dunbar-Nelson*, 4.

68. Hammonds, "Black (W)holes," 145.

69. Nash, *Black Body in Ecstasy*, 3.

70. V. Boyd, *Wrapped in Rainbows*, 131; Mitchell and Davis, *Literary Sisters*, 96.

71. Foucault, *History of Sexuality*; Halperin, *How to Do the History of Homosexuality*.

72. Mabel Hampton, interview by Joan Nestle, "Mabel Hampton's Story, July 1986 (Tape 4)," MHC, http://herstories.prattinfoschool.nyc/omeka/items/show/85.

73. Nestle, "I Lift My Eyes to the Hill," 267.

74. Quoted in J. Baker, *Josephine Baker*, 63–64.

75. Regarding women self-identifying as "queer," a woman at the Bally Hoo Café in 1933 Chicago was asked to dance by a male University of Chicago sociology student; she declined and told him "queer people despise" straight people. See Ernest W. Burgess Papers, box 98, folder 2, Special Collections Research Center, University of Chicago.

76. As Jafari S. Allen has noted, while the term "queer" might be problematic, "no term, even those that may seem self-evidently local, indigenous, or autochthonous, is perfectly stable or synchronous with dynamic self-identification on the ground." See Allen, "Black/Queer/Diaspora," 222.

77. In referring to "queer networks," I am taking a cue from the work of Tristan Cabello, "Queer Bronzeville."

78. Wirth, introduction to *Gay Rebel of the Harlem Renaissance*, 21.

CHAPTER 1

1. "Woman Rivals for Affection of Another Woman Battles with Knives, and One Has Head Almost Severed from Body," *New York Age*, November 27, 1926, 1.

2. "Woman Rivals for Affection."

3. Regarding the phenomenon of the "rent party," sociologist Ira De A. Reid explained in 1927 that "it has been the custom of certain portions of the Negro group living in southern cities to give some form of party when money was needed to supplement the family income." Reid, "Mrs. Bailey," 144.

4. This area is now where Lincoln Center was built on the Upper East Side of Manhattan. Scheiner, *Negro Mecca*, 19.

5. Osofsky, *Harlem*, 112–13, 120.

6. "City's Crime Spots Shown by Survey," *New York Times*, December 14, 1923.

7. Bessie, *Jazz Journalism*.

8. The Tenderloin, San Juan Hill/Columbus Hill, and Harlem were the three neighborhoods where the majority of southern migrants settled between 1900 and 1920. See Osofsky, *Harlem*, 34.

9. For example, in the first half of 1928, out of thirty-four homicides in Harlem, half of which took place between whites and half between African Americans, only one occurred between "women lovers" according to the article "More Homicides in Harlem Than Down on Bowery," *New York Amsterdam News*, July 18, 1928. Similarly, in the state of Illinois in 1926, Black men were charged with murdering fifty Black men and sixteen Black women, compared with white men who were charged with murdering sixty-five white men and twenty-seven white women. Black women were charged with killing ten Black men and two Black women, compared with white women who were charged with killing nine white men and ten white women. Black women therefore killed fewer women than any other demographic. See Zollmann, "Table 13: Color and Sex of Known Perpetrators," in *Illinois Crime Survey*, 624.

10. Despite the lack of "official evidence" of these subjects' queerness, they are still analyzed here as potential queer subjects. As lesbian historian Martha Vicinus notes, "Lesbian history has always been characterized by a 'not knowing' which could be its defining core." See Martha Vicinus, "Lesbian History," 57. Further, it does not seem likely that death reports and court records from the 1920s would explicate women's queer behavior; as Roderick Ferguson argues, "Epistemology is an economy of information privileged and information excluded," and "canonical and national formations rarely disclose what they have rejected." Hence, a lack of references to lesbianism should not imply its absence. See Ferguson, *Aberrations in Black*, xi.

11. Wiltenburg, "True Crime," 1377–80.

12. Duggan, "Trials of Alice Mitchell," 804. Kali Gross discusses this "copycat" murder and another similar incident between two Black women in 1905 Philadelphia in *Colored Amazons*.

13. On living conditions in Harlem and Bronzeville in the early Great Migration, see J. Johnson, *Black Manhattan*; Drake and Cayton, *Black Metropolis*; Osofsky, *Harlem*; Baldwin, *Chicago's New Negroes*; and Lewinnek, *Working Man's Reward*.

14. Dodge, *Whores and Thieves of the Worst Kind*, 103.

15. Frazier, "Sex Morality among Negroes," 450.

16. For example, journalists told Black migrant women not to be too friendly to white men, to abstain from "vile language," and to dress modestly for the theater and practice their "indoor voices" there. See "Things That Should Be Considered," *Chicago Defender*,

October 20, 1917; A. L. Jackson, "The Onlooker: Public Manners," *Chicago Defender*, December 3, 1921; and "Too Familiar," *Chicago Whip*, September 9, 1922.

17. Frazier, *Negro Family in Chicago*, 196–97.

18. Chauncey, *Gay New York*, 254–56; Hicks, *Talk with You Like a Woman*, 219.

19. "Dr. A. C. Powell Scores Pulp Evils," *New York Age*, November 16, 1929.

20. Wirth, *Gay Rebel of the Harlem Renaissance*, 22.

21. "Dr. Powell's Crusade against Abnormal Vice Is Approved," *New York Age*, November 23, 1929.

22. Gallon, *Pleasure in the News*, 148.

23. Martin, *Preaching on Wax*, 1.

24. J. M. Gates, "Manish Women" Okeh Records ad, *Baltimore Afro-American*, May 17, 1930.

25. One exception was the infamous case of Nathan Leopold and Richard Loeb, white gay male students at the University of Chicago who kidnapped and killed a boy in 1924. I have uncovered only one similar 1920s narrative between two white women, in 1921 Chicago. See "Girl Victims of Queer Love Lie Near Death," *Chicago Evening News*, April 28, 1921. No similar stories concerning Black gay men have been found.

26. Gallon, *Pleasure in the News*, 157.

27. K. Phillips, *Alabama North*, 39–40.

28. K. Phillips, *Alabama North*, 39–40; Chicago Commission on Race Relations, *Negro in Chicago*, 80.

29. On the factors that contributed to the early Great Migration, see Grossman, *Land of Hope*; Marks, *Farewell—We're Good and Gone*; Trotter, *Great Migration in Historical Perspective*; Griffin, *"Who Set You Flowin'?"*; Hahn, *A Nation under Our Feet*; Wilkerson, *Warmth of Other Suns*; and Hicks, *Talk with You Like a Woman*.

30. For example, one 1922 Chicago study found that "labor shortage was given as the reason for employing Negro women and girls by all of the firms employing them in large numbers." Chicago Commission on Race Relations, *Negro in Chicago*, 380.

31. Grossman, *Land of Hope*, 14; Wilkerson, *Warmth of Other Suns*, 10.

32. L. Brown, "African American Women and Migration," 210.

33. Carby, "Policing the Black Woman's Body," 741.

34. Grossman, *Land of Hope*, 94; K. Phillips, *Alabama North*, 40.

35. Kelly Miller, "Surplus Negro Women," *Southern Workman* 34 (1906): 524.

36. Clark-Lewis, "This Work Had an End," 198; Sacks, *Before Harlem*, 26.

37. Kelly Miller, "Surplus Negro Women," 523–24.

38. Kelly Miller, "Surplus Negro Women," 524.

39. Carby, "Policing the Black Woman's Body," 741; Hicks, *Talk with You Like a Woman*, 121.

40. Reckless, *Vice in Chicago*, 192.

41. Mumford, *Interzones*, 20.

42. Reckless, *Vice in Chicago*, 192.

43. Mumford, *Interzones*, 84.

44. Edgar M. Grey, "The Devil's Playground: Harlem an Easy Prey for Depraved Joy-Seeking Whites," *New York Amsterdam News*, July 6, 1927.

45. "Vice Runs Unchecked in 2nd Ward," *Chicago Defender*, July 10, 1920.

46. Chicago Commission on Race Relations, *Negro in Chicago*, 328.

47. Simmons, "'Modern Marriage' for African Americans," 277.

48. Farley, *Growth of the Negro Population*; M. Mitchell, *Righteous Propagation*, 10.

49. Vincent, *Black Power and the Garvey Movement*.

50. Douglas, *Terrible Honesty*, 324.

51. Summers, "'This Immoral Practice,'" 24.

52. M. Mitchell, *Righteous Propagation*, 80; Blain, *Set the World on Fire*, 12.

53. Corbould, *Becoming African Americans*, 22–23.

54. John Houghton, "The Plight of Our Race in Harlem, Brooklyn and New Jersey," *Negro World*, April 21, 1923.

55. Houghton, "Plight of Our Race in Harlem, Brooklyn and New Jersey."

56. Gallon, *Pleasure in the News*, 95–104.

57. Freud, *Three Essays on the Theory of Sexuality*.

58. Houghton, "Plight of Our Race in Harlem, Brooklyn and New Jersey."

59. Summers, "'This Immoral Practice,'" 34.

60. J. A. Rogers, "Books on Mingling of the Races Stir Paris," *Pittsburgh Courier*, July 14, 1928. Scholarly works that refute such simplistic notions include Wekker, *Politics of Passion*; and Tinsley, "Black Atlantic, Queer Atlantic."

61. Despite this, as Keisha Blain has shown, many women also worked within the Universal Negro Improvement Association to fight for equal rights for Black women. See Blain, *Set the World on Fire*.

62. Higginbotham, *Righteous Discontent*, 203.

63. "'Unusual Type,' Say Cops of Women Caught in Raid," *Chicago Defender*, December 9, 1922, 1. It is also notable that "Barney" was the given first name of one of the women there, suggesting a masculine gender presentation to match this traditionally male name, which would further fit the 1920s notion of a woman being an "unusual type."

64. "'Unusual Type.'"

65. Gertrude "Ma" Rainey, "Shave 'Em Dry," 1924, Paramount Records 12222-A.

66. "The Captive," *Variety*, October 6, 1926.

67. Somerville, *Queering the Color Line*; Carter, *Heart of Whiteness*.

68. However, *The Captive* was not the first Broadway play to deal with lesbianism; the play *God of Vengeance*, which ran briefly on Broadway in 1923, also focused on the topic but did not receive as much publicity, despite the fact that the production also led to an obscenity case. See Curtin, *We Can Always Call Them Bulgarians*.

69. Burton Davies, "Much Talked of 'Captive' Opens," *New York Morning Telegraph*, September 30, 1926.

70. F. Allen, *Only Yesterday*, 113.

71. "The Captive," *Variety*.

72. "Woman Rivals for Affection."

73. "A Rent Party Tragedy," *New York Age*, December 11, 1926.

74. "Woman Slain in Queer Love Brawl," *Chicago Defender*, December 1, 1928, 1.

75. See the 1900 census for Franklin County, Tennessee, accessed through Ancestry.com.

76. *Cook County Marriage Index, 1914–1942*, accessed through Ancestry.com.

77. *Illinois, Deaths and Stillbirths Index, 1916–1947*, accessed through Ancestry.com.

78. *Cook County Marriage Index, 1914–1942*, accessed through Ancestry.com.

79. See the "Homicide in Chicago 1870–1930" database, accessed February 10, 2023, https://homicide.northwestern.edu/.

80. George S. Schuyler, "Views and Reviews," *Pittsburgh Courier*, April 21, 1928.

81. Newton, "Mythic Mannish Lesbian," 559.

82. "Police Seize Novel by Radclyffe Hall," *New York Times*, January 12, 1929.

83. Taylor, "'I Made Up My Mind to Get It,'" 251–53.

84. Edgar M. Grey, "Are Women Lovers Harmful?," *Inter-State Tattler*, February 15, 1929.

85. Grey, "Are Women Lovers Harmful?"

86. Ellis, *Sexual Inversion*, 133.

87. Grey, "Are Women Lovers Harmful?"

88. "More Homicides in Harlem Than Down on Bowery," *New York Amsterdam News*, July 18, 1928.

89. "More Homicides in Harlem Than Down on Bowery."

90. "Woman Stabbed to Death, Man and Woman Held," *New York Age*, June 23, 1928.

91. "Negress Stabbed to Death," *Brooklyn Eagle*, June 20, 1928.

92. "Woman Kills Woman for Love of Woman," *New York Amsterdam News*, June 27, 1928, 1.

93. "Women Love Woman, One Kills Rival," *Indianapolis Recorder*, July 7, 1928, 1.

94. "Woman Slayer of Female Lover Found Guilty of Manslaughter," *New York Amsterdam News*, October 24, 1928, 1.

95. "Woman Gets Manslaughter Verdict in 'Queer Love' Case," *Pittsburgh Courier*, November 3, 1928.

96. "Four to Eight Year Sentence for Woman," *New York Amsterdam News*, November 14, 1928.

97. "Four to Eight Year Sentence for Woman."

98. Meyerowitz, *Women Adrift*, 112; Jakle and Sculle, *America's Main Street Hotels*, 112.

99. Edna Washington's death certificate no. 17332, *1928 Deaths Reported in Borough of Manhattan*, New York Municipal Archives.

100. Edna Washington's death certificate no. 17332, June 20, 1928; district attorney file, Alberta Mitchell murder trial, New York Municipal Archives. In 1930, 63 percent of African American women worked in domestic and personal service in the United States, up from 42 percent in 1910. See US Bureau of the Census, *Social and Economic Status of the Black Population*, 71.

101. See the 1930 US Census, New York State, Cayuga County, city of Auburn, District 8, accessed through Ancestry.com.

102. Lerner, *Dry Manhattan*, 256–57.

CHAPTER 2

1. While Bessie Smith was almost as popular with southern whites as she was with southern African Americans, northern whites thought she had a "crude and simplistic" sound. Nonetheless, her biographer Chris Albertson states she "ascended to a level that no other African-American artist of her time and genre has reached." See

Albertson, *Bessie*, 66, 7. Also on Smith see Oliver, *Story of the Blues*; Harrison, *Black Pearls*; A. Davis, *Blues Legacies and Black Feminism*; and M. Scott, *Blues Empress in Black Chattanooga*.

2. Albertson, *Bessie*, x.

3. Albertson, *Bessie*, 123.

4. S. T. Whitney, "Watch Your Step!," *New York Amsterdam News*, December 4, 1929.

5. Prior to the mid-1920s, the word "lesbian" rarely took on the connotation of female same-sex sexuality in the United States but was usually an innocuous term associated with the ancient Greek poet Sappho and matters of love in general. For example, in 1917, the Black newspaper the *Chicago Defender* announced an Atlantic City performance at an African Methodist Episcopal church by the Lesbian Rose Trio of Wilberforce University, which was a choir made up of both men and women. See "Doings Down along the Jersey Shore," *Chicago Defender*, March 17, 1917.

6. Whitney, "Watch Your Step!"

7. See, among other works, Lieb, *Mother of the Blues*; Harrison, *Black Pearls*; Mumford, *Interzones*; J. Brown, *Babylon Girls*; A. Davis, *Blues Legacies and Black Feminism*; Heap, *Slumming*; Wilson, *Bulldaggers, Pansies, and Chocolate Babies*; and A. Jones, "She Wolves."

8. Interview with Charles Elmore, Southern Oral History Program, Southern Historical Collection, Wilson Library, University of North Carolina at Chapel Hill; Abbott and Seroff, *Original Blues*, 202.

9. Cullen with Hackman and McNeilly, *Vaudeville Old and New*, 12

10. Cullen with Hackman and McNeilly, *Vaudeville Old and New*, 210; Packard, *American Nightmare*, 92–93.

11. Lieb, *Mother of the Blues*, 6.

12. The beginnings of an organized, nationwide American popular entertainment industry can be traced to the advent of blackface minstrelsy, which arose in the early nineteenth century, coinciding with the Industrial Revolution. Minstrel shows were generally performed by and for white working-class men beginning in the 1840s. Performances involved white men "blackening up" their faces by applying burnt cork to their skin in order to mimic and caricature Black men. As David Roediger argues, with the ascendancy of industrial capitalist modes of production, whites shored up their racial superiority by imbuing African Americans with qualities no longer useful in an industrial age of time management and self-control, such as overt eroticism and carefree leisure. By the end of the nineteenth century, Black performers such as Bert Williams and George Walker utilized the stereotypes of minstrelsy to underscore the artifice and constructedness of the form, as well as to critique the system of Jim Crow segregation from the stage. See Roediger, *Wages of Whiteness*; and Sotiropoulos, *Staging Race*.

13. Lieb, *Mother of the Blues*, xii–xiii.

14. Harrison, *Black Pearls*, 11.

15. Lieb, *Mother of the Blues*, xiii.

16. Scholars have often incorrectly stated the birth of TOBA as 1909 or 1910. Preston Lauterbach argues that January 1921 was the actual birth of TOBA, as the *Chicago Defender* asserts that the association was a "new organization" in the article "New Organization," *Chicago Defender*, January 29, 1921. See Lauterbach, *Chitlin' Circuit*, 304.

17. "New Organization," *Chicago Defender*; Knight, "He Paved the Way for T.O.B.A.," 171.

18. Lauterbach, *Chitlin' Circuit*, 304.

19. Jay Joslin, "Chair Firm Turned to Recording and Helped Launch Black Artists," *Milwaukee Sentinel*, December 11, 1984, John Steiner Collection, box 30, folder 6: History of Paramount, 1917–1989, Special Collections Research Center, University of Chicago Library.

20. Albertson, *Bessie*, 66; Waters with Samuels, *His Eye Is on the Sparrow*, 73, 166.

21. Harrison, *Black Pearls*, 4–25; Albertson, *Bessie*, 142.

22. Taylor and Cook, *Alberta Hunter*, 68.

23. Lieb, *Mother of the Blues*, 39.

24. "Musicians Quit; Ethel Waters Goes South," *Chicago Defender*, February 11, 1922.

25. Bogle, *Heat Wave*, 81.

26. Waters with Samuels, *His Eye Is on the Sparrow*, 159.

27. Albertson, *Bessie*, 156–58.

28. *Talking Machine World* 1 (January 1905): 3; K. Miller, *Segregating Sound*, 151.

29. W. C. Handy, author of the song "St. Louis Blues," is often described as the "Father of the Blues" for his pioneering songwriting and was also one of the founders of Black Swan Records. Muir, *Long Lost Blues*, 20, 96.

30. "Demands Records of Our Artists," *Chicago Defender*, November 11, 1916; Bradford, *Born with the Blues*, 115.

31. Samuel Charters and Leonard Kunstadt have argued that the record sold over a million copies in less than a year, but Adam Gussow has discredited this, stating the sales number is unreliable and may have been combined with sales of other formats, such as sheet music and piano rolls. See Charters and Kunstadt, *Jazz*, 91; and Gussow, "'Shoot Myself a Cop,'" 40.

32. For examples of historical scholarship on queer theater, see Curtin, *We Can Always Call Them Bulgarians*; D. Miller, *Place for Us*; Sinfield, *Out on Stage*; and Marra and Schanke, *Staging Desire*. On queer popular music scholarship, see J. Gill, *Queer Noises*; and Fuller and Whitesell, *Queer Episodes in Music and Modern Identity*.

33. Harbin, Marra, and Schanke, *Gay and Lesbian Theatrical Legacy*, 1; Sinfield, *Out on Stage*, 6.

34. A. Jones, "She Wolves," 294.

35. Ralph Matthews, "Love Laughs at Life in Harlem," *Baltimore Afro-American*, March 11, 1933; Ralph Matthews, "She Wolf: She Had Charm and Beauty but She Preyed on Her Own Sex, Part One," *Baltimore Afro-American*, November 17, 1934; Ralph Matthews, "She Wolf: She Had Charm and Beauty but She Preyed on Her Own Sex, Part Two," *Baltimore Afro-American*, November 24, 1934.

36. Matthews, "Love Laughs at Life in Harlem."

37. Matthews, "Love Laughs at Life in Harlem."

38. Albertson, *Bessie*, 35.

39. Perry Lichtenstein, "The Fairy and the Lady Lover," *Medical Review of Reviews* 27 (1921): 372.

40. Henry, *Sex Variants*, 724–26. See also the discussion of Marian J. in chapter 4.

41. Henry, *Sex Variants*, 783–84.

42. Quoted in J. Baker, *Josephine Baker*, 63–64.

43. Mabel Hampton, interview by Joan Nestle, "Mabel Hampton's Story, July 1986 (Tape 4)," MHC, http://herstories.prattinfoschool.nyc/omeka/items/show/85.

44. Nestle, "I Lift My Eyes to the Hill," 265.

45. Mabel Hampton, interview by Joan Nestle, "Mabel Hampton, Undated (Tape 1)," MHC, http://herstories.prattinfoschool.nyc/omeka/items/show/95.

46. Nestle, "I Lift My Eyes to the Hill," 266, 268.

47. Nestle, "I Lift My Eyes to the Hill," 267–68.

48. Mumford, *Interzones*; Coleman, "Cabarets and Revues," 9.

49. Waters with Samuels, *His Eye Is on the Sparrow*, 136.

50. "Correspondence with Harry H. Pace, Nov. 17, 1939," in Ottley and Weatherby, *Negro in New York*, 133.

51. Bogle, *Heat Wave*, 84–85.

52. Personal correspondence between Joan Nestle and Stephen Bourne, February 10, 1994, cited in Bourne, *Ethel Waters*, 26.

53. Bogle, *Heat Wave*, 516.

54. Mabel Hampton, interview by Joan Nestle, n.d., 9, Eric Garber Papers, Gay, Lesbian, Bisexual, and Transgender Historical Society, San Francisco.

55. Waters with Samuels, *His Eye Is on the Sparrow*, 137.

56. Waters with Samuels, *His Eye Is on the Sparrow*, 137.

57. Personal correspondence between Joan Nestle and Stephen Bourne, February 10, 1994, cited in Bourne, *Ethel Waters*, 26.

58. Suisman, *Selling Sounds*, 206; Muir, *Long Lost Blues*, 96.

59. Gaines, *Uplifting the Race*, 76; M. Mitchell, *Righteous Propagation*, 79.

60. This contract that supposedly kept Waters from marrying was never mentioned in her autobiography, and her biographer Donald Bogle doubts its existence. See Bogle, *Heat Wave*, 85.

61. "Ethel Must Not Marry," *Chicago Defender*, December 24, 1921.

62. J. Jones, *Labor of Love*, 73.

63. Simmons, "Companionate Marriage and the Lesbian Threat."

64. "Entertains Ethel Waters," *Chicago Defender*, February 4, 1922.

65. Taylor and Cook, *Alberta Hunter*, 52.

66. "Correspondence with Harry H. Pace, Nov. 17, 1939," in Ottley and Weatherby, *Negro in New York*, 234.

67. Bogle, *Heat Wave*, 80.

68. Waters with Samuels, *His Eye Is on the Sparrow*, 151.

69. Sotiropoulos, *Staging Race*, 64.

70. J. Scott, *Domination and the Arts of Resistance*, x–xii.

71. Sotiropoulos, *Staging Race*.

72. Bailey, "Conspiracies of Meaning."

73. Lieb, *Mother of the Blues*, xii; Van Der Tuuk, *Paramount's Rise and Fall*, 73; Carby, *Culture in Babylon*, 16; Harrison, *Black Pearls*, 35.

74. Lieb, *Mother of the Blues*, 17–18.

75. Lyrics transcribed by A. Davis, *Blues Legacies and Black Feminism*, 241. A much more sexually explicit song also titled "Shave 'Em Dry" was later recorded by Lucille Bogan in 1935.

76. Lyrics transcribed by A. Davis, *Blues Legacies and Black Feminism*, 201.

77. Another artist who sang about this topic was Lucille Bogan, who recorded the song "B. D. Woman's Blues" under the pseudonym of Bessie Jackson in 1935. B. D. stood for "bull dyke" or "bulldagger."

78. Kokomo Arnold's 1935 song "Sissy Man Blues," declared, "Lord, if you can't send me no woman, please send me some sissy man." Decca Records 7050.

79. Gertrude "Ma" Rainey, "Sissy Man Blues," 1926, Paramount Records 12384.

80. The long-standing rumor about Rainey and Bessie Smith having an affair will be addressed in the section on Smith.

81. Albertson, *Bessie*, 116.

82. This is the line that Rainey recorded, but her biographer Sandra Lieb points out that the lead sheet for the song contained the alternative line "Likes to watch while the women pass by." Lieb, *Mother of the Blues*, 207.

83. Gertrude "Ma" Rainey, "Prove It on Me Blues," 1928, Paramount Records 12668.

84. As queer theorist Eve Sedgwick notes, the modern conception of "coming out of the closet" did not exist until after the Stonewall Uprising in 1969, which is generally hailed as initiating the modern gay rights movement in the United States, so to speak of this act taking place in the 1920s is ahistorical, hence the term "proto-outing." See Sedgwick, *Epistemology of the Closet*, 14.

85. For example, Valerie Boyd writes that "Rainey parlayed the scandal into a hit record." There are also no accounts of how many copies "Prove It on Me Blues" sold, so to refer to it as a "hit" record may also be inaccurate. See V. Boyd, *Wrapped in Rainbows*, 128.

86. Dolan, "Extra!," 114.

87. Titon, *Early Downhome Blues*, 201. Somewhat similar to the "Prove It on Me Blues" ad, other 1920s race records ads showed Black men playing dice on the street and depicted male blues singers in prison, among other topics that concerned white and Black middle class and anti-vice organizations.

88. Carby, "Policing the Black Woman's Body."

89. Smith's actual birth year and date is debated and unknown but is most likely 1894 or 1895. Albertson, *Bessie*, 7–9.

90. Cullen with Hackman and McNeilly, *Vaudeville Old and New*, 1044.

91. Rodger, *Just One of the Boys*, 2018.

92. Lieb, *Mother of the Blues*, xii.

93. Lieb, *Mother of the Blues*, 18.

94. Alberston, *Bessie*, 14.

95. W. C. Handy, Handy Brothers Music Co., Inc. press release, February 7, 1948, box H-HD, Carl Van Vechten Papers, Beinecke Rare Book and Manuscript Library, Yale University, New Haven, CT.

96. Albertson, *Bessie*, 25, 174.

97. Suisman, *Selling Sounds*, 208.

98. Suisman, *Selling Sounds*, 222.

99. Albertson, *Bessie*, 145.

100. Albertson, *Bessie*, 102.

101. Albertson, *Bessie*, 142.

102. Albertson, *Bessie*, 142.

103. Albertson, *Bessie*, 142–43.

104. Lyrics transcribed by A. Davis, *Blues Legacies and Black Feminism*, 280.

105. J. Gill, *Queer Noises*, 36.

106. Chauncey, *Gay New York*, 249.

107. A. Davis, *Blues Legacies and Black Feminism*, 13.

108. The song "My Man Blues" (1925), for example, is a duet by Bessie Smith and Clara Smith where they resolve the issue of fighting over a man by agreeing to share him. See Atwater, *African American Women's Rhetoric*, 77.

CHAPTER 3

1. Box 82, folder "135–207 St," COFR. The letter "c——," might have stood for "cocksucker," but this was not yet a term regularly used in relation to gay men in African American communities in the 1920s, as the word "cock" often referred to female genitalia as well. For an example of the latter, see Lucille Bogan's version of the song "Shave 'Em Dry" from 1935.

2. This is significant because she reveals that some Black women self-identified with the term "bulldagger" during the era; it wasn't merely a negative label used by heterosexuals to denigrate queer women or specifically masculine queer women. As the woman in question was likely feminine in appearance—the investigator asked if she was a "normal, regular girl"—this also reveals that "bulldagger" was a term that some working-class queer African American women used regardless of their gender presentation.

3. Box 82, folder "135–207 St," COFR.

4. Mumford, *Interzones*; Heap, *Slumming*.

5. Lerner, *Dry Manhattan*.

6. Chauncey, *Gay New York*; Mumford, *Interzones*; Heap, *Slumming*.

7. Hughes, *Big Sea*, 228.

8. Langston Hughes noted of the Prohibition era, "Non-theatrical, non-intellectual Harlem was an unwilling victim of its own vogue. It didn't like to be stared at by white folks." See Hughes, *Big Sea*, 229.

9. Mumford, *Interzones*, 21.

10. Goldberg, *Discontented America*, 54.

11. In fact, the group's original name was the Committee of Fourteen for the Suppression of Raines Law Hotels in New York City. See Committee of Fourteen, *Social Evil in New York City*, xi, 1.

12. Gilfoyle, *City of Eros*, 303.

13. Gilfoyle, *City of Eros*, 304.

14. Robertson, "Harlem Undercover," 489.

15. Erenberg, *Steppin' Out*, 63–64.

16. Kelly Miller, "Cause of Prohibition Promises More Beneficial Results for the Race Than Any Other Movement as 1927 Dawns, He Holds," *New York Amsterdam News*, December 29, 1926.

17. Lerner, *Dry Manhattan*, 201–2.

18. Mumford, *Interzones*, 33–34.

19. M. Davis, *Jews and Booze*, 161–62. "Numbers runner" refers to an occupation that was part of an early form of gambling called "the numbers," which was one of the

few Black-dominated industries that white people sought to break into at this time. See White and Robertson, *Playing the Numbers*, 24–25.

20. Chicago Commission on Race Relations, *Negro in Chicago*, 202.

21. Kusmer, *Ghetto Takes Shape*, 50.

22. Muhammad, *Condemnation of Blackness*, 226.

23. Blair, *I've Got to Make My Livin'*, 2.

24. Committee of Fourteen, "Night Club and Speak Easy Problem," 11.

25. COF general secretary Frederick Whitin to Philip Payton, May 29, 1916, box 23, folder "135th St to 213th Street," COFR, cited in Robertson, "Harlem Undercover," 490.

26. Robertson, "Harlem Undercover," 494.

27. Robertson, "Harlem Undercover," 486.

28. Robertson, "Harlem Undercover," 488.

29. Robertson, "Harlem Undercover," 487.

30. Robertson, White, Garton, and White, "Disorderly Houses," 461.

31. Robertson, "Harlem Undercover," 499.

32. Reid, "Mrs. Bailey," 144.

33. "A Rent Party Tragedy," *New York Age*, December 11, 1926.

34. "Rent Party Tragedy."

35. Frank Byrd, "Harlem Rent Parties," August 23, 1938, WPA Federal Writers' Project Collection, Manuscript Division, Library of Congress, Washington, DC, http://lcweb2.loc.gov/mss/wpalh2/21/2101/21011010/21011010.pdf.

36. "Rent Parties in Harlem Attract White Patrons," *Atlanta Daily World*, October 26, 1932.

37. Blair, *I've Got to Make My Livin'*, 180.

38. J. Wilson, *Bulldaggers, Pansies, and Chocolate Babies*, 12.

39. White and Robertson, *Playing the Numbers*, 229.

40. Bill Graves, "House-Rent Parties," in Komara, *Encyclopedia of the Blues*, 468.

41. Chauncey, *Gay New York*.

42. James, *Doin' Drugs*, 38; "Black Belts Nite Life," *Variety*, October 16, 1929.

43. "Black Belts Nite Life."

44. Wolcott, *Remaking Respectability*, 108.

45. Albertson, *Bessie*, 140. As will be further discussed later in this chapter, "in the life" was an expression that referred both to queer African American life as well as to the underworld of prostitution, gambling, drugs, and other illicit activities.

46. Albertson, *Bessie*, 140.

47. Albertson, *Bessie*, 141–42.

48. Before the 1910s, it was not considered respectable for women to patronize saloons or bars, where they would be assumed to be sex workers. This began to change with the rise of cabarets in the 1910s. See Gilfoyle, *City of Eros*, 247–48; and Blair, *I've Got to Make My Livin'*, 176.

49. Tye, *Rising from the Rails*. See Albertson, *Bessie*, 140; and M. Harris, *Rise of Gospel Blues*, 51.

50. Blair, *I've Got to Make My Livin'*, 176.

51. A white newspaper noted of the buffet flat, "It's peculiar to Harlem, yet few white visitors to that Negro haven in New York City ever hear of it and practically none get

into one." See *Amsterdam (NY) Evening Recorder*, December 11, 1933; and Blair, *I've Got to Make My Livin'*, 281n85.

52. The following accounts of Black women running buffet flats do not mention any outside parties that helped run or fund their events: Frank Byrd, "Buffet Flat," in Bascom, *Renaissance in Harlem*, 68–71; Wolcott, *Remaking Respectability*, 118, 194; Blair, *I've Got to Make My Livin'*, 175–85.

53. Lerner, *Dry Manhattan*, 3.

54. Bricktop with Haskins, *Bricktop*, 70.

55. Bricktop with Haskins, *Bricktop*, 34.

56. Investigator Report, 1928, box 37, COFR.

57. Bricktop with Haskins, *Bricktop*, 67.

58. Garvin Bushell quoted in Gussow, *Seems Like Murder in Here*, 220.

59. "Speakeasy Fad Spreading Fast; Expensive Nite Clubs Belted by It," *Variety*, January 15, 1930.

60. Thorpe, "'House Where Queers Go'"; Chauncey, *Gay New York*.

61. Mumford, *Interzones*, 84.

62. White and Robertson, *Playing the Numbers*, 16.

63. Garber, "Spectacle in Color," 323.

64. Box 82, folder "Sa-Su," COFR.

65. "LFL Coming Out Stories," June 21, 1981, 9, box 3, MHC.

66. Box 82, folder "Sa-Su," COFR.

67. Segrave, *Jukeboxes*, 45–46.

68. Buckman, *Let's Dance*, 213–15.

69. "Bandits Hold Up Elks' Speakeasy: $138 Taken in Seventh Avenue Resort—Man Shot," *New York Amsterdam News*, October 12, 1927. This article notes that the bartender was "Frank Autullo, white." Another article noted that both Black men and white women were socializing at the Elks during a robbery. See "Two Negros Rob Café," *New York Sun*, October 5, 1927.

70. Nestle, "I Lift My Eyes to the Hill," 267.

71. Nestle, "I Lift My Eyes to the Hill," 267.

72. Ted Yates, "Around the Town," *Baltimore Afro-American*, September 8, 1934.

73. Kneeland with Davis, *Commercialized Prostitution*, 15; J. Jones, *Labor of Love*, 2.

74. Jack Moore, "Harlem Browns Busy!," *Broadway Brevities*, September 19, 1932, cited in Heap, *Slumming*, 259.

75. Coyle and Van Dyke, "Sex, Smashing, and Storyville," 65.

76. Hicks, *Talk with You Like a Woman*, 211.

77. Hicks, "'Bright and Good Looking Colored Girl,'" 419.

78. Hicks, "'Bright and Good Looking Colored Girl'"; Carby, "Policing the Black Woman's Body," 740, 751–52.

79. Hicks, *Talk with You Like a Woman*, 420.

80. Mabel Hampton, interview by Joan Nestle, "Mabel Hampton's Story, July 1986 (Tape 4)," MHC, http://herstories.prattinfoschool.nyc/omeka/items/show/85.

81. Nestle, "I Lift My Eyes to the Hill," 265.

82. Inmate no. 3696, Recommendation for Parole, January 13, 1925, New York State Reformatory for Women at Bedford, cited in Hicks, *Talk with You Like a Woman*, 428.

83. Nestle, "I Lift My Eyes to the Hill," 265–66.

84. See Peiss, *Cheap Amusements*; and Clement, *Love for Sale*.

85. L. Harris, *Sex Workers, Psychics, and Number Runners*, 28.

86. Nestle, "I Lift My Eyes to the Hill," 266–67.

87. Robertson, White, Garton, and White, "Disorderly Houses," 444.

88. L. Harris, "'Women and Girls in Jeopardy.'"

89. "Stool Pigeon Dancey, Out on Bail on Serious Charge Still Perniciously Active," *New York Age*, August 23, 1924.

90. "Dancey Out Again and at His Old Tricks; Girls Are Warned," *New York Age*, October 11, 1924.

91. Hicks, *Talk with You Like a Woman*; Muhammad, *Condemnation of Blackness*.

92. "Framing Women in Harlem," *New York Age*, December 6, 1930.

93. Court of General Sessions Probation Department Case File no. 10900 (1928), New York Municipal Archives, cited in Robertson, White, Garton, and White, "Disorderly Houses," 455.

94. Joan Nestle argues that as sex workers were the first "policed community of outlaw women"—similar to the policing that queer women would endure by the mid-twentieth century—"they were forced to develop a subculture of survival and resistance." See Nestle, "Lesbians and Prostitutes," 169.

95. Kunzel, *Fallen Women, Problem Girls*, 195n102.

96. George Schuyler, "Lights and Shadows of the Underworld," *Messenger*, August 1923, 798.

97. Schuyler, "Lights and Shadows of the Underworld," 799.

98. As discussed in chapter 1, in 1906 Howard University professor Kelly Miller wrote about the notion of "surplus women," which he saw as a unique danger befalling the growing Black districts of the urban North. See Miller, "Surplus Negro Women," *Southern Workman* 34 (1906): 524.

99. The article referred to prostitutes as "prosties" and to feminine gay men as "nances."

100. "Deep Harlem," *Variety*, October 10, 1928.

101. S. T. Whitney, "Timely Topics," *New York Amsterdam News*, October 6, 1928.

102. S. T. Whitney, "Watch Your Step!," *New York Amsterdam News*, December 4, 1929.

103. W. Smith, *Music on My Mind*, 32.

104. W. Smith, *Music on My Mind*, 192.

105. Woolston, *Prostitution in the United States*, 49, 94.

106. Beam, *In the Life*, 12.

107. Garber, "Gladys Bentley," 53.

108. Garber, "Gladys Bentley," 53, 58.

109. Garber, "Gladys Bentley," 55.

110. Wilbur Young, "Sketches of Colorful Harlem Characters: Gladys Bentley," *Negroes of New York*, WPA Writers' Project, 1939, Schomburg Center for Research in Black Culture, New York, NY.

111. Sobol, "On the Old Harlem Express," 53.

112. Garber, "Gladys Bentley," 56; J. Wilson, *Bulldaggers, Pansies, and Chocolate Babies*, 175.

113. Young, "Sketches of Colorful Harlem Characters."

114. Gladys Bentley, "Worried Blues," 1928, Okeh Records 8610.

115. Gladys Bentley, "How Much Can I Stand?," 1928, Okeh Records 8643.

116. W. E. Thomas, "Just a Fairy Tale," *Baltimore Afro-American*, September 30, 1933.

117. Malcolm Fulcher, "Believe Me," *Baltimore Afro-American*, June 3, 1933.

118. Hughes, *Big Sea*, 225–26.

119. Chinitz, "Rejuvenation through Joy," 61.

120. Chappell, *Restaurants of New York*, 119–20.

121. Douglas, *Terrible Honesty*, 282–83.

122. For example, a 1926 *Vanity Fair* article by Carl Van Vechten that introduced many white readers to the "Empress of the Blues" noted, "If Bessie Smith is crude and primitive, she represents the true folk-spirit of the race." He also referred to her live performances as bringing forth "the perversely complicated spell of African voodoo." See Carl Van Vechten, "Negro 'Blues' Singers," *Vanity Fair*, March 1926, 67, 107, 108.

123. Heap, *Slumming*, 102.

124. "New York Cops Hit Vulgar Dance in Cafes; New York Police Launch Drive on Harlem Cafes," *Chicago Defender*, March 17, 1934.

125. "New York Cops Hit Vulgar Dance in Cafes"; "New York Police's War on Cafes Ends," *Chicago Defender*, April 7, 1934.

126. "New York Cops Hit Vulgar Dance in Cafes."

127. "The Reminiscences of George S. Schuyler," Oral History Research Office, Columbia University, cited in Osofsky, *Harlem*, 149.

128. Osofsky, *Harlem*, 14.

129. *Chicago Defender*, January 29, 1929, cited in Drake and Cayton, *Black Metropolis*, 83.

130. Drake and Cayton, *Black Metropolis*, 83.

131. Drake and Cayton, *Black Metropolis*, 517.

132. Katznelson, *When Affirmative Action Was White*.

133. Gray, *Black Female Domestics*, 109.

134. Chauncey, *Gay New York*, 301, 353–54.

135. Chauncey, *Gay New York*, 308.

136. Chauncey, *Gay New York*, 334–35.

137. McGirr, *War on Alcohol*, 246.

138. Chauncey, *Gay New York*, 337.

139. Chauncey, *Gay New York*, 337.

140. Chauncey, *Gay New York*, 339.

141. Albertson, *Bessie*, 219; Reed, "African American Cultural Expression," 16.

142. Vere E. Johns, "Lafayette Theatre," *New York Age*, April 14, 1934.

143. Johns, "Lafayette Theatre." Bellevue was an infamous New York mental hospital, and "alienist" was an early twentieth-century term for psychiatrist.

144. Vere E. Johns, "In the Name of Art," *New York Age*, April 28, 1934.

145. Ralph Matthews, "Love Laughs at Life in Harlem," *Baltimore Afro-American*, March 11, 1933; Ralph Matthews, "She Wolf: She Had Charm and Beauty but She Preyed on Her Own Sex, Part One," *Baltimore Afro-American*, November 17, 1934; Ralph Matthews, "She Wolf: She Had Charm and Beauty but She Preyed on Her Own Sex, Part Two," *Baltimore Afro-American*, November 24, 1934.

146. Matthews, "She Wolf, Part One."

147. Matthews, "She Wolf, Part Two."

148. Matthews, "She Wolf, Part Two."

149. Marcus Wright, "The Talk of the Town," *New York Age*, May 26, 1934. Also see Marcus Wright, "The Talk of the Town," *New York Age*, August 11, 1934; and Marcus Wright, "The Talk of the Town," *New York Age*, November 10, 1934.

150. Kenton Jackson, "'Queers' Big Factor in Commercialized Vice Ring," *Philadelphia Tribune*, August 23, 1934.

151. "Raphael Picture for Women Only," *Baltimore Afro-American*, November 14, 1936.

152. While it is difficult to trace the emergence of new identity categories, the fact that COF investigators spoke to women self-identified as "bulldaggers" in these spaces serves as important evidence that some Black women claimed such queer identities by the late 1920s.

153. W. Smith, *Music on My Mind*, 156.

154. Murphy, "Bootlegging Mothers and Drinking Daughters," 176.

CHAPTER 4

1. Dunbar-Nelson, *Give Us Each Day*, 191 (August 25, 1927, diary entry).

2. Edna Thomas was originally a friend of Rachel West, Dorothy West's mother, who chaperoned her friend's daughter on various trips. See Mitchell and Davis, *Literary Sisters*, 10.

3. G. Gill, *White Grease Paint on Black Performers*, 74.

4. Sterling A. Brown, "More Odds," *Opportunity*, June 1932, 189.

5. Hull, introduction to *Give Us Each Day*, 22–23.

6. Mitchell and Davis, introduction to *Where the Wild Grape Grows*, 36–37.

7. Mitchell and Davis, introduction to *Where the Wild Grape Grows*, 36–37.

8. White, *Too Heavy a Load*, 128–29; Hine, "Rape and the Inner Lives of Black Women."

9. Carby, *Reconstructing Womanhood*, 39.

10. Hunter, *To 'Joy My Freedom*, 34.

11. Hine, "Rape and the Inner Lives of Black Women," 912.

12. The dearth of such sources has been in part because, as Dunbar-Nelson's biographer Akasha (Gloria) Hull points out, "diary keeping has not been compatible with the conditions of the lives of the vast majority of Black women." Hull, introduction to *Give Us Each Day*, 14.

13. Hull, *Color, Sex, and Poetry*, 96; E. Alexander, *Lyrics of Sunshine and Shadow*, 22.

14. Hull, introduction to *Give Us Each Day*, 14–15.

15. Hull, introduction to *Give Us Each Day*, 22.

16. Personal correspondence from Alice Dunbar to Edwina Kruse, 1907, cited in Hull, *Color, Sex, and Poetry*, 63.

17. Hull, introduction to *Give Us Each Day*, 22.

18. Hull, introduction to *Give Us Each Day*, 22–23.

19. Hull, introduction to *Give Us Each Day*, 23.

20. Hull, introduction to *Give Us Each Day*, 25.

21. Logan, *Homelands and Waterways*, 489.

22. Dunbar-Nelson chose to live as a Black woman but passed as white on occasion, once even bragging about it in her diary. She also appeared in at least one ad for a skin bleaching product. See Green, *Love, Activism, and the Respectable Life of Alice Dunbar-Nelson*, 102; and Roberts, *Pageants, Parlors, and Pretty Women*, 79.

23. Dunbar-Nelson, *Give Us Each Day*, 254–55 (August 16, 1928, diary entry).

24. Dunbar-Nelson, *Give Us Each Day*, 254 (August 15, 1928, diary entry).

25. "Mrs. Dingle Must Produce Sorority Fund," *Chicago Defender*, May 12, 1934.

26. Dunbar-Nelson, *Give Us Each Day*, 266–67 (September 26–27, 1928, diary entries).

27. Green, *Love, Activism, and the Respectable Life of Alice Dunbar-Nelson*, 113.

28. Dunbar-Nelson, *Give Us Each Day*, 249–50 (August 1, 1928, diary entry), 266 (September 21, 1928, diary entry).

29. Logan, *Homelands and Waterways*, 492.

30. Jackson started the first Black intellectual newsweekly on the West Coast, titled *Flash*, in 1928; then became the political editor of the *California Eagle* in 1931; and later served as the first Hollywood correspondent for the Associated Negro Press in the 1930s. See Hughes-Watkins, "Fay M. Jackson and the Color Line," 120.

31. Green, *Love, Activism, and the Respectable Life of Alice Dunbar-Nelson*, 215.

32. Dunbar-Nelson, *Give Us Each Day*, 359 (March 18, 1930, diary entry).

33. Dunbar-Nelson, *Give Us Each Day*, 359 (March 19, 1930, diary entry).

34. Dunbar-Nelson, *Give Us Each Day*, 360 (March 20, 1930, diary entry).

35. Dunbar-Nelson, *Give Us Each Day*, 362 (March 29, 1930, diary entry).

36. Dunbar-Nelson, *Give Us Each Day*, 362 (March 29, 1930, diary entry).

37. Dunbar-Nelson, *Give Us Each Day*, 366 (April 15, 1930, diary entry).

38. Dunbar-Nelson, *Give Us Each Day*, 374 (June 17, 1930, diary entry).

39. Hull, introduction to *Give Us Each Day*, 24–25.

40. For example, West is not mentioned in Schwarz's *Gay Voices of the Harlem Renaissance*.

41. Mitchell and Davis, *Literary Sisters*, 39.

42. Sherrard-Johnson, *Dorothy West's Paradise*, 126.

43. Wirth, *Gay Rebel of the Harlem Renaissance*, 15.

44. V. Boyd, *Wrapped in Rainbows*, 122.

45. Richard Bruce Nugent to Dorothy West, December 5, 1928, "Correspondence. Incoming personal, 1916, 1926–1929," MC 676, folder 2.14, Dorothy West Papers, Schlesinger Library, Radcliffe Institute, Harvard University, Cambridge, MA.

46. Helene Johnson to Dorothy West, February 24, 1931, in V. Mitchell, *This Waiting for Love*, 111.

47. Dorothy West to Countee Cullen, March 18, 1931, Countee Cullen Papers, Amistad Research Center, Tulane University, cited in Mitchell and Davis, *Literary Sisters*, 111.

48. David Streitfeld, "Dorothy West, Renaissance Woman," *Washington Post*, July 6, 1995.

49. Mitchell and Davis, *Literary Sisters*, 19, 109.

50. Dorothy West to Countee Cullen, Sunday, n.d., 1931, Countee Cullen Papers, cited in Mitchell and Davis, *Literary Sisters*, 112.

51. J. Jones, "So the Girl Marries," 58. Thomas H. Wirth argues that while Cullen and Jackman were gay best friends, there is no evidence that they actually had a romantic relationship. See Wirth, introduction to *Gay Rebel of the Harlem Renaissance*, 29–30.

52. Countee Cullen to Dorothy West, April 16, 1931, Dorothy West Collection, Howard Gotlieb Archival Research Center at Boston University, cited in Mitchell and Davis, *Literary Sisters*, 112.

53. Companionate marriage was the new modern notion that a husband and wife should be equal partners and both should get their emotional and sexual needs met through their union. See Simmons, *Making Marriage Modern*; and Dorothy West to Countee Cullen, Sunday, n.d., 1931, Countee Cullen Papers, cited in Mitchell and Davis, *Literary Sisters*, 112.

54. "State Stars Embark for Russia to Make Picture," *Chicago Defender*, June 18, 1932.

55. Dorothy West to Langston Hughes, October 27, 1932, in West, *Where the Wild Grape Grows*, 189.

56. Mitchell and Davis, *Literary Sisters*, 143.

57. Dorothy West interview by Joyce Rickson in Sherrard-Johnson, *Dorothy West's Paradise*, 45.

58. Emma Garman, "Feminize Your Canon: Dorothy West," July 11, 2018, *Paris Review*, www.theparisreview.org/blog/2018/07/11/feminize-your-canon-dorothy-west.

59. Hassan, *Loren Miller*, 63.

60. Rowley, *Richard Wright*, 118; Walker, *Richard Wright*, 91.

61. Mitchell and Davis, introduction to *Where the Wild Grape Grows*, 38.

62. Mitchell and Davis, *Literary Sisters*, 48. It appears Minus's mother was either widowed or divorced by the time her daughter was in college. Mitchell and Davis, introduction to *Where the Wild Grape Grows*, 38.

63. Mitchell and Davis, introduction to *Where the Wild Grape Grows*, 38.

64. Donyel Hobbs Williams, "'Mattie' Marian Minus (1913–1973)," in Tracy, *Writers of the Black Chicago Renaissance*, 242.

65. Williams, "'Mattie' Marian Minus," 244.

66. Marian Minus to Dorothy West, October 21, 1936, "Correspondence. From other writers and artists, 1923–1942," MC 676, folder 2.13, Dorothy West Papers.

67. "Publication in N.Y. Debut," *Atlanta Daily World*, November 2, 1937.

68. Dorothy West to Countee Cullen, July 4, 1933, Countee Cullen Papers, cited in Mitchell and Davis, *Literary Sisters*, 130. This idea for a queer-friendly salon may have been inspired by West's friends and mentors Elisabeth Marbury and Elsie de Wolfe, an American lesbian couple who went to Paris and had a salon where "the Hemingways and the Fitzgeralds and all would come." See Guinier, "Interview with Dorothy West, May 6, 1978," 169.

69. Mitchell and Davis, *Literary Sisters*, 131.

70. Dorothy West to Rachel West, n.d., "Correspondence. Incoming personal, 1916, 1929–1942," MC 676, folder 1.16, Dorothy West Papers.

71. Dorothy West to Rachel West, n.d., "Correspondence. Incoming personal, 1916, 1929–1942," MC 676, folder 1.16, Dorothy West Papers.

72. Mitchell and Davis, *Literary Sisters*, 18.

73. Bundles, *On Her Own Ground*, 238.

74. "Walker Studio Manager Held: Lloyd Thomas Charged with Renting Premises for Dances," *New York Amsterdam News*, July 28, 1926.

75. Mitchell and Davis, *Literary Sisters*, 28.

76. "Edna Thomas New Head of WPA Negro Theatre," *New York Age*, May 20, 1939; Astrid Haas, "The Lafayette Players," in Wintz and Finkleman, *Encyclopedia of the Harlem Renaissance: K–Y*, 677.

77. Thompson, "Lafayette Players," 262.

78. "Mrs. Edna Lewis Thomas, Well-Known Socially, Joins Lafayette Players," *New York Age*, November 6, 1920.

79. "Mrs. Edna Lewis Thomas, Well-Known Socially, Joins Lafayette Players."

80. "Edna Lewis Thomas Stars in 'Turn to the Right' at Lafayette," *New York Age*, June 11, 1921.

81. Hutchinson, *In Search of Nella Larsen*, 447.

82. Mitchell and Davis, *Literary Sisters*, 21.

83. Minton, *Departing from Deviance*, 60–61.

84. Henry, *Sex Variants*, v, xi.

85. Terry, "Seductive Power of Science," 275; Henry, *Sex Variants*, xii.

86. Not all sexologists at the time agreed with this line of thinking. For example, the German sexologist Magnus Hirschfeld wrote about variations of LGBTQ people and was also an early activist fighting for their equal rights.

87. Henry, *Sex Variants*, 674.

88. Henry, *Sex Variants*, 567.

89. Henry, *Sex Variants*, 563.

90. Henry, *Sex Variants*, 566–67.

91. Mitchell and Davis, *Literary Sisters*, 121.

92. G. Gill, *White Grease Paint on Black Performers*, 74.

93. Mitchell and Davis, *Literary Sisters*, 120; Henry, *Sex Variants*, 566.

94. Thelma Berlack-Boozer, "Rich British Woman Forsook Own People to Reside in Harlem," *New York Amsterdam News*, September 24, 1938.

95. Berlack-Boozer, "Rich British Woman Forsook Own People to Reside in Harlem."

96. These include scholars Jonathan Ned Katz, Henry Minton, and Thomas Wirth.

97. Nugent, "On Georgette Harvey," *Gay Rebel of the Harlem Renaissance*, 211–14; "Miss G. Harvey, Actress, Singer," *New York Times*, February 18, 1952; S. Wilson, *Making of "Gone with the Wind,"* 83.

98. Nugent, "On Georgette Harvey," 211.

99. Nugent, "On Georgette Harvey," 213.

100. Barranger, *Gambler's Instinct*, 79.

101. "Director of 'Porgy and Bess' is Feted by Georgette Harvey," *New York Age*, November 2, 1935.

102. Henry, *Sex Variants*, 720.

103. Henry, *Sex Variants*, 726.

104. Hughes, *Big Sea*, 245.

105. Lewis, *When Harlem Was in Vogue*, 167.

106. Bundles, *On Her Own Ground*, 283.

107. Lowry, *Her Dream of Dreams*, 435, 439.

108. Jerry, "New York: Social Whirl," *Baltimore Afro-American*, November 15, 1930.

109. Levi Hubert, "7th Ave.," *Baltimore Afro-American*, November 29, 1930.

110. William Pickens, "The Bookshelf: 'The Dark Tower,'" *Chicago Defender*, January 28, 1928.

111. Mabel Hampton gave extensive oral histories with the Lesbian Herstory Archives, documenting a rare, first-person perspective on her life as a working-class Black queer woman in the 1920s–30s. See MHC, http://herstories.prattinfoschool.nyc/omeka /collections/show/29.

112. Mabel Hampton, interview by Joan Nestle, "Mabel Hampton Interviews (Tape 1)," MHC, http://herstories.prattinfoschool.nyc/omeka/items/show/95.

113. Hughes, *Big Sea*, 244.

114. Hughes, *Big Sea*, 247.

115. "Mme. Walker Dies," *Baltimore Afro-American*, August 22, 1931.

116. Bundles, *On Her Own Ground*, 90–91.

117. Maurice Dancer, "Harlem: Night by Night," *Pittsburgh Courier*, August 19, 1933.

118. "Aide to Late Mme. Walker Seeks Back Pay," *Chicago Defender*, August 5, 1933.

119. "'Perjury!' Says Judge in Mme. Walker Wage Suit," *Chicago Defender*, August 26, 1933.

120. As Rachel Cleves notes, distinctive queer marriage forms began to appear in the United States during the late nineteenth century. One of these was the "Boston marriage"—a committed relationship between two elite, educated, cosmopolitan women, which was tolerated due to its gendered and classed associations of sexlessness. See Cleves, "'What, Another Female Husband?,'" 1077.

121. Mary Burrill wrote some of the first anti-lynching plays in the 1910s. See Stephens, "Anti-Lynch Plays by African American Women."

122. K. Anderson, "'Brickbats and Roses,'" 285.

123. Beemyn, *Queer Capital*, 79; Miller and Pruitt-Logan, *Faithful to the Task at Hand*, 76.

124. Box 90–2, folder 24, LDSP.

125. Miller and Pruitt-Logan, *Faithful to the Task at Hand*, 232.

126. Beemyn, *Queer Capital*, 48.

127. Lucy Diggs Slowe to J. Stanley Durkee, May 31, 1922, box 90–1, folder 1, LDSP.

128. Perkins, "Lucy Diggs Slowe," 98.

129. Emmett J. Scott on behalf of the Howard University Board of Trustees to Lucy Diggs Slowe, June 19, 1925, box 90–2, folder 90, LDSP.

130. Lucy Diggs Slowe to Abraham Flexner, June 2, 1933, box 90–3, folder 58, LDSP.

131. Lindsey, *Colored No More*, 48.

132. Beauboeuf-Lafontant, "New Howard Woman," 25.

133. Lindsey, *Colored No More*, 37.

134. Abraham Flexner to Lucy Diggs Slowe, May 12, 1933, box 90–3, folder 57, LDSP; box 90–1, folder 1: Biographical data, LDSP.

135. Lucy Diggs Slowe to Abraham Flexner, May 14, 1933, box 90–3, folder 57, LDSP.

136. Box 90–1, folder 7: List of persons who sent letters with flowers upon the occasion of Dean Slowe's death, LDSP.

137. Mollie T. Barrien to Mary P. Burrill, box 90–1, folder 2: Letters of condolence A–E, LDSP.

138. Box 90–1, folder 2: Letters of condolence A–E, LDSP.

139. Faderman, *Odd Girls and Twilight Lovers*, 93.

140. Box 90–1, folder 9: Tributes to Dean Slowe A–F, LDSP.

141. Mary Burrill to T. L. Hungate, chairman of Howard University Board of Trustees, October 30, 1937, box 90–2, folder 36, LDSP.

142. Box 90–1, folder 1: Biographical data, LDSP.

143. Rasheed, "Lucy Diggs Slowe," 211–12; Miller and Pruitt-Logan, *Faithful to the Task at Hand*, 232; *1940 United States Federal Census*, accessed through Ancestry.com.

144. Box 90–1, folder 10: Tributes to Dean Slowe G–N, LDSP.

145. Lindsey, *Colored No More*, 27.

CONCLUSION

1. "Have We a New Sex Problem Here?," *Chicago Whip*, November 27, 1920.

2. Harry Levette, "Coast Codgings," *Chicago Defender*, July 22, 1933; "Coast Hot Shots," *Chicago Defender*, September 29, 1934.

3. Henry, *Sex Variants*, 908–16.

4. A. Davis, *Blues Legacies and Black Feminism*, 13.

5. Albertson, *Bessie*, xii, 115.

6. Albertson, *Bessie*, 125.

7. Kellner, *Harlem Renaissance*, 31; Driscoll, "Gladys Bentley," 48.

8. Nestle, "Excerpts from the Oral History of Mabel Hampton," 934.

9. Anderson, "Last Hired, First Fired."

10. The gendered terms "stud" and "a stud and her lady" were used in the midcentury Buffalo, New York, African American lesbian community, as were "butch" and "fem," which were identity categories used by many queer white working-class women. See Kennedy and Davis, *Boots of Leather*, 7. Further, a 1940s–50s study of queer San Francisco also found that most women in this community called themselves gay women, and some, depending on their race and class, also or either used the terms "stud," "butch," "fem," and "girl." N. Boyd, *Wide-Open Town*, 261n7. And regarding the spelling of "fem" or "femme," queer feminine working-class women first became known as "fems," which later often became spelled "femmes" instead.

11. Kennedy and Davis, *Boots of Leather*, 10.

12. Nestle, "I Lift My Eyes to the Hill," 267.

13. Kennedy and Davis, *Boots of Leather*, 321–22.

BIBLIOGRAPHY

PRIMARY SOURCES

Manuscript and Archival Collections

Borough of Manhattan Death Records, New York Municipal Archives, New York City.
Burgess, Ernest W. Papers. Special Collections Research Center. University of Chicago Library.
Committee of Fourteen Records. Manuscripts and Archives Division. New York Public Library, New York.
Garber, Eric. Papers. Gay, Lesbian, Bisexual, and Transgender Historical Society, San Francisco, CA.
Hampton, Mabel. Collection. Lesbian Herstory Archives, Brooklyn, NY.
Hunter, Alberta. Papers. Schomburg Center for Research in Black Culture. New York Public Library, New York City.
Slowe, Lucy Diggs. Papers. Moorland-Spingarn Research Center. Howard University, Washington, DC.
Smith, Ada "Bricktop." Papers. Stuart A. Rose Manuscript, Archives, and Rare Book Library. Emory University, Atlanta, GA.
Southern Oral History Program. Southern Historical Collection. Wilson Library. University of North Carolina at Chapel Hill.
Steiner, John. Collection. Special Collections Research Center. University of Chicago Library
Van Vechten, Carl. Papers. Beinecke Rare Book and Manuscript Library. Yale University, New Haven, CT.
West, Dorothy. Papers. Schlesinger Library. Radcliffe Institute. Harvard University, Cambridge, MA.
WPA Federal Writers' Project Collection. Manuscript Division, Library of Congress, Washington, DC.

Periodicals

Amsterdam (NY) Evening Recorder
Atlanta Daily World

Baltimore Afro-American
Brooklyn Eagle

Chicago Defender
Chicago Evening News
Chicago Whip
The Crisis
Current Opinion
Indianapolis Recorder
Inter-State Tattler
Medical Review of Reviews
Messenger
The Nation
Negro World
New York Age

New York Amsterdam News
New York Morning Telegraph
New York Sun
New York Times
Opportunity
Philadelphia Tribune
Pittsburgh Courier
Southern Workman
Talking Machine World
Vanity Fair
Variety
Washington Post

Books, Chapters, and Journal Articles

Allen, Frederick Lewis. *Only Yesterday*. New York: Harper and Row, 1931.

Bessie, Simon Michael. *Jazz Journalism: The Story of the Tabloid Newspapers*. New York: E. P. Dutton, 1938.

Bradford, Perry. *Born with the Blues*. New York: Oak Publications, 1965.

Bricktop, with James Haskins. *Bricktop*. New York: Atheneum, 1983.

Chappell, George. *The Restaurants of New York*. New York: Greenberg, 1925.

Chicago Commission on Race Relations. *The Negro in Chicago: A Study of Race Relations and a Race Riot*. Chicago: University of Chicago Press, 1922.

Committee of Fourteen. *The Social Evil in New York City: A Study of Law Enforcement by the Research Committee of the Committee of Fourteen*. New York: Andrew H. Kellog, 1910.

———. "The Night Club and Speak Easy Problem." In *Annual Report of the Committee of Fourteen*. New York: printed by the authors, 1928.

Drake, St. Clair, and Horace R. Cayton. *Black Metropolis: A Study of Negro Life in a Northern City*. New York: Harper and Row, 1945.

Dunbar-Nelson, Alice. *Give Us Each Day: The Diary of Alice Dunbar-Nelson*. Edited by Akasha (Gloria) Hull. New York: W. W. Norton, 1984.

Ellis, Havelock. *Sexual Inversion*. Vol. 2 of *Studies in the Psychology of Sex*. Philadelphia: F. A. Davis, 1904.

Frazier, E. Franklin. *The Negro Family in Chicago*. Chicago: University of Chicago Press, 1932.

———. "Sex Morality among Negroes." *Religious Education* 23, no. 5 (December–January 1928): 447–50.

Freud, Sigmund. *Three Essays on the Theory of Sexuality*. Translated by James Strachey. New York: Basic Books, 1975.

Hall, Radclyffe. *The Well of Loneliness*. 1928. Hertfordshire, UK: Wordsworth Editions Limited, 2005.

Henry, George W. *Sex Variants: A Study of Homosexual Patterns*. 1941. New York: Paul B. Hoeber, 1948.

Hughes, Langston. *The Big Sea*. 1940. New York: Hill and Wang, 1993.

Johnson, Charles S., ed. *Ebony and Topaz: A Collectanea.* New York: National Urban League, 1927.

Johnson, James Weldon. *Black Manhattan.* New York: Da Capo, 1930.

Kneeland, George Jackson, with Katherine Bement Davis. *Commercialized Prostitution in New York City.* Publications of the Bureau of Social Hygiene. New York: Century, 1913.

Krafft-Ebing, Richard von. *Psychopathia Sexualis.* 1886. New York: Arcade Publishing, 1998.

McKay, Claude. *Home to Harlem.* 1928. New York: Harper and Brothers, 1987.

Nugent, Richard Bruce. *Gay Rebel of the Harlem Renaissance: Selections from the Work of Richard Bruce Nugent.* Edited and with an introduction by Thomas H. Wirth. Durham, NC: Duke University Press, 2002.

Otis, Margaret. "A Perversion Not Commonly Noted." *Journal of Abnormal Psychology* 8 (June–July 1913): 113–16.

Ottley, Roi, and William J. Weatherby, eds. *The Negro in New York: An Informal Social History.* New York: New York Public Library, 1967.

Powell, Adam Clayton, Sr. *Against the Tide: An Autobiography.* New York: R. R. Smith, 1938.

Reckless, Walter. *Vice in Chicago.* Chicago: University of Chicago Press, 1933.

Smith, Willie "The Lion." *Music on My Mind: The Memoirs of an American Pianist.* New York: Doubleday, 1964.

Sobol, Louis. "On the Old Harlem Express." *The Longest Street.* New York: Crown, 1968.

Reid, Ira De A. "Mrs. Bailey Pays the Rent." In *Ebony and Topaz: A Collectanea*, edited by Charles S. Johnson, 144–48. New York: National Urban League, 1927.

US Bureau of the Census. *Negro Population 1790–1915.* Washington, DC: Department of Commerce, 1918.

US Bureau of the Census. "Summary of the Population of the United States and Outlying Possessions, by Color, or Race and Sex: 1920." *Fourteenth Census of the United States, Volume 3: Population.* Washington DC: Department of Commerce, 1922.

US Bureau of the Census. *The Social and Economic Status of the Black Population in the United States: An Historical View, 1790–1978.* Washington, DC: Department of Commerce, 1980.

Van Vechten, Carl. *The Splendid Drunken Twenties: Selections from the Day Books, 1922–30.* Edited by Bruce Kellner. Champaign: University of Illinois Press, 2003.

Waters, Ethel, with Charles Samuels. *His Eye Is on the Sparrow.* New York: Doubleday, 1951.

West, Dorothy. *Where the Wild Grape Grows: Selected Writings, 1930–1950.* Edited by Verner D. Mitchell and Cynthia Davis. Amherst: University of Massachusetts Press, 2004.

Woolston, Howard B. *Prostitution in the United States, Volume One.* New York: Century, 1921.

Zollmann, Carl. *The Illinois Crime Survey.* Chicago: Blakely Printing, 1929.

SECONDARY SOURCES

Books

Abbot, Lynn, and Doug Seroff. *The Original Blues: The Emergence of the Blues in African American Vaudeville.* Oxford: University of Mississippi Press, 2017.

————. *Ragged but Right: Black Traveling Shows, "Coon Songs," and the Dark Pathway to Blues and Jazz*. Jackson: University of Mississippi Press, 2007.

Albertson, Chris. *Bessie*. New Haven: Yale University Press, 2003.

Alexander, Eleanor. *Lyrics of Sunshine and Shadow: The Courtship and Marriage of Paul Laurence Dunbar and Alice Ruth Moore*. New York: New York University Press, 2001.

Alexander, Ruth. *The Girl Problem: Female Sexual Delinquency in New York, 1900–1930*. Ithaca, NY: Cornell University Press, 1998.

Anderson, Paul Allen. *Deep River: Music and Memory in Harlem Renaissance Thought*. Durham, NC: Duke University Press, 2001.

Atwater, Deborah F. *African American Women's Rhetoric: The Search for Dignity, Personhood, and Honor*. Lanham, MD: Lexington Books, 2009.

Baker, Houston. *Blues Ideology and Afro-American Literature: A Vernacular Theory*. Chicago: University of Chicago Press, 1984.

Baker, Jean-Claude. *Josephine Baker: The Hungry Heart*. Lanham, MD: Cooper Square Press, 2001.

Baldwin, Davarian. *Chicago's New Negroes: Modernity, the Great Migration, and Black Urban Life*. Chapel Hill: University of North Carolina Press, 2007.

Barranger, Milly S. *A Gambler's Instinct: The Story of Broadway Producer Cheryl Crawford*. Carbondale: Southern Illinois University Press, 2010.

Bascom, Lionel C., ed. *A Renaissance in Harlem: Lost Voices of an American Community*. New York: William Morrow, 1999.

Beam, Joseph, ed. *In the Life: A Black Gay Anthology*. Boston: Alyson Publications, 1986.

Beauboeuf-Lafontant, Tamara. *To Live More Abundantly: Black Collegiate Women, Howard University, and the Audacity of Dean Lucy Diggs Slowe*. Athens: University of Georgia Press, 2022.

Beemyn, Genny. *A Queer Capital: A History of Gay Life in Washington, D.C.* New York: Routledge, 2014.

Bérubé, Allan. *Coming Out under Fire: The History of Gay Men and Women in World War II*. New York: Free Press, 1990.

————. *My Desire for History: Essays in Gay, Community, and Labor History*. Edited with an introduction by John D'Emilio and Estelle B. Freedman. Chapel Hill: University of North Carolina Press, 2011.

Blain, Keisha N. *Set the World on Fire: Black Nationalist Women and the Global Struggle for Freedom*. Philadelphia: University of Pennsylvania Press, 2018.

Blair, Cynthia M. *I've Got to Make My Livin': Black Women's Sex Work in Turn-of-the-Century Chicago*. Chicago: University of Chicago Press, 2010.

Bogle, Donald. *Bright Boulevards, Bold Dreams: The Story of Black Hollywood*. New York: Ballantine Books, 2006.

————. *Heat Wave: The Life and Career of Ethel Waters*. New York: HarperCollins, 2011.

Bourne, Stephen. *Ethel Waters: Stormy Weather*. Lanham, MD: Scarecrow Press, 2007.

Boyd, Nan Alamilla. *Wide-Open Town: A History of Queer San Francisco to 1965*. Berkeley: University of California Press, 2003.

Boyd, Valerie. *Wrapped in Rainbows: The Life of Zora Neale Hurston*. New York: Simon and Schuster, 2003.

Brooks, Tim. *Lost Sounds: Blacks and the Birth of the Recording Industry, 1890–1919*. Champaign: University of Illinois Press, 2004.

Brown, Jayna. *Babylon Girls: Black Women Performers and the Shaping of the Modern*. Durham, NC: Duke University Press, 2008.

Brown, Kathleen M. *Good Wives, Nasty Wenches, and Anxious Patriarchs: Gender, Race, and Power in Colonial Virginia*. Chapel Hill: University of North Carolina Press, 1996.

Buckman, Peter. *Let's Dance: Social, Ballroom and Folk Dancing*. New York: Penguin, 1979.

Bundles, A'Lelia. *On Her Own Ground: The Life and Times of Madam C. J. Walker*. New York: Simon and Schuster, 2001.

Camp, Stephanie. *Closer to Freedom: Enslaved Women and Everyday Resistance in the Plantation South*. Chapel Hill: University of North Carolina Press, 2004.

Canaday, Margot. *The Straight State: Sexuality and Citizenship in Twentieth-Century America*. Princeton: Princeton University Press, 2009.

Carby, Hazel. *Culture in Babylon: Black Britain and African America*. New York: Verso, 1999.

———. *Reconstructing Womanhood: The Emergence of the Afro-American Woman Novelist*. New York: Oxford University Press, 1987.

Carter, Julian B. *The Heart of Whiteness: Normal Sexuality and Race in America, 1880–1940*. Durham, NC: Duke University Press, 2007.

Celello, Kristin. *Making Marriage Work: A History of Marriage and Divorce in the Twentieth Century*. Chapel Hill: University of North Carolina Press, 2009.

Chapman, Erin D. *Prove It on Me: New Negroes, Sex, and Popular Culture in the 1920s*. New York: Oxford University Press, 2012.

Charters, Samuel, and Leonard Kunstadt. *Jazz: A History of the New York Scene*. Garden City, NY: Doubleday, 1962.

Chauncey, George. *Gay New York: Gender, Urban Culture, and the Making of the Gay Male World, 1890–1940*. New York: Basic Books, 1994.

Chesler, Ellen. *Woman of Valor: Margaret Sanger and the Birth Control Movement in America*. New York: Anchor Books, 1992.

Chude-Sokei, Louis. *The Last "Darky": Bert Williams, Black-on-Black Minstrelsy, and the African Diaspora*. Durham, NC: Duke University Press, 2006.

Clark-Lewis, Elizabeth. *Living In, Living Out: African American Domestics in Washington, D.C., 1910–1940*. Washington: Smithsonian, 1994.

Clement, Elizabeth. *Love for Sale: Courting, Treating, and Prostitution in New York City, 1900–1945*. Chapel Hill: University of North Carolina Press, 2006.

Cook, James W., Lawrence B. Glickman, and Michael O'Malley, eds. *The Cultural Turn in U.S. History: Past, Present, and Future*. Chicago: University of Chicago Press, 2008.

Cooper, Brittney. *Beyond Respectability: The Intellectual Thought of Race Women*. Champaign: University of Illinois Press, 2017.

Corbould, Clare. *Becoming African Americans: Black Public Life in Harlem, 1919–1939*. Cambridge, MA: Harvard University Press, 2009.

Cullen, Frank, with Florence Hackman and Donald McNeilly. *Vaudeville Old and New*. Vol. 1. New York: Routledge, 2007.

Curtin, Kaier. *We Can Always Call Them Bulgarians: The Emergence of Lesbians and Gay Men on the American Stage*. Boston: Alyson Publications, 1987.

Davis, Angela. *Blues Legacies and Black Feminism: Gertrude "Ma" Rainey, Bessie Smith, and Billie Holiday*. New York: Pantheon Books, 1998,

Davis, Janet. *The Circus Age: Culture and Society under the Big Top*. Chapel Hill: University of North Carolina Press, 2002.

Davis, Marni. *Jews and Booze: Becoming American in the Age of Prohibition*. New York: New York University Press, 2012.

D'Emilio, John. *Sexual Politics, Sexual Communities*. Chicago: University of Chicago Press, 1983.

D'Emilio, John, and Estelle B. Freedman. *Intimate Matters: A History of Sexuality in America*. New York: Harper and Row, 1988.

Dodge, L. Mara. *Whores and Thieves of the Worst Kind: A Study of Women, Crime, and Prisons, 1835–2000*. DeKalb: Northern Illinois University Press, 2002.

Douglas, Ann. *Terrible Honesty: Mongrel Manhattan in the 1920s*. New York: Farrar, Straus and Giroux, 1995.

Duggan, Lisa. *Sapphic Slashers: Sex, Violence, and American Modernity*. Durham, NC: Duke University Press, 2000.

Dumenil, Lynn. *The Modern Temper: American Culture and Society in the 1920s*. New York: Hill and Wang, 1995.

Erenberg, Lewis. *Steppin' Out: New York Nightlife and the Transformation of American Culture*. Chicago: University of Chicago Press, 1984.

Faderman, Lillian. *Odd Girls and Twilight Lovers: A History of Lesbian Life in Twentieth-Century America*. New York: Penguin, 1991.

———. *Surpassing the Love of Men: Romantic Friendship and Love between Women from the Renaissance to the Present*. New York: William Morrow, 1981.

———. *To Believe in Women: What Lesbians Have Done for America—A History*. New York: Houghton Mifflin Harcourt, 1999.

Farley, Reynolds. *Growth of the Negro Population*. Chicago: Markham, 1970.

Farrar, Hayward. *The Baltimore "Afro-American," 1892–1950*. Westport, CT: Greenwood Press, 1998.

Ferguson, Roderick. *Aberrations in Black: Toward a Queer of Color Critique*. Minneapolis: University of Minnesota Press, 2004.

Foucault, Michel. *The History of Sexuality*. Vol. 1, *An Introduction*. New York: Pantheon Books, 1978.

Frank, Miriam. *Out in the Union: A Labor History of Queer America*. Philadelphia: Temple University Press, 2014.

Freeland, David. *Automats, Taxi Dances, and Vaudeville: Excavating Manhattan's Lost Places of Leisure*. New York: New York University Press, 2009.

Fuller, Sophie, and Lloyd Whitesell, eds. *Queer Episodes in Music and Modern Identity*. Champaign: University of Illinois Press, 2002.

Gaines, Kevin. *Uplifting the Race: Black Leadership, Politics and Culture in the Twentieth Century*. Chapel Hill: University of North Carolina Press, 1996.

Gallon, Kim. *Pleasure in the News: African American Readership and Sexuality in the Black Press*. Urbana: University of Illinois Press, 2020.

George-Graves, Nadine. *The Royalty of Negro Vaudeville: The Whitman Sisters and the Negotiation of Race, Gender, and Class in African American Theater, 1900–1940*. New York: St. Martin's Press, 2000.

Giddings, Paula. *When and Where I Enter: The Impact of Black Women on Race and Sex in America*. New York: William Morrow, 1996.

Gilfoyle, Timothy. *City of Eros: New York City, Prostitution, and the Commercialization of Sex, 1790–1920*. New York: W. W. Norton, 1992.

Gill, Glenda Eloise. *White Grease Paint on Black Performers: A Study of the Federal Theatre of 1935–1939*. New York: Peter Lang, 1988.

Gill, John. *Queer Noises: Male and Female Homosexuality in Twentieth-Century Music*. Minneapolis: University of Minnesota Press, 1995.

Gilman, Sander L. *Difference and Pathology: Stereotypes of Sexuality, Race, and Madness*. Ithaca: Cornell University Press, 1985.

Glenn, Susan. *Female Spectacle: The Theatrical Roots of Modern Feminism*. Cambridge, MA: Harvard University Press, 2000.

Goldberg, David J. *Discontented America: The United States in the 1920s*. Baltimore: Johns Hopkins University Press, 1999.

Gordon, Linda. *Woman's Body, Woman's Right: Birth Control in America*. New York: Penguin, 1977.

Gray, Brenda Clegg. *Black Female Domestics during the Depression in New York*. New York: Garland, 1993.

Green, Tara T. *Love, Activism, and the Respectable Life of Alice Dunbar-Nelson*. New York: Bloomsbury, 2022.

Greenberg, Cheryl Lynn. *"Or Does it Explode?": Black Harlem in the Great Depression*. New York: Oxford University Press, 1991.

Greenidge, Kerri K. *The Grimkes: The Legacy of Slavery in an American Family*. New York: W. W. Norton, 2022.

Griffin, Farah Jasmine. *"Who Set You Flowin'?": The African-American Migration Narrative*. New York: Oxford University Press, 1995.

Gross, Kali. *Colored Amazons: Crime, Violence, and Black Women in the City of Brotherly Love, 1880–1910*. Durham, NC: Duke University Press, 2006.

Grossman, James. *Land of Hope: Chicago, Black Southerners, and the Great Migration*. Chicago: University of Chicago Press, 1989.

Gussow, Adam. *Seems Like Murder in Here: Southern Violence and the Blues Tradition*. Chicago: University of Chicago Press, 2002.

Hahn, Steven. *A Nation under Our Feet: Black Political Struggles in the Rural South from Slavery to the Great Migration*. Cambridge, MA: Belknap, 2003.

Halperin, David. *How to Do the History of Homosexuality*. Chicago: University of Chicago Press, 2002.

Harbin, Billy J., Kim Marra, and Robert A. Schanke, eds. *The Gay and Lesbian Theatrical Legacy: A Biographical Dictionary of Major Figures in American Stage History in the Pre-Stonewall Era*. Ann Arbor: University of Michigan Press, 2007.

Harris, LaShawn. *Sex Workers, Psychics, and Number Runners: Black Women in New York City's Underground Economy*. Champaign: University of Illinois Press, 2016.

Harris, Michael W. *The Rise of Gospel Blues: The Music of Thomas Andrew Dorsey in the Urban Church*. New York: Oxford University Press, 1992.

Harrison, Daphne Duval. *Black Pearls: Blues Queens of the 1920s*. New Brunswick: Rutgers University Press, 1988.

Hart, Lynda. *Fatal Women: Lesbian Sexuality and the Mark of Aggression*. Princeton: Princeton University Press, 1994.

Hartman, Saidiya. *Wayward Lives, Beautiful Experiments: Intimate Histories of Social Upheaval*. New York: W. W. Norton, 2019.

Hassan, Amina. *Loren Miller: Civil Rights Attorney and Journalist*. Oklahoma City: University of Oklahoma Press, 2015.

Hay, Samuel A. *African American Theatre: An Historical and Critical Analysis*. Cambridge: Cambridge University Press, 1994.

Heap, Chad. *Slumming: Sexual and Racial Encounters in American Nightlife, 1885–1940*. Chicago: University of Chicago Press, 2008.

Hicks, Cheryl D. *Talk with You Like a Woman: African American Women, Justice, and Reform in New York, 1890–1935*. Chapel Hill: University of North Carolina Press, 2010.

Higginbotham, Evelyn Brooks. *Righteous Discontent: The Women's Movement in the Black Baptist Church, 1880–1920*. Cambridge, MA: Harvard University Press, 1993.

Hill, Errol, and James V. Hatch. *A History of African American Theatre*. Cambridge: Cambridge University Press, 2003.

Hobson, Janell. *Venus in the Dark: Blackness and Beauty in Popular Culture*. New York: Routledge, 2005.

Hull, Akasha (Gloria). *Color, Sex and Poetry: Three Women Writers of the Harlem Renaissance*. Bloomington: Indiana University Press, 1987.

———, ed. Introduction to *Give Us Each Day: The Diary of Alice Dunbar-Nelson*, 13–32. New York: W. W. Norton, 1984.

Hunter, Tera. *To 'Joy My Freedom: Southern Black Women's Lives and Labors after the Civil War*. Cambridge, MA: Harvard University Press, 1997.

Hutchinson, George. *In Search of Nella Larsen: A Biography of the Color Line*. Cambridge, MA: Harvard University Press, 2006.

Inness, Sherrie A. *The Lesbian Menace: Ideology, Identity, and the Representation of Lesbian Life*. Amherst: University of Massachusetts Press, 1997.

Jakle, John A., and Keith A. Sculle. *America's Main Street Hotels: Transiency and Community in the Early Auto Age*. Knoxville: University of Tennessee Press, 2009.

James, William H. *Doin' Drugs: Patterns of African American Addiction*. Austin: University of Texas Press, 1996.

Johnson, E. Patrick. *Black. Queer. Southern. Women: An Oral History*. Chapel Hill: University of North Carolina Press, 2018.

Johnson, Mae G., and E. Patrick Johnson, eds. *Black Queer Studies: A Critical Anthology*. Durham, NC: Duke University Press, 2005.

Jones, Jacqueline. *Labor of Love, Labor of Sorrow: Black Women, Work, and the Family from Slavery to the Present*. 1985, rev. ed. New York: Basic Books, 2010.

Katznelson, Ira. *When Affirmative Action Was White: An Untold History of Racial Inequality in Twentieth-Century America*. New York: W. W. Norton, 2005.

Kellner, Bruce. *The Harlem Renaissance: A Historical Dictionary for the Era*. Westport, CT: Greenwood Press, 1984.

Kennedy, Elizabeth Lapovsky, and Madeline D. Davis. *Boots of Leather, Slippers of Gold: The History of a Lesbian Community*. New York: Routledge, 1993.

Komara, Edward, ed. *Encyclopedia of the Blues*. Vol. 1. New York: Routledge, 2005.

Krasner, David. *A Beautiful Pageant: African American Theatre, Drama, and Performance in the Harlem Renaissance, 1910–1927*. New York: Palgrave Macmillan, 2002.

———. *Resistance, Parody, and Double Consciousness in African American Theatre, 1895–1910*. New York: St. Martin's Press, 1997.

Kunzel, Regina. *Fallen Women, Problem Girls: Unmarried Mothers and the Professionalization of Social Work, 1890–1945*. New Haven: Yale University Press, 1995.

———. *Criminal Intimacy: Prison and the Uneven History of Modern American Sexuality*. Chicago: University of Chicago Press, 2008.

Kusmer, Kenneth. *A Ghetto Takes Shape: Black Cleveland, 1870–1930*. Urbana: University of Illinois Press, 1976.

Lauterbach, Preston. *The Chitlin' Circuit and the Road to Rock 'n' Roll*. New York: W. W. Norton, 2011.

Lawson, R. A. *Jim Crow's Counterculture: The Blues and Black Southerners, 1890–1945*. Baton Rouge: Louisiana State University Press, 2010.

Lerner, Michael. *Dry Manhattan: Prohibition in New York City*. Cambridge, MA: Harvard University Press, 2007.

Levine, Lawrence. *Highbrow/Lowbrow: The Emergence of Cultural Hierarchy in America*. Cambridge, MA: Harvard University Press, 1988.

Lewinnek, Elaine. *The Working Man's Reward: Chicago's Early Suburbs and the Roots of American Sprawl*. New York: Oxford University Press, 2014.

Lewis, David Levering. *When Harlem Was in Vogue*. New York: Knopf, 1981.

Lieb, Sandra R. *Mother of the Blues: A Study of Ma Rainey*. Amherst: University of Massachusetts Press, 1981.

Lindquis, Malinda Alaine. *Black Social Science and the Crisis of Manhood, 1890–1970: We Are the Supermen*. New York: Routledge, 2012.

Lindsey, Treva. *Colored No More: Reinventing Black Womanhood in Washington, D.C.* Champaign: University of Illinois Press, 2017.

Logan, Adele. *Homelands and Waterways: The American Journey of the Bond Family*. New York: Vintage, 2000.

Lowry, Beverly. *Her Dream of Dreams: The Rise and Triumph of Madam C. J. Walker*. New York: Vintage, 2004.

Marks, Carole. *Farewell—We're Good and Gone: The Great Black Migration*. Bloomington: Indiana University Press, 1989.

Martin, Lerone A. *Preaching on Wax: The Phonograph and the Shaping of Modern African American Religion*. New York: New York University Press, 2014.

Marra, Kim, and Robert A. Schanke, eds. *Staging Desire: Queer Readings of American Theater History*. Ann Arbor: University of Michigan Press, 2002.

May, Elaine Tyler. *Barren in the Promised Land: Childless Americans and the Pursuit of Happiness*. Cambridge, MA: Harvard University Press, 1995.

McGirr, Lisa. *The War on Alcohol: Prohibition and the Rise of the American State*. New York: W. W. Norton, 2016.

Meyerowitz, Joanne. *How Sex Changed: A History of Transsexuality in the United States*. Cambridge, MA: Harvard University Press, 2002.

———. *Women Adrift: Independent Wage Earners in Chicago, 1880–1930*. Chicago: University of Chicago Press, 1988.

Miller, Carroll L. L., and Anne S. Pruitt-Logan. *Faithful to the Task at Hand: The Life of Lucy Diggs Slowe*. Albany: State University of New York Press, 2012.

Miller, D. A. *Place for Us: Essay on the Broadway Musical*. Cambridge, MA: Harvard University Press, 1998.

Miller, Karl Hagstrom. *Segregating Sound: Inventing Folk and Pop Music in the Age of Jim Crow*. Durham, NC: Duke University Press, 2010.

Minton, Henry. *Departing from Deviance: A History of Homosexual Rights and Emancipatory Science in America*. Chicago: University of Chicago Press, 2001.

Mitchell, Michelle. *Righteous Propagation: African Americans and the Politics of Racial Destiny after Reconstruction*. Chapel Hill: University of North Carolina Press, 2004.

Mitchell, Verner D., ed. *This Waiting for Love: Helene Johnson, Poet of the Harlem Renaissance*. Amherst: University of Massachusetts Press, 2000.

Mitchell, Verner D., and Cynthia Davis, eds. Introduction to *Where the Wild Grape Grows: Selected Writings, 1930–1950*, by Dorothy West, 3–38. Amherst: University of Massachusetts Press, 2004.

———. *Literary Sisters: Dorothy West and Her Circle, a Biography of the Harlem Renaissance*. New Brunswick: Rutgers University Press, 2012.

Morgan, Jennifer L. *Laboring Women: Reproduction and Gender in New World Slavery*. Philadelphia: University of Pennsylvania Press, 2004.

Muhammad, Khalil Gibran. *The Condemnation of Blackness: Race, Crime, and the Making of Modern Urban America*. Cambridge, MA: Harvard University Press, 2010.

Muir, Peter C. *Long Lost Blues: Popular Blues in America, 1850–1920*. Champaign: University of Illinois Press, 2010.

Mumford, Kevin. *Interzones: Black/White Sex Districts in Chicago and New York in the Early Twentieth Century*. New York: Columbia University Press, 1997.

———. *Not Straight, Not White: Black Gay Men from the March on Washington to the AIDS Crisis*. Chapel Hill: University of North Carolina Press, 2016.

Murdock, Catherine Gilbert. *Domesticating Drink: Women, Men and Alcohol in America, 1870–1940*. Baltimore: Johns Hopkins University Press, 1998.

Nasaw, David. *Going Out: The Rise and Fall of Public Amusements*. Cambridge, MA: Harvard University Press, 1993.

Nash, Jennifer C. *The Black Body in Ecstasy: Reading Race, Reading Pornography*. Durham, NC: Duke University Press, 2014.

Ogbar, Jeffrey O. G., ed. *The Harlem Renaissance Revisited: Politics, Arts, and Letters*. Baltimore: Johns Hopkins University Press, 2010.

Okrent, Daniel. *Last Call: The Rise and Fall of Prohibition*. New York: Simon and Schuster, 2010.

Oliver, Paul. *The Story of the Blues*. Boston: Northeastern University Press, 1969.

Osofsky, Gilbert. *Harlem: The Making of a Ghetto; Negro New York, 1890–1930*. New York: Harper and Row, 1963.

Packard, Jerrold. *American Nightmare: The History of Jim Crow*. New York: St. Martins Griffin, 2003.

Peck, Garrett. *The Prohibition Hangover: Alcohol in America from Demon Rum to Cult Cabernet*. New Brunswick: Rutgers University Press, 2009.

Peiss, Kathy. *Cheap Amusements: Working Women and Leisure in Turn-of-the-Century New York*. Philadelphia: Temple University Press, 1986.

Phillips, Kimberly L. *Alabama North: African-American Migrants, Community, and Working-Class Activism in Cleveland, 1915–1945*. Champaign: University of Illinois Press, 1999.

Rafter, Nicole Hahn. *Partial Justice: Women in State Prisons, 1800–1935*. Boston: Northeastern University Press, 1990.

Roberts, Blain. *Pageants, Parlors, and Pretty Women: Race and Beauty in the Twentieth-Century South*. Chapel Hill: University of North Carolina Press, 2014.

Rodger, Gillian. *Just One of the Boys: Female-to-Male Cross-Dressing on the American Variety Stage*. Champaign: University of Illinois Press, 2018.

Roediger, David. *The Wages of Whiteness: Race and the Making of the American Working Class*. New York: Verso, 1991.

Rowley, Hazel. *Richard Wright: The Life and Times*. Chicago: University of Chicago Press, 2008.

Rupp, Leila. *A Desired Past: A Short History of Same-Sex Love in America*. Chicago: University of Chicago Press, 1999.

———. *Sapphistries: A Global History of Love between Women*. New York: New York University Press, 2009.

Sacks, Marcy S. *Before Harlem: The Black Experience in New York City before World War I*. Philadelphia: University of Pennsylvania Press, 2006.

Scheiner, Seth M. *Negro Mecca: A History of the Negro in New York City, 1865–1920*. New York: New York University Press, 1965.

Schwarz, A. B. Christa. *Gay Voices of the Harlem Renaissance*. Bloomington: Indiana University Press, 2003.

Scott, James C. *Domination and the Arts of Resistance: Hidden Transcripts*. New Haven: Yale University Press, 1990.

Scott, Michelle R. *Blues Empress in Black Chattanooga: Bessie Smith and the Emerging Urban South*. Champaign: University of Illinois Press, 2008.

———. *TOBA Time: Black Vaudeville and the Theater Owners' Booking Association in Jazz-Age America*. Champaign: University of Illinois Press, 2023.

Sedgwick, Eve Kosofsky. *Epistemology of the Closet*. Berkeley: University of California Press, 1990.

Segrave, Kerry. *Jukeboxes: An American Social History*. Jefferson, NC: McFarland, 2002.

Sherrard-Johnson, Cherene. *Dorothy West's Paradise: A Biography of Class and Color*. New Brunswick: Rutgers University Press, 2012.

Simmons, Christina. *Making Marriage Modern: Women's Sexuality from the Progressive Era to World War II*. New York: Oxford University Press, 2009.

Sinfield, Alan. *Out on Stage: Lesbian and Gay Theatre in the Twentieth Century*. New Haven: Yale University Press, 1999.

Smith, Barbara. *All the Women Are White, All the Blacks Are Men, but Some of Us Are Brave: Black Women's Studies*. New York: Feminist Press of City University of New York, 1993.

Smith-Rosenberg, Carroll. *Disorderly Conduct: Visions of Gender in Victorian America*. New York: Oxford University Press, 1985.

Snyder, Robert. *Voice of the City: Vaudeville and Popular Culture in New York*. New York: Oxford University Press, 1989.

Somerville, Siobhan. *Queering the Color Line: Race and the Invention of Homosexuality in America*. Durham, NC: Duke University Press, 2000.

Sotiropoulos, Karen. *Staging Race: Black Performers in Turn of the Century America.* Cambridge, MA: Harvard University Press, 2006.

Stansell, Christine. *American Moderns: Bohemian New York and the Creation of a New Century.* New York: Henry Holt, 2001.

Starr, Paul. *The Creation of the Media: Political Origins of Modern Communications.* New York: Basic Books, 2004.

Stearns, Marshall, and Jean Stearns. *Jazz Dance: The Story of American Vernacular Dance.* New York: Macmillan, 1968.

Stevenson, Brenda. *Life in Black and White: Family and Community in the Slave South.* New York: Oxford University Press, 1996.

Suisman, David. *Selling Sounds: The Commercial Revolution in American Music.* Cambridge, MA: Harvard University Press, 2009.

Summers, Martin. *Manliness and Its Discontents: The Black Middle Class and the Transformation of Masculinity, 1900–1930.* Chapel Hill: University of North Carolina Press, 2004.

Taylor, Frank C., and Gerald Cook. *Alberta Hunter: A Celebration in Blues.* New York: McGraw-Hill, 1987.

Terry, Jennifer. *An American Obsession: Science, Medicine, and Homosexuality in Modern Society.* Chicago: University of Chicago Press, 1999.

Titon, Jeff Todd. *Early Downhome Blues: A Musical and Cultural Analysis.* Chapel Hill: University of North Carolina Press, 1994.

Tracy, Steven C., ed. *Writers of the Black Chicago Renaissance.* Champaign: University of Illinois Press, 2012.

Trotter, Joe William, ed. *The Great Migration in Historical Perspective: New Dimensions of Race, Class, and Gender.* Bloomington: Indiana University Press, 1991.

Tye, Larry. *Rising from the Rails: Pullman Porters and the Making of the Black Middle Class.* New York: Henry Holt, 2004.

Ullman, Sharon. *Sex Seen: The Emergence of Modern Sexuality in America.* Berkeley: University of California Press, 1997.

Van Der Tuuk, Alex. *Paramount's Rise and Fall: A History of the Wisconsin Chair Company and Its Recording Activities.* Denver: Mainspring Press, 2003.

Vicinus, Martha. *Intimate Friends: Women Who Loved Women, 1778–1928.* Chicago: University of Chicago Press, 2004.

Vincent, Theodore G. *Black Power and the Garvey Movement.* Berkeley: Ramparts, 1972.

Vogel, Shane. *The Scene of Harlem Cabaret: Race, Sexuality, Performance.* Chicago: University of Chicago Press, 2009.

Walker, Margaret. *Richard Wright: Daemonic Genius.* New York: Harper, 2000.

Ware, Susan. *Holding Their Own: American Women in the 1930s.* Boston: Twayne, 1982.

Warner, Michael. *Publics and Counterpublics.* New York: Zone Books, 2002.

Watson, Steven. *The Harlem Renaissance: Hub of African-American Culture, 1920–1930.* New York: Pantheon Books, 1995.

Wekker, Gloria. *The Politics of Passion: Women's Sexual Culture in the Afro-Surinamese Diaspora.* New York: Columbia University Press, 2006.

White, Deborah Gray. *Too Heavy a Load: Black Women in Defense of Themselves, 1894–1994.* New York: W. W. Norton, 1999.

White, Shane, and Stephen Robertson. *Playing the Numbers: Gambling in Harlem between the Wars*. Cambridge, MA: Harvard University Press, 2010.

Whitely, Sheila, and Jennifer Rycenga, eds. *Queering the Popular Pitch*. New York: Routledge, 2006.

Wilkerson, Isabel. *The Warmth of Other Suns: The Epic Story of America's Great Migration*. New York: Random House, 2010.

Williams, Heather. *Help Me to Find My People: The African American Search for Family Lost in Slavery*. Chapel Hill: University of North Carolina Press, 2012.

Wilson, James F. *Bulldaggers, Pansies, and Chocolate Babies: Performance, Race, and Sexuality in the Harlem Renaissance*. Ann Arbor: University of Michigan Press, 2010.

Wilson, Steve. *The Making of "Gone with the Wind."* Austin: University of Texas Press, 2014.

Wintz, Cary D., and Paul Finkleman, eds. *Encyclopedia of the Harlem Renaissance: K–Y*. New York: Routledge, 2004.

Wirth, Thomas H., ed. Introduction to *Gay Rebel of the Harlem Renaissance: Selections from the Work of Richard Bruce Nugent*, 1–61. Durham, NC: Duke University Press, 2002.

Wolcott, Victoria. *Remaking Respectability: African American Women in Interwar Detroit*. Chapel Hill: University of North Carolina Press, 2001.

Chapters, Journal Articles, and Dissertations

Allen, Jafari S. "Black/Queer/Diaspora at the Current Conjuncture." *GLQ* 18, no. 2–3 (2012): 211–48.

Anderson, Karen T. "Last Hired, First Fired: Black Women Workers during World War II." *Journal of American History* 69, no. 1 (June 1982): 82–97.

———. "'Brickbats and Roses': Lucy Diggs Slowe, 1883–1937." In *Lone Voyagers: Academic Women in Coeducational Universities, 1870–1937*, edited by Geraldine Jonçich Clifford, 283–307. New York: Feminist Press, 1989.

Bailey, Peter. "Conspiracies of Meaning: Music-Hall and the Knowingness of Popular Culture." *Past and Present* 144 (August 1994): 138–71.

Bean, Annemarie. "Black Minstrelsy and Double Inversion, circa 1890." In *African American Performance and Theater History*, edited by Harry Justin Elam and David Krasner, 171–91. New York: Oxford University Press, 2001.

Beauboeuf-Lafontant, Tamara. "The New Howard Woman: Dean Lucy Diggs Slowe and the Education of a Modern Black Femininity." In *Meridians: Feminism, Race, Transnationalism* 17 (September 2018): 25–48.

Brown, Leslie. "African American Women and Migration." In *The Practice of U.S. Women's History: Narratives, Intersections, and Dialogues*, edited by S. Jay Kleinberg, Eileen Boris, and Vicki L. Ruiz, 201–20. New Brunswick: Rutgers University Press, 2007.

Cabello, Tristan. "Queer Bronzeville: Race, Sexuality and Culture in Black Chicago, 1920–1985." PhD diss., Northwestern University, 2011.

Carby, Hazel. "Policing the Black Woman's Body in an Urban Context." *Critical Inquiry* 18 (Summer 1992): 738–55.

Carlston, Erin G. "'A Finer Differentiation': Female Homosexuality and the American Medical Community, 1926–1940." In *Science and Homosexualities*, edited by Vernon A. Rosario, 177–96. New York: Routledge, 1997.

Carter, Julian. "Normality, Whiteness, Authorship: Evolutionary Sexology and the Primitive Pervert." In *Science and Homosexualities*, edited by Vernon A. Rosario, 155–76. New York: Routledge, 1997.

Chauncey, George. "From Sexual Inversion to Homosexuality: Medicine and the Changing Conceptualization of Female Desire." *Salmagundi* 58–59 (Fall 1982–Winter 1983): 114–46.

Chenier, Elise. "Love-Politics: Lesbian Wedding Practices in Canada and the United States from the 1920s to the 1970s." *Journal of the History of Sexuality* 27, no. 2 (May 2018): 294–321.

Chinitz, David. "Rejuvenation through Joy: Langston Hughes, Primitivism, and Jazz." *American Literary History* 9, no. 1 (Spring 1997): 60–78.

Clark-Lewis, Elizabeth. "This Work Had an End: African-American Domestic Workers in Washington D.C., 1910–1940." In *To Toil the Livelong Day: America's Women at Work, 1780–1980*, edited by Carol Groneman and Mary Beth Norton, 196–212. Ithaca: Cornell University Press, 1987.

Cleves, Rachel Hope. "'What, Another Female Husband?': The Prehistory of Same-Sex Marriage in America." *Journal of American History* 101 (March 2015): 1055–81.

Coleman, Bud. "Cabarets and Revues." In *The Queer Encyclopedia of Music, Dance, and Musical Theater*, edited by Claude J. Summers, 9. San Francisco: Cleis Press, 2004.

Cook, Blanche Wiesen. "The Historical Denial of Lesbianism." *Radical History Review* 20 (Spring–Summer 1979): 60–65.

Coyle, Katy, and Nadiene Van Dyke. "Sex, Smashing, and Storyville." In *Carryin' On in the Gay and Lesbian South*, edited by John Howard, 54–72. New York: New York University Press, 1997.

Dalsgård, Katrine. "Alive and Well and Living on the Island of Martha's Vineyard: An Interview with Dorothy West, October 29, 1988." *Langston Hughes Review* 12 (Fall 1993): 28–44.

D'Emilio, John. "Capitalism and Gay Identity." In *Powers of Desire: The Politics of Sexuality*, edited by Ann Snitow, Christine Stansell, and Sharon Thompson, 100–13. New York: Monthly Review Press, 1983.

DeSantis, Alan D. "Selling the American Dream Myth to Black Southerners: The Chicago *Defender* and the Great Migration of 1915–1919." *Western Journal of Communication* 62 (1997): 63–71.

Dolan, Mark K. "Extra! *Chicago Defender* Race Records Ads Show South from Afar." *Southern Cultures* 13 (Fall 2007): 106–24.

Dorman, Jacob S. "Back to Harlem: Abstract and Everyday Labor during the Harlem Renaissance." In *The Harlem Renaissance Revisited: Politics, Arts, and Letters*, edited by Jeffrey O. G. Ogbar, 74–90. Baltimore: Johns Hopkins University Press, 2010.

Driscoll, Anne K. "Gladys Bentley." In *Harlem Renaissance Lives from the African American National Biography*, edited by Evelyn Brooks Higginbotham and Henry Louis Gates Jr., 47–48. New York: Oxford University Press, 2009.

Duggan, Lisa. "The Discipline Problem: Queer Theory Meets Gay and Lesbian History." *GLQ* 2, no. 3 (1995): 179–91.

———. "The Trials of Alice Mitchell: Sensationalism, Sexology, and the Lesbian Subject in Turn-of-the-Century America." *Signs* 18, no. 4 (Summer 1993): 798–814.

Erenberg, Lewis. "From New York to Middletown: Repeal and the Legitimization of Nightlife in the Great Depression." *American Quarterly* 38 (Winter 1986): 761–78.

Faderman, Lillian. "The Morbidification of Love between Woman by 19th-Century Sexologists." *Journal of Homosexuality* 4 (Fall 1978): 73–90.

Garber, Eric. "Gladys Bentley: The Bulldagger Who Sang the Blues." *Out/Look* 1 (Spring 1988): 52–61.

———. "A Spectacle in Color: The Lesbian and Gay Subculture of Jazz Age Harlem." In *Hidden from History: Reclaiming the Gay and Lesbian Past*, edited by Martin Duberman, Martha Vicinus, and George Chauncey, 318–31. New York: Basic Books, 1989.

Gilman, Sander L. "Black Bodies, White Bodies: Toward an Iconography of Female Sexuality in Late Nineteenth-Century Art, Medicine and Literature." *Critical Inquiry* 12 (Fall 1985): 204–42.

Guinier, Genii. "Interview with Dorothy West, May 6, 1978." In *The Black Women Oral History Project*, edited by Ruth Edmonds Hill, 143–224. Westport, CT: Meckler, 1991.

Gussow, Adam. "'Shoot Myself a Cop': Mamie Smith's 'Crazy Blues' as Social Text." *Callaloo* 25, no. 1 (Winter 2002): 8–44.

Haag, Pamela. "In Search of the Real Thing: Ideologies of Love, Modern Romance, and Women's Sexual Subjectivity in the U.S., 1920–40." In *American Sexual Politics: Sex, Gender, and Race since the Civil War*, edited by John C. Fout and Maura Shaw Tantillo, 161–91. Chicago: University of Chicago Press, 1992.

Hammonds, Evelynn. "Black (W)holes and the Geometry of Black Female Sexuality." In *Feminism Meets Queer Theory*, edited by Elizabeth Weed and Naomi Schor, 136–56. Bloomington: Indiana University Press, 1997.

Hansen, Karen V. "'No *Kisses* Is Like Youres': An Erotic Friendship between Two African-American Women during the Mid-Nineteenth Century." *Gender and History* 7 (August 1995): 153–82.

Harris, LaShawn. "'Women and Girls in Jeopardy by His False Testimony': Charles Dancy, Urban Policing, and Black Women in New York City during the 1920s." *Journal of Urban History* 44, no. 3 (May 2018): 457–75.

Hicks, Cheryl D. "'Bright and Good Looking Colored Girl': Black Women's Sexuality and 'Harmful Intimacy' in Early-Twentieth-Century New York." *Journal of the History of Sexuality* 18, no. 3 (September 2009): 418–56.

Higginbotham, Evelyn Brooks. "African-American Women's History and the Metalanguage of Race." *Signs* 17, no. 2 (Winter 1992): 251–74.

Hine, Darlene Clark. "Rape and the Inner Lives of Black Women in the Middle West: Preliminary Thoughts on the Culture of Dissemblance." *Signs* 14 (Summer 1989): 912–20.

Hughes-Watkins, Lae'l. "Fay M. Jackson and the Color Line: The First African American Foreign Correspondent for the Associated Negro Press." *Journal of Pan African Studies* 3 (September 2009): 119–34.

Hull, Akasha (Gloria). "Researching Alice Dunbar-Nelson: A Personal and Literary Perspective." In *Lesbian Subjects: A Feminist Studies Reader*, edited by Martha Vicinus, 15–20. Bloomington: Indiana University Press, 1996.

Jones, Anastasia. "She Wolves: Feminine Sapphists and Liminal Sociosexual Categories in the U.S. Urban Entertainment Industry, 1920–1940." *Journal of the History of Sexuality* 26, no. 2 (May 2017): 294–317.

Jones, Jacqueline C. "So the Girl Marries: Class, the Black Press, and the Du Bois-Cullen Marriage of 1928." In *The Harlem Renaissance Revisited: Politics, Arts, and Letters*, edited by Jeffrey O. G. Ogbar, 45–62. Baltimore: Johns Hopkins University Press, 2010.

Knight, Athelia. "He Paved the Way for T.O.B.A." *Black Perspective in Music* 15 (Autumn 1987): 153–81.

Murphy, Mary. "Bootlegging Mothers and Drinking Daughters: Gender and Prohibition in Butte, Montana." *American Quarterly* 46 (June 1994): 174–94.

Nestle, Joan. "Excerpts from the Oral History of Mabel Hampton." *Signs* 18, no. 4 (Summer 1993): 925–35.

———. "I Lift My Eyes to the Hill: The Life of Mabel Hampton as Told by a White Woman." In *Queer Representations: Reading Lives, Reading Cultures*, edited by Martin Duberman, 258–75. New York: New York University Press, 1997.

———. "Lesbians and Prostitutes: An Historical Sisterhood." In *A Restricted Country*, 154–75. San Francisco: Cleis Press, 2003.

Newton, Esther. "The Mythic Mannish Lesbian: Radclyffe Hall and the New Woman." *Signs* 9 (Summer 1984): 557–75.

Oosterhuis, Harry. "Richard von Krafft-Ebing's 'Step-Children of Nature': Psychiatry and the Making of Homosexual Identity." In *Sexualities in History: A Reader*, edited by Kim M. Phillips and Barry Reay, 271–92. New York: Routledge, 2002.

Penn, Donna. "Queer: Theorizing Politics and History." *Radical History Review* 62 (Spring 1995): 24–42.

Perkins, Linda M. "Lucy Diggs Slowe: Champion of the Self-Determination of African-American Women in Higher Education." *Journal of African American History* 81, no. 1–4 (Winter/Autumn 1996): 89–104.

Phillips, Danielle Taylor. "Moving with the Women: Tracing Racialization, Migration, and Domestic Workers in the Archive." *Signs* 38, no. 2 (Winter 2013): 379–404.

Pinson, Luvenia. "The Black Lesbian: Times Past—Time Present." *Womanews*, May 1980, 8.

Potter, Sarah. "'Undesirable Relations': Same-Sex Relationships and the Meaning of Sexual Desire at a Woman's Reformatory during the Progressive Era." *Feminist Studies* 30 (Summer 2004): 394–415.

Rasheed, Lisa R. "Lucy Diggs Slowe, Howard University Dean of Women, 1922–1937: Educator, Administrator, Activist." PhD diss., Georgia State University, 2009.

Reed, Christopher Robert. "African American Cultural Expression in Chicago before the Renaissance: The Performing, Visual, and Literary Arts, 1893–1933." In *The Black Chicago Renaissance*, edited by Darlene Clark Hine and John McCluskey, 3–20. Champaign: University of Illinois Press, 2012.

Richardson, Matt. "No More Secrets, No More Lies: African American History and Compulsory Heterosexuality." *Journal of Women's History* 15, no. 3 (Autumn 2003): 63–76.

Robertson, Stephen. "Harlem Undercover: Vice Investigators, Race, and Prostitution, 1910–1930." *Journal of Urban History* 35, no. 4 (May 2009): 486–504.

Robertson, Stephen, Shane White, Stephen Garton, and Graham White. "Disorderly Houses: Residences, Privacy, and the Surveillance of Sexuality in 1920s Harlem." *Journal of the History of Sexuality* 21, no. 3 (September 2012): 443–66.

Robinson, Paul. "Freud and Homosexuality." In *Whose Freud? The Place of Psychoanalysis in Contemporary Culture*, edited by Peter Brooks and Alex Woloch, 144–49. New Haven: Yale University Press, 2000.

Rupp, Leila. "Imagine My Surprise: Women's Relationships in Historical Perspective." *Frontiers* 5, no. 3 (Autumn 1980): 61–70.

Simmons, Christina. "Companionate Marriage and the Lesbian Threat." *Frontiers* 4, no. 3 (Autumn 1979): 54–59.

———. "'Modern Marriage' for African Americans, 1920–1940." *Canadian Review of American Studies* 30, no. 3 (2000): 273–300.

Smith-Rosenberg, Carroll. "The Female World of Love and Ritual: Relations between Women in Nineteenth-Century America." *Signs* 1, no. 1 (Autumn 1975): 1–29.

Stephens, Judith L. "Anti-Lynch Plays by African American Women: Race, Gender, and Social Protest in American Drama." *African American Review* 26, no. 2 (Summer 1992): 329–39.

Stevenson, Brenda. "Distress and Discord in Virginia Slave Families, 1830–1860." In *In Joy and in Sorrow: Women, Family, and Marriage in the Victorian South, 1830–1900*, edited by Carol K. Rothrock Bleser, 103–24. New York: Oxford University Press, 1991.

Summers, Martin. "'This Immoral Practice': The Prehistory of Homophobia in Black Nationalist Thought." In *Gender Nonconformity, Race, and Sexuality*, edited by Toni Lester, 21–43. Madison: University of Wisconsin Press, 2002.

Taylor, Leslie A. "'I Made Up My Mind to Get It': The American Trial of *The Well of Loneliness*, New York City, 1928–29." *Journal of the History of Sexuality* 10, no. 2 (April 2001): 250–86.

Terry, Jennifer. "Anxious Slippages between 'Us' and 'Them': A Brief History of the Scientific Search for Homosexual Bodies." In *Deviant Bodies: Critical Perspectives on Difference in Science and Popular Culture*, edited by Jennifer Terry and Jacqueline Urla, 129–69. Bloomington: Indiana University Press, 1995.

———. "The Seductive Power of Science in the Making of Deviant Subjectivity." In *Science and Homosexualities*, edited by Vernon Rosario, 271–96. New York: Routledge, 1997.

Thompson, Mary Francesca. "The Lafayette Players: 1915–1932." PhD diss., University of Michigan, 1972.

Thorpe, Rochella. "'A House Where Queers Go': African-American Lesbian Nightlife in Detroit, 1940–1975." In *Inventing Lesbian Cultures in America*, edited by Ellen Lewin, 40–61. Boston: Beacon Press, 1996.

Tinsley, Omise'eke Natasha. "Black Atlantic, Queer Atlantic: Queer Imaginings of the Middle Passage." *GLQ* 14, no. 2–3 (2008): 191–215.

Vicinus, Martha. "Lesbian History: All Theory and No Facts or All Facts and No Theory?" *Radical History Review* 60 (Fall 1994): 57–75.

Wiltenburg, Joy. "True Crime: The Origins of Modern Sensationalism." *American Historical Review* 109, no. 5 (December 2004): 1377–404.

INDEX

Page numbers in italics refer to illustrations.

laws, respectability and, 41

leaders, race, 103. *See also* authorities; racial uplift; respectability

leaders, religious, 23, 25–26. *See also* authorities

Lee-Rayford, Narka, 110

Leghorn, Azelia, 35

Lesbian Herstory Archives, 88

lesbianism: awareness of, 121, 127; Black community and, 38, 39; Black press and, 34, 46, 135, 138–39; in *The Captive*, 35; as choice, 38; conceptions of, 33; depictions of, 43, 44, 138–39; as immature form of development, 30; knowledge of, 37; negative ideas around, 87; popular interest in, 42; prostitution associated with, 102; representations of, 23–26, 34, 35; rhetorical violence of, 35; theories of, 37–38; as threat to male authorities, 127; use of terms, 18, 32, 46, 157n5; violence and, 42; visibility of, 6, 91–92, 93, 95, 97. *See also* Black lady lovers

Lieb, Sandra, 66–67

literary community, 114, 117

literary journals, 5, 113, 114, 117

literary networks, 114, 116, 117, 132. *See also* West, Dorothy

living arrangements, 11, 12, 41, 42, 43–44, 106, 132–34; ambiguity of, 128; boardinghouses, 11, 41, 68, 70; Great Depression and, 106, 121, 124, 133; Slowe's, 126–27, 128–29; suspicion of sex work and, 88, 90; Thomas's, 117, 119; Walker's, 124

Locke, Alain, 117

London, Helene Ricks, 111–12

lynching, 10, 26, 77

Mabley, Jackie "Moms," 86

marital status, 88. *See also* marriage, traditional; women, single

marriage, same-sex, 127, 138

marriage, traditional, 43, 71, 106, 136, 152n59; Black lady lovers and, 1, 110,

111, 112, 114; Dunbar-Nelson and, 108–9; middle-class Black women and, 110; respectability and, 111, 114, 136, 137; same-sex relationships and, 36; Bessie Smith's, 67–68, 71; Thomas's, 120; West and, 114–15

masculinist ideology, 11, 30–31, 127, 129

Mason, Margaret, 90

Matthews, Ralph, 50–51, 100

McGirr, Lisa, 98

meeting spaces. *See* spaces

men, Black, 10, 11. *See also* authorities

men, gay, 38, 61, 80, 83, 107

men, relationships with, 43. *See also* marriage, traditional

Mencken, Helen, 54

Messenger (periodical), 90

middle class: Black, 8, 105, 106, 107, 109–10, 111; white, 97. *See also* class, social; Dunbar-Nelson, Alice; press, Black; Slowe, Lucy Diggs; Thomas, Edna; Walker, Ruby; West, Dorothy

migrants, southern, 1, 5, 42; in Black press, 22, 43; blues and, 55; in entertainment industry, 51, 53; immorality perceived among, 2, 24, 29, 65; predatory older lesbians and, 70; Prohibition and, 77; rent parties and, 79; representations of lady lovers and, 25; single migrant women, 26–29, 65; as social problem, 65; as threat, 27, 140; views of, 27; violence and, 15, 22; white perception of, 29; work opportunities for, 27. *See also* Great Migration

Miller, Kelly, 27–28, 77, 91

Minus, Marian, 5, 105, 113, 116–17, 132

Mitchell, Alberta, 39–41, 42

Mitchell, Alice, 23, 39, 41

mobility, 3, 4, 71, 132, 135, 136. *See also* Great Migration; migrants, southern

mobility, upward, 97

modernity, 3, 4

Moore, Fred, 78

morality, 77, 88. *See also* respectability

motherhood, 106, 114, 116, 132, 137–38

movement, freedom of, 71. *See also* mobility

Moynihan, Daniel Patrick, 12

Mumford, Kevin, 84

murders, 11, 23, 24, 35–37, 36, 39–41, 153n9. *See also* violence

Murray, Pauli, 117

music, 84–85, 92–97. *See also* blues

music industry, 15; Black lady lovers in, 136; segregation of, 5. *See also* blues; entertainment industry; performers; record industry

Nash, Jennifer C., 14

nationalism, Black, 3, 26, 30, 31, 43

Negro Family in Chicago, The (Frazier), 24–25

Negro World (newspaper), 3, 29, 30

neighborhoods, Black: vice in, 7, 28–29, 82, 88, 103; white ownership of real estate in, 84

Nelson, Robert, 109, 111

Nestle, Joan, 88

New Deal, 96, 97, 98, 113. *See also* reformers

New Negro era, 11, 107, 129

newspapers, Black. *See* press, Black; *and titles of individual newspapers*

New Woman, 129

New York Age (newspaper), 6, 21, 25, 101; on Bentley, 99; on bootleg alcohol, 78; on false arrests for solicitation, 89–90; murder coverage in, 39; on rent parties, 79; on Thomas, 118; on violence, 34–35

New York Amsterdam News (newspaper), 28, 99; depiction of Black lady lovers in, 138–39; on murders, 39, 40, 41; on queer women in theater, 46; Thomas's relationship in, 120–21; Whitney's columns in, 91–92

New York City: Black population of, 26; Columbus Hill, 22, 33. *See also* Harlem

nightlife: in Harlem, 73, 79, 94; queer, 76. *See also* clubs; speakeasies; vice districts

Nugent, Richard Bruce, 19, 106, 113–14, 122, 123

obscenity trials, 37

Opportunity (periodical), 107

ostracization, social, 123

otherness, 32, 96

Otis, Margaret, 10

Pace, Harry, 55–57, 67. *See also* Black Swan Records

Paramount Records, 59–60, 62, 63, 71

performance: Black queer women and, 50; live, 92–97. *See also* entertainment industry

performers, 46, 47, 136; buffet flats and, 80; mobility of, 4, 71; queer, critics of, 46, 97, 135–36; sexology case studies of, 52; white women and, 52. *See also* entertainment industry; music industry; record industry; Thomas, Edna; West, Dorothy

pervert, female, 91

Philadelphia Tribune (newspaper), 101

phonographs, 84–85

physicians, female, 129–30

Pittsburgh Courier (newspaper), 41, 31, 37, 41, 126

Plessy v. Ferguson, 26

police, corruption and, 90

policing, 79, 82, 83, 138. *See also* surveillance

popular culture, 46, 65. *See also* blues; entertainment industry; performers; record industry

Porgy, 113–14, 118, 122

Porgy and Bess, 122

Powell, Adam Clayton, Sr., 6–7, 25

predators, women, 30, 31, 51, 70, 100–101

press, Black, 2, 4, 9; Black lady lovers and, 12, 24, 26, 31, 43, 44, 138–39; dissemination of, 4–5; on Harlem performers, 70; journalistic integrity of, 42; lesbianism and, 34, 46, 135, 138–39; on "perverted love," 11; on queer love brawls, 15; queer networks and, 15, 33; on queer presence in entertainment industry, 46, 50–51, 135–36; southern migrants and, 22, 29; terminology used by, 18; Thomas's relationship in, 120–21; on vice districts, 28–29; violence in, 3, 21–22, 24, 31–44; Walker in, 124, 125, 126; Waters in, 57; on women-only parties, 63. *See also titles of individual newspapers*

primitivism, 8, 95–96

prisons: Black women in, 10, 88–90, 138; interracial queer relationships in, 10–11, 52

privacy, 89, 125, 135. *See also* gatherings; residential sites

procreation, 38. *See also* birth control; birth rates; children

Progressive Era, 77. *See also* reformers

Prohibition, 4, 16, 77, 133, 140; alcohol during, 82, 83; enforcement of, 77; leisure during, 76; live performance during, 92–97; queer networks during, 7–8, 16, 74; rent parties and, 79; repeal of, 98, 99, 102; sex work during, 87, 88, 92, 138; spaces and, 75, 76, 77–78, 140; violence during, 43; visibility of queer behaviors and identities during, 103; white illegal activity and, 78. *See also* gatherings; speakeasies; vice districts

prostitution. *See* sex work

Prostitution in the United States (Woolston), 92

"Prove It on Me Blues" (Rainey), 15–16, 62–65, 64, 71, 136

Pullman porters, 4–5, 82

queer, use of term, 18–19, 37, 152n75, 152n76

queer communities, 133. *See also* queer networks; spaces

queerness: pathologized, 9, 47, 140; prostitution associated with, 7, 85–86, 87, 90, 92, 102; referencing, 70; vice associated with, 16, 74; views of, 12; visibility of, 5, 47, 107. *See also* gay men; homosexuality; lesbianism

queer networks, 3, 4, 19, 22, 40, 44, 135; Black press and, 15, 33; building, 70; college-educated Black lady lovers and, 5–6; Dark Tower, 110, 124–25, 126, 136; during Prohibition, 7–8, 16, 74; emergence of, 11, 30, 32, 33, 102, 136; entertainment industry and, 45, 50–54, 71, 86; foundation provided by, 139; Great Migration and, 3; identity categories and, 139; narratives describing, 23; performers and, 72; as political, 8; visibility of, 46. *See also* buffet flats; gatherings; rent parties; spaces

race leaders, 103. *See also* authorities

race pride, 107

race records, 5, 46, 54, 150n11; Black Swan Records, 47, 54, 55–58, 67, 71. *See also* entertainment industry; music industry; record industry

race work, 97, 113. *See also* club movement, Black women's; racial uplift; respectability

racial ideologies, 88

racial uplift, 7, 8, 25, 30, 54, 56, 67, 100, 108, 113, 127, 130

Raines law, 76–77

Rainey, Gertrude "Ma," 15, 32, 47–48, 49, 50, 59–66; clothing worn by, 63, 65; lyrics of, 69; marketing of, 62–65; "Prove It on Me Blues," 15–16, 62–65, 64, 71, 136; sexual fluidity and ambiguity of, 65–66; Smith and, 66–67; style of, 48

Rainey, William "Pa," 48, 60

rape, 8, 108

record industry: Black market for, 49–50; Black Swan Records, 47, 54, 55–58, 67, 71; marketing by, 62–65, 71; race records, 46, 54; white-run record companies, 67, 71. *See also* blues; entertainment industry; performers

recording artists, 15. *See also* blues; entertainment industry; performers

reformers, 77, 78, 96; COF, 16, 73, 74, 75, 76–79, 83, 86; single Black female southern migrants and, 65. *See also* New Deal; Prohibition

Reid, Ira De A., 79

religious authorities, 23, 138. *See also* authorities

rent parties, 16, 21, 22, 75, 79–80, 81, 101, 102, 139, 140; vs. pay parties, 85; violence at, 34. *See also* queer networks; spaces; vice districts

rents, 79, 91, 97

residential sites, 16, 22, 75, 77. *See also* buffet flats; gatherings; rent parties

respectability, 2, 14, 17, 30, 91, 108, 110; Black Swan Records and, 56, 67; Black women migrants as threats to, 27; documentation and, 13; entertainment industry and, 122; gender roles and, 2; laws and, 41; marriage and, 111, 114, 136, 137; middle class and, 111; nonconformity and, 31; racial uplift and, 127, 130; single women and, 90; Slowe and, 128; West and, 114

Richardson, Matt, 13

Rickson, Joyce, 116

Robinson, Fay Jackson, 111–12

Robinson, Ida May, 1, 3

Rogers, J. A., 31

Russell, Maud, 18, 53

Schuyler, George, 90, 97

segregation, 27, 47, 49, 88, 140; of music industry, 5; "separate but equal," 26; transportation and, 15, 68

sex, nonreproductive, 3, 29–30, 31, 38, 74

sex circuses, 87

sex delinquency, 90

sex economy, 92. *See also* sex work

sexology, 9, 26, 34, 37; case studies of Black queer masculine performers, 52; Ellis, 9, 37, 38; Henry, 119, 121–23, 136–37; terminology from, 42

"sex perversion," 6, 99

sex problem, Black lady lovers as, 1, 3, 24, 31, 35, 38, 135, 138

sex ratios, 27–28, 91

sexual agency, 17, 101

sexual autonomy, 8, 11, 17

sexual deviance, 140

sexual entertainments, 80

sexuality: Black women's, 8, 14, 108, 140; changing notions of, 4; control of, 98; history of, 14; norms of, 6

sexuality, ambiguous, 69

sexuality, fluid, 4, 51–52, 65, 70

sexual subjectivities, 36

Sex Variants (Henry), 119, 121–23, 136–37

sex work, 65, 74, 75, 79, 81–82, 90–92, 102, 138, 164n94; Black women and, 78, 88, 90, 103; brothels, 76–77, 82; buffet flats and, 80, 87; documentation of, 85; during Prohibition, 87, 88, 92, 138; false arrests for, 88–90, 138; during Great Depression, 138; marital status and, 88; queerness associated with, 7, 85–86, 87, 90, 92, 102; speakeasies and, 78; treating, 89; visibility of, 91–92. *See also* buffet flats; speakeasies; vice districts

sharecropping system, 5, 27

Simpson, Lillian, 51

sissies, 61, 69

slavery, 5, 8, 107

Slowe, Lucy Diggs, 5, 6, 16, 17, 107, 126–33, 136, 140. *See also* students, female

slummers, 7–8, 74–75, 78, 82, 83, 95, 96; decline of, 97; drugs and, 81; in Harlem clubs, 93–94, 94; at rent parties, 80

Smith, Ada "Bricktop," 82, 83

Smith, Bessie, 2, 4, 5, 15, 45, 47, 48, 49, 50, 62, 66–70; African Americans' views of, 95; ambiguous sexuality of, 69; at buffet flats, 81; desire for children, 137–38; "Foolish Man Blues," 69, 71; lyrics of, 69; marriage of, 67–68, 71; Rainey and, 66–67; style of, 48

Smith, Mamie, 50

Smith, Maud, 67

Printed in the USA
CPSIA information can be obtained
at www.ICGtesting.com
CBHW030107030824
12615CB00006B/290